D0875958

Schubert

SCHUBERT

Critical and Analytical Studies

Edited by Walter Frisch

UNIVERSITY OF NEBRASKA PRESS

Lincoln and London

Acknowledgments for the use of copyrighted material
appear on pages vii–viii.
Music autography by Helen M. Jenner
Copyright 1986 by the University of Nebraska Press
Manufactured in the United States of America
The paper in this book meets the guidelines for permanence
and durability of the Committee on Production Guidelines
for Book Longevity of the Council on Library Resources.

Library of Congress Cataloging in Publication Data
Main entry under title:
Schubert : critical and analytical studies.
Includes index.
Contents: Sonata form in Schubert: the first movement
of the G-major string quartet, op. 161 (D.887) / Carl
Dahlhaus; translated by Thilo Reinhard—Schubert's
promissory note: an exercise in musical hermeneutics /
Edward T. Cone—Dance music as high art: Schubert's
twelve Ländler, op. 171 (D. 790) / David Brodbeck—
[etc.]
    1. Schubert, Franz, 1797–1828—Criticism and
interpretation—Addresses, essays, lectures.   I. Frisch,
Walter.
ML410.S3S2985   1986   780'.92'4   85-8445
ISBN 0-8032-1971-7

Contents

Acknowledgments

This collection would not have come about without the efforts and talents of many people. I am especially grateful to Thomas Baker, Ellin Feld, Anthony Newcomb, Ernest Sanders, and Robert Winter who gave generously of their time to help polish my translations from the German.

Permission is also gratefully acknowledged to reprint or translate the following selections:

Edward T. Cone, "Schubert's Promissory Note: An Exercise in Musical Hermeneutics," © 1982 by The Regents of the University of California. Reprinted from *19th-Century Music 5*, no. 3 (Spring 1982):233–41, by permission of the Regents. Revisions by the author for this reprinting.

Carl Dahlhaus, "Die Sonatenform bei Schubert: Der erste Satz des G-dur-Quartetts D 887," *Musica* 32 (1978):125–30.

Arnold Feil, "'Moment musical,' F-moll, op. 94, nr. 3 (D 780)," chapter 6 of *Studien zu Schuberts Rhythmik* (Munich: Fink, 1966), pp. 83–87.

Arnold Feil, "*Im Dorfe* aus der *Winterreise*," from chapter 3 of *Franz Schubert: Die schöne Müllerin. Winterreise* (Stuttgart: Philipp Reclam jun., 1975), pp. 34–44.

Thrasybulos Georgiades, "Lyrik als musikalische Struktur (*Über allen Gipfeln*)," from chapter 1 of *Schubert: Musik und Lyrik* (Göttingen: Vandenhoeck und Ruprecht, 1967), pp. 17–31.

Joseph Kerman, "A Romantic Detail in Schubert's *Schwa-*

Introduction

Among the major composers of the Austro-German tradition, Schubert has received less than his fair share of enlightening criticism and analysis, especially in English. Too often he has fallen prey to the discursive, chatty kind of commentary that skims the surface of the music, picking up striking details but failing to delve for any deeper structural features. Perhaps the only extended studies in English that transcend the limitations of this style are those by Richard Capell, Donald Tovey, and (translated from the German) Hans Gal.[1] Denser, more substantial work has emanated from Austria and Germany, beginning at least as long ago as 1928 (the centenary year of Schubert's death), when there appeared renowned studies by Paul Mies and Felix Salzer.[2] But these and later efforts in German have had surprisingly little impact on Anglo-American scholars. Although the most recent *Schubertjahr*, 1978, stimulated a considerable amount of publication, the most remarkable achievement, a full revision of the Deutsch catalogue, was primarily philological, not analytical or critical.[3]

By "analysis" and "criticism" I mean approaches that concentrate primarily on the technical and/or aesthetic dimensions of the music. Analysis normally focuses on the technical, internal relationships of an individual work. Criticism broadens the analytical perspective by taking in other forces that impinge on a work—different pieces by the same composer or by other composers, historical and cultural matters, and source-related issues. Criticism often involves comparisons and explicit value judgments. Although they will (and should) be informed by music theory, analysis and criticism will never seek simply to validate a theoretical approach. The structural and expressive aspects of the music itself always remain at the heart of the endeavor. As Edward T. Cone has put it succinctly, "the critic seeks to impart to others something of his own vivid experience of the concrete musical values he finds in the works that interest him."[4]

The present volume assembles some of the more stimulating recent commentary of this kind from both the English and German traditions. Of the twelve selections, five have been written especially for this collection by younger American scholars (Brodbeck, Frisch, Kinderman, Kramer, Newcomb). Four others appear here in English for the first time (Dahlhaus, two by Feil, Georgiades). Three additional essays were first published in American journals and have been revised or updated by their authors for this reprinting (Cone, Kerman, Lewin). The authors concentrate primarily on individual pieces (or on a group of related pieces) drawn from the repertory of songs, piano, and chamber music that many of us regularly hear, play, and teach.

Perhaps one reason Schubert's works have remained critically impoverished is that although they form part of the mainstream of the Viennese Classical/Romantic tradition, their "concrete values" are not easily elucidated by the methods developed for other composers. This point is made in the opening article of the collection, by Carl Dahlhaus. He claims that Schubert's "lyric-epic" approach to large-scale form demands different modes of understanding than does Beethoven's "dramatic-dialectical" style, even though the two composers share certain compositional techniques. Dahlhaus demonstrates how the massive first movement of the G-Major String Quartet combines a thematic process of Beethovenian logic and continuity with a sense of time that is uniquely Schubertian—indeed, a kind of timelessness, or "tendency toward the boundless." To achieve this synthesis, Schubert draws together techniques normally associated with two different forms, sonata and variation.

Dahlhaus's essay on the quartet is especially valuable for being one of the few extended discussions of a single piece by a scholar known mainly for his historical or philosophical work.

As in his broader endeavors, Dahlhaus takes a strongly dialectical approach; yet his precise analysis comes closer than many others to accounting for Schubert's "heavenly lengths."

One special analytical challenge in Schubert studies is presented by the shorter piano pieces and the Lieder, which deviate even more sharply from the Beethoven/Classical paradigm. It is these smaller-scale but equally rich works that occupy most of the writers in the present volume.

Edwart T. Cone and Arnold Feil examine individual *Moments musicaux* from very different perspectives. Cone's approach to no. 6, in A-flat, is pitch-oriented. He demonstrates how a small, apparently insignificant chromatic detail introduced near the beginning becomes a "promissory note," which is "redeemed" later when it affects the larger harmonic and melodic dimensions of the piece. Cone's "congeneric" or internal analysis is amplified by an "extrageneric" one, in which the purely musical process is taken as a representation of Schubert's feelings about his incurable venereal disease. Feil makes little reference to specific pitches (or ailments) in his account of no. 3, in F minor. He focuses almost exclusively on rhythm—with rhythm conceived in its broadest sense, as the way a piece unfolds in time. In Feil's analysis the ostensibly simple phrase structure of the *Moment musical* is unveiled as a subtle alternation and juxtaposition of two different two-bar gestures, or, as he calls them, "figures of motion."

One potentially significant analytical issue raised by Schubert's shorter piano works (but not treated by Feil or Cone) is the extent to which they form part of a larger whole. No one today will seriously accept Schumann's theory that the Impromptus of op. 142 (D. 935) are really the movements of a sonata. But are there in fact musical links between the individual pieces of a group? In his essay, David Brodbeck argues that, unlike many of the random collections of dances, the twelve Ländler of op. 171 (D. 790) cohere by means of numerous harmonic and melodic relationships. Moreover, the first piece has certain introductory features and the final one elements of closure, a fact that suggests Schubert conceived of these dances as a unified set—as did Brahms, who saw to their posthumous publication in 1864.

Two articles explore a tantalizing but underdeveloped

area of Schubert criticism—the relationship between the instrumental music and the Lieder. Joseph Kerman and William Kinderman deal not with the kind of self-borrowing found in the "Trout" Quintet, the "Death and the Maiden" Quartet, or the "Wanderer" Fantasy, but rather with more a profound transference of compositional and expressive techniques. Kerman shows how in the piano introductions to several songs from 1828, Schubert enhances the initial statement of the tonic harmony with strongly Romantic and evocative chromatic neighbor chords. Such harmonic devices also assume an important role in the late instrumental works, he argues: what began as a literary-poetic inspiration in the Lieder has become a more abstract or (in Kerman's words) "purely musical" phenomenon. Kinderman suggests that the juxtaposition of minor and major key areas so characteristic of certain songs—especially in *Winterreise*—is a musical representation of a conflict between the tragic reality of the poem and an illusory world imagined or remembered by the protagonist. Like Kerman, Kinderman argues that this technique, developed in the Lieder (he also cites *Erlkönig* and *Ihr Bild*), carries over as "latent symbolism" into Schubert's mature instrumental works, in particular the Fantasy in F minor, op. 103 (D. 940).

The five other articles in this volume are concerned exclusively with the Lieder. The analysis by Thrasybulos Georgiades is taken from his book *Schubert: Musik und Lyrik*, perhaps the most important and original study on Schubert to appear since World War II. English and American readers will probably never have encountered anything quite like his style of analysis—at once intensely detailed and rigorous, and at the same time boldy (even wildly) imaginative. In the introductory chapter excerpted here, Georgiades treats a single brief song, the *Wandrers Nachtlied* (D. 768). By a close examination of the syntax of both the poem and the music, he shows that Schubert does not merely "set" Goethe's lyric or capture its atmosphere, but penetrates beneath its surface—its imagery and semantic meaning—to the very bedrock of linguistic structure. The song thus becomes "the musical sounding of language," or "language as music."

Although too little known in America, Georgiades's writings have had some impact on German critics, most notably his own former pupil Arnold Feil. Feil's discussion likewise probes well beneath the musical surface of *Im Dorfe* from *Winterreise*, here to the rhythmic-metrical foundation. The techniques of analysis applied to the purely instrumental F-Minor *Moment musical* prove to be highly adaptable to Lieder. Feil demonstrates how the central image of the Müller poem—that of the wanderer emotionally bound to the town, and then finally breaking free—is transformed by Schubert into "musical motion" and is actually composed as "musical structure."

Though working outside the German tradition, David Lewin is the American analyst who comes closest to the techniques of Georgiades and Feil: he too unveils a musical structure that conveys the text at a very basic level. Through successive proportional reductions of the metrical, harmonic, and melodic framework of *Auf dem Flusse*, he shows how the deep structure of the song reflects the two principal, related images of Müller's poem, the stream surging beneath its frozen crust and the protagonist's feelings swelling within his heart.

Anthony Newcomb's essay, written partly in response to Lewin's, suggests that the expressive and structural crux of the song is not the stream/heart image, but the power of memory. Newcomb traces a musical process in which the protagonist's gradual recollection of his former happiness is overcome by his realization of the hopelessness of his present situation. The song begins with the "frozen motion" of the opening bars, which gradually thaws and reaches a climax in the animated rhythm and high vocal tessitura of the final stanza.

The notion of a continuous, developmental musical process (perhaps derived from Beethoven, as Dahlhaus argues) is both attractive and appropriate in analyzing songs that are through-composed (*Wandrers Nachtlied*), or have an A B A' (*Im Dorfe*) or modified strophic form (*Auf dem Flusse*). But what of simple strophic songs, for which Schubert demonstrated such an affinity? The question is addressed in my own essay on *Nähe des Geliebten* (D. 162). After tracing the history of other folklike settings of this Goethe lyric, I suggest how Schubert transforms that tradition by maintaining the larger strophic design, but fashioning an individual musical strophe with extraordinary inner tension and development.

Like Dahlhaus's opening essay, the final one, by Lawrence

Kramer, elaborates a dialectical viewpoint on Schubert's musical language. Kramer claims that Schubert songs often manifest "clashing perspectives" between Classical principles of continuity and more disjunct, unpredictable Romantic tendencies. He analyzes four songs in which the Classical "horizon" (Husserl's term) of traditional harmonic procedures is obscured or overwhelmed by a Romantic "presentational" structure, which creates its own norms and expectations.

It is hoped that the colloquy represented in this collection of articles will stimulate further detailed study of Schubert's music. Only from more "close readings" of this kind can we begin to shape a larger picture of Schubert's musical personality. The best analysis and criticism will always move outward from the particular to the general, but will never stop striving to articulate those "concrete values" that form the core of the music.

Walter Frisch

Notes

1. Richard Capell, *Schubert's Songs* (London: Benn, 1928); Donald F. Tovey, "Franz Schubert" and "Tonality in Schubert," both in *Essays and Lectures on Music* (London: Oxford University Press, 1949); Hans Gal, *Franz Schubert and the Essence of Melody* (1974; repr. New York: Crescendo, 1977).

2. Paul Mies, *Schubert der Meister des Liedes* (Berlin: M. Hesse, 1928); Felix Salzer, "Die Sonatenform bei Schubert," *Studien zur Musikwissenschaft* 15 (1928):86–125.

3. O. E. Deutsch, *Franz Schubert. Thematisches Verzeichnis seiner Werke in chronologischer Folge*, rev. Walther Dürr, Arnold Feil, et al. (Kassel: Bärenreiter, 1978). The major volume in English to emerge (belatedly) from the Schubert year was *Schubert Studies: Problems of Style and Chronology*, ed. E. Badura-Skoda and P. Branscombe (Cambridge: Cambridge University Press, 1982). There is no mention of analysis or criticism in the title, and too little evidence of it within the book. A notable exception to the generally low level of recent critical commentary can be found in the work of James Webster, who drew on both Tovey and Salzer in his "Schubert's Sonata Form and Brahms's First Maturity," *19th-Century Music* 2 (1978):18–35; and 3 (1979):52–71.

4. Edward T. Cone, review of Leonard Meyer, *Explaining Music*, in *Journal of the American Musicological Society* 27 (1974):335. For a magisterial account of the distinctions between criticism, analysis, and theory (and a review of the most important literature), see Joseph Kerman, *Contemplating Music: Challenges to Musicology* (Cambridge, Mass.: Harvard University Press, 1985), chapters 3 and 4.

Sonata Form in Schubert:
The First Movement of the G-Major String Quartet, op. 161 (D. 887)

◆

CARL DAHLHAUS
Translated by Thilo Reinhard

I

Despite biographical documentation, the opinion that, as an instrumental composer, Schubert stands "in Beethoven's shadow" is considered folly among the initiated. It is evident that we should not sacrifice historical fairness to a norm based on aesthetics or on compositional techniques—thus, that Schubert's lyric-epic sonata form ought not to be measured by the standards of Beethoven's dramatic-dialectic form. Yet it is difficult to understand the relationship between the theory of sonata form, which was extracted from Beethoven's oeuvre, and analyses of Schubert's work that also aspire to the realm of theory, instead of merely describing the musical surface or relying on a hermeneutic that, by dealing only with the most basic issues, pays the price of remaining hypothetical and metaphorical.

The first movement of the G-Major String Quartet (D. 887), composed in 1826 and published posthumously in 1851 as op. 161, may be regarded as epic or novelistic—in the sense used by Theodor W. Adorno in his book on Mahler—despite the numerous tremolos that characterize almost half the movement, and whose agitation hardly seems suited to the idea of epic composure. Both the principal and subsidiary groups of the exposition comprise a series of variations. Each variation breaks off more because of the constraint of sonata principles—a constraint that Schubert called to mind late enough—than because it points beyond itself and pushes ahead to the next "station" of the form. The "periods [*Zeiten*] of the form," as August Halm called them, seem to be dissolved into a timelessness: the musical moment extends immeasurably. This occurs most clearly in the subsidiary theme, which invites endless lingering, but also to a lesser degree in the principal group.

This is not to deny a functional differentiation among the variants of the main idea, whose framework is governed by the chromatic descending fourth G–F♯–F♮–E–E♭–D, the lament progression of the Baroque tradition. The four sections of the principal group can be easily characterized as antecedent (bars 15–23), consequent (bars 24–32), elaboration (bars 33–53), and transition (bars 54–63). The melodic gesture of the consequent appears as a reply to the antecedent, of which it forms a partial inversion. In the elaboration (bars 33–42), the superimposition of the rhythmic pattern of the "introduction" (bars 1–4)—which is in fact thematic, as shall be shown—and the harmonic model of the main idea can be understood as a musical chain of logic: as an expression of the idea that form is a process in which later elements grow of necessity from earlier ones. And in the fourth variant, the replacement of the falling sequence of the main idea (G–F♯/F♮–E/E♭–D) by an ascending one (G–F♯/A–G♯/B–A♯; bars 54–59) leads to a tonally remote F-sharp major, from which the D major of the subsidiary group, the traditional key, emerges in sharp relief: convention achieved by surprise.

The functional differentiation of parts, which obeys the rule of sonata form, nevertheless alters little in the basic design of successive variations, which form a cycle insofar as they draw circles, ever expanding circles, around the theme. The variation principle as such is not goal-oriented, but rather resembles a commentary "meandering" about the theme, illuminating it from different sides. And in the subsidiary group—which comprises almost a hundred bars (in a "very moderate" Allegro), thus exceeding by far every normal dimension—the four appearances of the theme are joined in the form of a circle, so that the second variation (the third appearance) is diverted to B-flat major and the third and last returns to D major. Variations 1 and 2 become longer than the theme because of a developmental extension—a sequence based on a five-bar model

(bars 90–94) referring back to the beginning of the theme—
and an epilogue (100–109), which combines liquidation of the
model with a delayed cadence. And the additional material
after variation 3 (bars 154–68) appears on the one hand as an
epilogue to the subsidiary theme (because of the analogy to 1
and 2) and on the other as the closing group of the entire
exposition.

Despite its excessive length, the development section is
little more than a paraphrase of the principal group. The antecedent is in E-flat major (bars 180–89), the consequent in E
major (bars 201–9), the elaboration at first in E minor (bars
210–31), and then in A minor (bars 234–55). A developmental
model, derived from blending the conclusion of the exposition
(bar 167) and the lament bass (bars 15–20), serves to introduce
both the antecedent and consequent (bars 168–79 and 189–200)
and is also inserted into the elaboration (bars 218–27 and
242–51). This model certainly modifies the fundamental character of the development—that of a paraphrase of the exposition by means of modulations—but does not erase it. In other
words, the development consists of further links in the chain of
variations, now involving changes of tonality. And because the
principle of variation includes the idea of an irreversible process, even the recapitulation—despite its implied tonal restora-
tion and its avoidance of interpolations—continues to transform the themes. (Since he omits variation 2, which digresses
to remote tonal areas, Schubert begins the subsidiary theme in
the subdominant; in this way he retains the effect of harmonic
surprise in the last variation, where the tonic emerges as something unexpected.)

The affinity for double variation, essential to the form of
the G-Major Quartet, can be traced back to the early history of
sonata form and continues to play a role in its later development. The treatment of the development section as a tonally
extended variation of the main theme, whose contours it delin-
eates, is related to the origin of sonata form in the suite. And in
Haydn's ever more apparent tendency toward thematic concentration, thus toward filling the functionally differentiated
stations or "periods" of the form with similar thematic material, we can recognize another condition for the proximity
of sonata and variation forms. The practice continues after

Schubert as well: in Brahms and Mahler we observe the tendency to transform symphonic sonata form, now presented in an extreme fashion, into a cycle of variations on two theme groups in regular alternation. It can therefore be said without exaggeration that the first movement of Schubert's G-Major Quartet belongs to a tradition of sonata form—a tradition, however, that deviates substantially from the evolutionary path dictated by Beethoven.

II

The tendency toward variation cycle, whereby Schubert's quartet movement deviates from Beethoven's model of sonata form, would nevertheless hardly have been possible without the profound changes in the structure of the variation chain—and in the very notion of variation—wrought by Beethoven's epochmaking "Eroica" Variations, op. 35. (Beethoven spoke of a "completely new way.") The distance from Beethoven reveals at the same time a dependence upon him.

In a literal sense it is inadequate—or at least misleading—to speak of a "theme" being varied in the principal group of the exposition of the G-Major Quartet. As in the "Eroica" Variations, the nucleus of the movement is really a "thematic configuration." The melody, bass, and harmonic-metrical scheme of Beethoven's op. 35 form nearly equal components of the "theme"; although tightly linked, they are taken up and varied independently in some of the variations. In Schubert, too, the thematic configuration embraces a multitude of elements, whose linkage and separation create a thematic process—one that evades the simple notions of statement and elaboration. The "theme" of the principal group is not a clearly outlined structure serving as a point of reference for thematic-motivic development, but rather an embodiment of characteristics that are "thematic" inasmuch as they represent starting points of a musical chain of logic. Nowhere, however, do these combine to form a shape that could be considered "the theme."

Although they function syntactically as a kind of introduction (because of their relaxed construction), bars 1–14 belong fundamentally to the exposition. The major-minor shift in the first chord, the rhythmic pattern of the opening bars,

Example 1

Example 2

and even the half-step figure of bar 5, which is separated off from bar 4—all these are "thematic" (ex. 1). The isolated half step then evolves into the ending of the melodic gesture of the principal theme (the counterpoint to the lament bass) by means of augmentation and transformation into a whole step (ex. 2). The stressed upbeat of bar 15 has been anticipated in bar 3. And the major-minor alternation extends ultimately into both the second and fourth reworkings of the principal theme: in bar 25 the minor variant (G–B♭) of the major third (G–B♮), though still recognizable, is embedded within a diminished-seventh chord (C♯–E–G–B♭); in bar 54 the major-minor shift emerges openly, once again transferred from the beginning of the introduction to the principal idea. (Like "introduction," the expression "principal idea," actually synonomous with "theme," is used here for lack of a more appropriate term. It is justified by the musical syntax if not by the substance: although bars 15–23 differ from 1–14 in their tighter organization, they form no basic thematic shape, but rather one element among others comprising the thematic configuration, a configuration whose first components have already been presented in the "introduction," on the other side of the "principal idea.")

What distinguishes the modification of a thematic configuration from the variation of a clearly delineated theme can be seen most effectively in the third and fourth versions of the principal idea. Bars 33–42 represent unmistakably a variant of bars 15–19, despite the fact that they adopt neither the melodic gesture of bars 15–19 nor the descending chromatic fourth of the bass. All that has been taken over from the principal idea, it appears, is the harmonic model, the chord progression G–D–F–C–E♭, which is now stretched to twice its length, following the example of figural variation. The rhythmic pattern, however, is derived from the introduction (bars 1–4); and the superimposition of introduction and principal idea creates retroactively a relationship between the parts, through which they reveal themselves as elements of a thematic configuration. Still, one can speak of a variant of the principal idea. On the one hand, the lament bass is perceptibly implied by the harmonic progression G–D–F–C–E♭, and on the other hand the rhythm of bar 3 represents the model for bar 15: therefore, the association between first and third versions of the principal idea is close enough to justify the notion of a transformed model.

The fourth version, finally, is based upon a two-bar phrase, imitated in stretto (bars 54–59). The major-minor alternation derives, as already mentioned, from the opening bars; bars 2 and 4 of the rhythmic pattern are contracted, or bars 43–44 (which are in themselves related to bars 2 and 4 through the mediation of bars 34 and 36) imitated in varied form; bars 43–46 are the model for imitation at the distance of a bar; and the harmonic design appears as a reflection of the principal idea, whose falling sequence (the linear progression G–F♯–F♮–E♮–E♭–D=the chord progression G–D–F–C–E♭–G) is reshaped into an ascending one (the linear progression G–F♯–A–G♯–B–A♯=the chord progression G–D–A–E–B–F♯). (Of the elements into which the lament bass can be divided—the falling half step, the sequential technique, and the direction of the sequence—two have been preserved. Thus it does not seem inappropriate to speak of a variant.)

The wealth of relationships, which renders the principal theme of the exposition comparable to a tightly knit web, can be described only if we abandon the notion of a theme—as a clearly outlined rhythmic-diastematic-harmonic shape—for that of thematic elements. We must operate instead with such categories as "alternation between major and minor third" (independent of the scale degree from which the intervals are reckoned), "rhythmic pattern" (separated from the diastematic structure), or "sequence of descending half steps" (without a specified direction of the sequence). Schubert is a composer whose musical imagination is to an exceptional degree tied to the sensuous phenomenon. It is thus surprising to find him having recourse to "abstract" elements—disengaged from the "concrete" theme or motive in which rhythmic, diastematic, and harmonic structures have grown together.

III

The concept of thematic process, which not coincidentally was invented for Beethoven's music and only later transferred to Classical-Romantic instrumental music, embraces two elements: the "logical" element of motivic-thematic derivation and the "pathetic" one of a development pressing constantly forward. Because of their inseparable amalgamation in Beethoven, it could scarcely be believed they were not associated as a matter of course. The compelling force of Beethoven's sonata form arises from the fact that the logic of musical discourse, which extracts later events from earlier ones through motivic work, developing variation, and contrasting derivation, is of the same significance as the energy that maintains the music in a state of nearly permanent intensification by means of contracted phrases, accelerated harmonic rhythm, and concentrated accents. (The tension lets up only in the arcadian moments when the music, as it were, draws a breath.) Yet Schubert's G-Major Quartet shows that consistent musical logic—the weaving of a tight fabric of motivic relaionships—is quite reconcilable with a relaxed pace and a musical attitude that, despite its agitation, remains devoid of pathos. Although the concept of a thematic process normally calls to mind the homogeneous image of both insistent energy and compelling logic, these two characteristics are in fact separable. (It would be a mistake to invoke the terminological strategem which claims that a logic spinning its web inconspicuously, instead of by inexorable syllogisms, cannot be counted as "logic," but only as mere motivic "association.")

When Schubert has the rhythm of the subsidiary theme (bar 65) emerge gradually during the principal group (bars 2, 34, 43, and 51), nothing prevents us from speaking of "contrasting derivation" [*kontrastierende Ableitung*]. The same holds true when the chromatic descending fourth, which underlies the principal idea as a *basso ostinato*, returns in the subsidiary theme as a middle voice (bars 65–69: D–C♯–C♮–B–A♯–A♮). (In the reprise of the subsidiary theme, bars 344–46, the implied chromaticism stands out clearly as a lyrical counterpoint in the bass.) To be sure, the contrasting derivation presents itself less ostentatiously than in Beethoven's F-Minor Sonata, op. 2, no. 1, in which the subsidiary theme is at once an inversion of the principal theme and a reversal of its character, so that the aesthetic transformation is in precise correlation to the technical one. But there is no reason to withhold from Schubert's procedure the term "contrasting derivation," which was coined by Arnold Schmitz for Beethoven's music. In both cases the thematic ideas display unmistakable interdependence as well as extreme diversity. And the fact that Schubert adopted the technical idea from Beethoven (the term "contrasting derivation" refers only to this specific compositional procedure) points up all the more clearly the aesthetic difference (which the nomenclature alone is hardly adequate to confirm).

The chromaticism of Schubert's subsidiary theme appears as a reflection or echo of the principal idea. The connection between the themes seems to derive not from the principal idea, whose structure determines that of the subsidiary theme (by analogy to a consequent), but rather from the subsidiary theme itself, which seizes upon a trait of the principal idea like a reminiscence. In Schubert, unlike in Beethoven, the most lasting impression is made by remembrance, which turns from later events back to earlier ones, and not by goal-consciousness, which presses on from earlier to later. (The preponderance of one factor should not, however, be taken for an exclusive status, which is impossible according to the psychology of form.) The teleological energy characteristic of Beethoven's contrasting derivation is surely not absent in Schubert, but it is perceptibly weaker. Conversely, Schubert's procedure gains an element of the involuntary: the link between the themes is not deliberately brought about; it simply happens. (This distinction is to be regarded as a statement not about the real, completed compositional process, but about the intentional, present aesthetic subject that the listener perceives as standing behind the music.)

Insofar as the character of reminiscence predominates, the contrasting derivation is similar in nature to variation technique, into which the sonata form of the G-Major Quartet dissolves. For Schubert's variation principle too is distinguished less by the dramatic emergence of consequences (like Beethoven's "completely new way" in the "Eroica" Variations) than by a certain placidity among the relationships. That an "introduction" proves in retrospect to be "thematic" means something different than in Beethoven's "Tempest" Sonata, op. 31, no. 2. In Beethoven the rhapsodic, prelude-like opening later reveals itself to have been a rudimentary expression of a principal and a subsidiary theme, which grow from the initial shapes with irresistible power. In Schubert the elements of the "introduction"—the rhythmic pattern, the isolated half step, and the major-minor alternation—are related in the way that images of recollection overlap with one another.

The wealth of motivic relationships in Schubert is as appropriate to a sonata form that tends toward variation cycle as it is to Beethoven's dialectically developmental forms. In fact, the affinity to a series of variations can be confirmed by appealing to the aesthetics of reception: the more intricate the structure that grows out of motivic relationships, the simpler the form that constitutes the supportive framework. It is precisely the simplicity of a succession of variations that renders comprehensible remote relationships that would scarcely be discernible in a rhapsodic development section, because in a variation one expects certain connections to occur at certain points. The elements of the fourth version of the principal idea in the G-Major Quartet—the major-minor alternation, the rhythmic pattern of bars 2 and 4, and the sequence model of bars 15–20 appearing in retrograde—would hardly reveal their origin if both the principal of variation and the incorporation of characteristics of the "introduction" had not already been impressed upon the listener by earlier variants.

IV

The bass of the principal idea, the falling chromatic fourth, appears in the G-Major Quartet harmonized as G–D⁶–F–C⁶–E♭–G, which deviates from the tradition of the *passus duriusculus*, as it was called in the seventeenth century. Whereas Beethoven's C-Minor Variations present the same lament bass in a tonally coherent form (see ex. 3), Schubert's version evades any labeling according to function (the difference between cadential and sequential harmony is independent of that between minor and major). The chord progression G–D–F–C originates in a scheme that is encountered more frequently as a rising sequence (C–F–D–G) than a falling one. The progression E♭–G disrupts the predictable scheme, yanking the sequence forcefully back from its progression, or regression, into the infinite: E♭–B♭⁶–D♭–A♭⁶. . .

Yet it was precisely the step into or back from the infinite to which Schubert, with his genius for letting things run their course, was drawn. And while in the exposition of the G-Major Quartet he inserts the chromatic sequence syntactically into the quadrature of phrase construction—though not without violence—and preserves at least tonally the outward appearance of closure (by means of the abrupt return to G), in the development section he ignores syntactical and tonal considerations. The descending chromatic progression of bars 168–77, generated by blending the end of the exposition and the lament bass of the principal theme (and repeated in bars 189–98, transposed up a half step), spans no less than a tenth (if one ignores the octave transfer). And the impression left by the development section is one of a largely limitless continuation, which breaks off as if by chance, not because a goal has been reached.

The harmonization of the lament bass in the exposition inspires extreme consequences in the development section: from the fragmentary juxtaposition of keys in whole-tone

Example 3

Example 4

transpositions (G: I–V^6, F: I–V^6, E♭: I) Schubert extracts a
whole-tone scale, which emerges from the interior of the sequential harmony, so to speak, and yet can no longer be justified by appeal to a traditional harmonic model (see ex. 4).

The whole-tone scale, a perplexing phenomenon in the
1820s (although the G-Major Quartet was not performed in
public until 1850), is partly, though not entirely, disguised as a
chromatic scale; upon close listening it emerges unmistakably
as the framework. And if one reckons from the neighbor notes
in between the whole steps, a pattern of 1 + 4 + 4 bars crys-
tallizes in bars 168–77 (see arrows in ex. 4): D is the final note
of the exposition, and the actual whole-tone scale, which
spans an eleventh, therefore comprises (as a model with sequence) two tritones (C–F♯ and E–B♭). But in distinction to
the chromatic descending fourth from which it originated, the
tritone progression by way of whole tones is an "extraterritorial" phenomenon within harmonic tonality. (The sequential harmony forms the intermediate link: in part tonally intan-
gible, in part integrated by custom.) Out of the sequential
harmony that Schubert impressed upon the lament bass—
and that represents the alternative to the cadential harmony of
Beethoven's C-Minor Variations—arises finally a succession of
whole tones, which descends into a tonal abyss.

The chromaticism of the development section, the endless
motion that ceases somewhere without making the turning
point its goal, is of the same nature as the succession of variations into which Schubert dissolves sonata form in the G-Major
Quartet. A tendency toward the boundless is perceptible in
both, no matter whether Schubert yields to it or represses it
under the constraint of formal principles.

What appears as involuntary occurrence nevertheless represents the outward manifestation of precise calculation; there is no question of unreflective composing. Without intense rationality, the progression from sequential harmony to a tonally extraterritorial whole-tone scale articulated in tritones would be as unthinkable as the wealth of motivic relationships, which, embedded within the framework of the variation cycle, vindicate it as the formal scheme of a sonata-allegro movement.

Schubert's Promissory Note:
An Exercise in Musical Hermeneutics

◆

EDWARD T. CONE

Hermeneutics is defined by the *Shorter Oxford English Dictionary* as "the art or science of interpretation, esp. of Scripture." It was toward the end of the last century that Hermann Kretschmar applied the word to the verbal elucidation of musical meaning, but musical hermeneutics was an art (or science) that, under one rubric or another, had long been practiced. Music, it was generally agreed, had meaning. It was an art of expression; therefore it should be possible to determine what it expressed and how. Kretschmar, with his detailed attempts at exact explanation, thus represented what might be called the dogmatic climax of a long tradition.

At the very time he was writing, however, a more formalistic view, expounded by critics like Gurney and Hanslick and furthered by theorists like Schenker, was gaining support. Indeed, for a time the purists were successful in discrediting hermeneutical methods and results—although their victories may have been due less to the force of their own logic than to a widespread reaction against the excesses of ultra-realistic program music on the one hand and of literalistic "interpretations" on the other. As a result, even those who still defended the possibility and relevance of musical expression were loath to define its nature in any specific terms.

Today, however, when it is once more acceptable to admit an interest in the subject matter and iconography of a painting, it has become increasingly feasible to discuss the putative meaning of a musical composition without evoking immediate derision. There have been a number of recent books that try, from various points of view, to come to grips with the problems involved.[1]

To be sure, not all discussions of musical meaning rely on the concept of expression. Wilson Coker, following certain semiologists, conveniently distinguished between two types of meaning: *congeneric* and *extrageneric*.[2] The first of these refers to relationships entirely within a given medium. As applied to music, it includes the significance that each part of a composition possesses through its connections with other parts of the same composition, and the significance that inheres in the composition as a whole through its employment of a recognizable sonic vocabulary organized in an appropriate manner. Congeneric meaning thus depends on purely musical relationships: of part to part within a composition, and of the composition to others perceived to be similar to it. It embraces the familiar subjects of syntax, formal structure, and style. And in fact, when the lucubrations of the recent school of musical semiologists are shorn of their pretentious jargon, that is all they are usually discussing—syntax, form, and style (and by no means always originally or even sensibly).

What will chiefly concern us, however, is extrageneric meaning: the supposed reference of a musical work to non-musical objects, events, moods, emotions, ideas, and so on. Here, obviously, we have returned, under another name, to the realm of hermeneutics, and to the problem of musical expression. On this subject there is still wide divergence of opinion; even those who vigorously defend the concept often disagree as to its nature, its range, and its limits. Whereas the relative stability of congeneric interpretations has tempted some analysts to claim that their conclusions are objectively demonstrable, it is hard to reach any consensus about the expressive or other extrageneric significance of even the simplest composition, save perhaps in the broadest terms. Writers who are clear and precise on congeneric meaning often become very fuzzy when they turn to extrageneric, even while insisting on its importance.

Coker, for example, discusses the Funeral March from the *Eroica* Symphony in terms that, with very slight modification, could equally well be applied to, say, the Funeral March from Chopin's Sonata in B-Flat Minor:

> The first part . . . is dominated by an unmistakably mournful attitude, to which the second part . . . contrasts a prevalent mood of comfort with an alleviation of sorrow and even moments of exultation. . . . The lament of the song is conveyed in gestures striving to ascend only to fall back. . . , as under the weight of sorrow. The tone of mourning is established by a number of effects: the very slow, fixed pace of the underlying march rhythm; the minor key and the long initial reiteration of the tonic triad . . . ; the prevailing lower registers . . . in fairly dense sonorities; . . . and the suppressed dynamic levels.[3]

One could continue further, omitting (as above) only the telltale measure numbers and remarks on instrumentation; for this account of extrageneric meaning, like many others, deals primarily in surface generalities. A slow, plodding pace; narrowly circumscribed melodies; somber—usually minor—harmonies in a low register: these are the immediately apprehensible characteristics of the musical surface that identify the typical funeral march, whether by Beethoven or by Chopin.

As the example shows, it is easy to assume that one has explained content when in fact one has only defined genre. Marches and dances, nocturnes and scherzi—the names suggest gestures, affects, or moods, to which certain musical characteristics are thought to be appropriate—usually broad features of tempo, meter, rhythm, mode, and the like. And such features in turn are, it is true, often accepted as defining basic types of expression. But generalizations are not enough, for surely, if a musical composition expresses anything at all, the importance of the expression must reside in its uniqueness to that composition, not in what the composition shares with a dozen others of the same genre. Specificity: that is what Mendelssohn was getting at in his oft-quoted statement: "The thoughts which are expressed to me by music that I love are not too indefinite to be put into words, but on the contrary, too definite."[4]

Surface generalities, then, can tell us only as much about

the content of a piece of music as the subject of a picture—
e.g., a Crucifixion or a still life—can tell us about its content.
Chardin and Cézanne both painted oranges and apples, but
what each expressed in his pictures was his personal vision
of the fruit. In the same way, Beethoven and Chopin produced widely differing versions of the same subject, the funeral march.[5]

Subject matter again is what is described, in a more detailed way, by the motivic vocabularies of the various types of
Figurenlehre, whether in earlier or in more recent formulations.
More detailed, and often more mechanical—yet not more specific, as Coker reveals when he employs the method to explain
the effect of the Trio of the Funeral March, which "clearly contrasts to the first [part] by giving a relief from distress and a
more encouraging attitude. Emphasis is on ascending gestures
in triads . . . and in steadfast scales rising."[6]

No; the locus of expression in a musical composition is
completely defined by neither its wider surfaces nor its more
detailed motivic contours alone, but by its comprehensive design, which includes *all* the sonic elements and relates them
to one another in a significant temporal structure. In other
words, extrageneric meaning can be completely explained
only in terms that take account of congeneric meaning. If verbalization of true content—the specific expression uniquely
embodied in a work—is possible at all, it must depend in large
part on close structural analysis.[7]

That analysis is all most of us need, most of the time. For
surely the best that can be said for the verbalization of content
is what Mendelssohn went on to add, in the quoted letter:
"And so I find in every effort to express such thoughts, that
something is right but at the same time, that something is lacking in all of them." Nevertheless, those of us who do believe in
the existence and relevance of extrageneric meaning ought to
find it uncomfortable to be in the position of insisting on the
validity of a concept that cannot be precisely defined, and instances of which are at best problematic. Once in a while we
should try to derive from the structural analysis of a composition an account of its expressive content. That is what I propose to do in the case of Schubert's *Moment musical* in A-flat,
op. 94, no. 6 (see Appendix, ex. A).

Since a complete analysis of even such a short piece—let alone a detailed treatment of its expressive content—would take much more than the available space, I shall limit my discussion to salient features that are special to this composition, and I shall try to show how their congeneric interrelations account for their extrageneric significance. I shall therefore assume agreement about certain formal aspects of the piece, taking it as established that the *Moment musical* consists of a three-part song form in A-flat major with a Trio in the subdominant, D-flat major. Its phrase articulations, harmonic progressions, and motivic manipulations are clearly defined. The opening statement consists of two balancing eight-bar phrases, each articulated 2 + 2 + 4, the antecedent cadencing on the dominant and the consequent on the tonic. The soprano line establishes the fifth degree, E♭, reaffirms it by the tonicization of V, and descends to A♭ for an authentic cadence. A pattern of suspensions set up at the outset suggests a meter of $^6_4$ underlying the notated $^3_4$; moreover it produces a little rhythmic a a b a pattern in each large phrase. All then is in order: a period exhibiting exact parallelism.

But does it? There is an arpeggiated upbeat in bar 4 that is not duplicated at the corresponding point in the consequent (bar 12). This prepares for a much more momentous element of imbalance: the descent of the bass into a lower register and the *fp* that marks the tonicization of V in bar 7. These characteristics of range and dynamics are echoed, not at the corresponding cadence at the end of the consequent, but at its midpoint, bars 10–12. Here too is a tonicization, this one effected by two chromatics: a B♮, which, like the earlier D♮, resolves normally upward, and an E♮. The arrival of the latter, replacing a previous E♭ as the resolution of the suspended F, produces another half cadence, this one on V/vi. But now the E♮ moves down to E♭, pulling an implied tonicization of vi back into the original key.

The result is to make of the prominent E♮ what I call, if the pun may be forgiven, a promissory note. It has strongly suggested an obligation that it has failed to discharge—in the present case, its function as a leading tone. Now, I do not wish to suggest that all incomplete tonicizations represent promises to be kept during the future course of the composition in

which they occur. The persistence of such an implication
depends not only on the specific context in which the progression occurs, but also on wider influences of style, both
personal and historical. I suspect, for example, that the development of nineteenth-century harmony might be analyzed
largely in terms of the increasing freedom shown by composers in their dealings with promissory situations—in the development of more and more unorthodox methods of repayment,
even in the eventual refusal to recognize the debt. (As we shall
see, that is almost the case with Schubert in the *Moment musical*.)

Normally, in music of the eighteenth and early nineteenth
centuries, promissory status is demanded, or at least requested,
by a note—or more accurately, though less paronomastically,
an entire chord—that has been blocked from proceeding to an
indicated resolution, and whose thwarted condition is under-
lined both by rhythmic emphasis and by relative isolation.
Rhythmic emphasis, of course, results from the stressed position of the chord within (or outside of) a phrase, from special
agogic or dynamic inflection, or from a combination of those.
Isolation is effected not only by the motivic detachment that
often separates such a chord from its surroundings, but also by
harmonic novelty. The promissory chord is promoted, so to
speak, by an insurrection that tries, but fails, to turn the course
of the harmony in its own new direction.

Although such chords are temporarily deprived of their
expected resolutions, the result is not, properly speaking, a deceptive cadence. What makes the standard deceptive cadence
work is the fact that the dominant chord is *almost* properly resolved; indeed, the voice leading binds it even more tightly to
its successor than in the typical authentic cadence. A promissory chord, on the other hand, is separated from what follows by a sudden switch in direction, of voice leading as well
as of harmony—and most often by a break in the rhythmic
flow, too. The combination of emphasis and separation draws
special attention to the unresolved chord and enables it to establish its influence so powerfully that it seems to require later
attention, the most obvious form of which is a prominent resolution so stated as to remind the acute listener of its connection with the promissory chord.

Closely related to the promissory situation—and, indeed, often similarly treated—is the half cadence, usually on V/vi, that sometimes concludes the development of a Classical sonata-form movement, or the entire slow movement of a Baroque sonata or concerto. Unlike the typical promissory chord, however, which appears early in a movement or a section, the secondary dominant in this case normally appears at the end of a progression that has already clarified its syntactic function. Its resolution, supplied in advance as it were, is clearly understood and requires no later confirmation (although, to be sure, that may be forthcoming anyway[8]). Look, for example, at the end of the development of the opening Allegro of Beethoven's Quartet in D, op. 18, no. 3. The reiterated V/vi in bars 154–56 is the climax of a passage in which the tonality of vi (F-sharp minor) is explicitly formulated, and in which the responsibilities of its dominant have in a sense already been discharged. The composer even gives one ample time to think that over, as he sustains the cello's C♯ for two bars before transforming it into the leading tone of the true tonic, D, and quitting the F-sharp-minor tonality for good.

Contrast now the opening Allegro of the same composer's Piano Sonata in F, op. 10, no. 2. Here the smooth progress of the movement is very soon (bars 16–18) interrupted by a sudden half cadence on V/iii—a threefold statement in an emphatic *forte*, rhythmically and motivically separate from its surroundings. What follows is a new theme in the dominant that leaves the unresolved V/iii hanging as an obvious promissory chord. It should therefore cause no surprise to find the development section beginning with a sudden shift to the mediant (almost as if the entire dominant section of the exposition had been a parenthesis). To be sure, the development might have started that way in any case; but the virtue of the promissory technique is rarely to elicit a harmony that would otherwise be missing—rather, it is to draw temporally separated sections of a work into more intimate and more interesting connection.

In the *Moment musical* no. 6, isolation and emphasis work together to produce a strong promissory effect. The pattern of rests has, from the outset, separated each motive from its fellows. That separation is exaggerated in the case that interests us, where the *subito forte*, the octave shift in the bass, and the octave doubling all draw special attention. (Contrast bars 4–8, where the descent in the bass is arpeggiated, the doublings are introduced gradually, and the *forte* occurs during the rise and fall of the $<$ *fp* $>$.)

The move toward F minor is hardly unprepared. That chord is foreshadowed in the opening: subtly embedded in the first downbeat, more frankly stated in the vi$_4^6$ of bar 3. But both of those are treated as suspensions and fail as functional harmonies. The half cadence of bars 10–12, with its strongly dominant-seeking French sixth, uncovers the concealed submediant influence. So when the concluding phrase member, dutifully remembering the demands of the true dominant of bars 7–8 suppresses the tendency toward vi and turns the E♮ downward to E♭, the E♮ remains in the ear as a troubling element of which one expects to hear more.

It is not surprising, therefore, that E♮ dominates the contrasting section of the song form. But unlike the development of the Beethoven sonata, which legitimized the foreign leading tone by an immediate reference to its tonic, this one is by no means eager to do likewise. It prefers rather to dwell on the promissory note and to investigate further its peculiar connection with E♭. The first step is to restate E♮ as F♭. In so doing, the music enlists the two other previously heard chromatic tones, B♮ (C♭) and D♮, sounding all three together in a German sixth (bars 16–17). The E♮–E♭ contrast is thus explained by reinterpretation as 6–5 in A-flat minor—a detail stated three times during the initial phrase of the development: first in the bass, next in an inner voice, and finally in the exposed soprano.

That phrase, constructed in the 2 + 2 + 4 model of its predecessors, terminates on a half cadence in A-flat minor, and its consequent at first seems to promise the expected conventional balance. But no: the F♭ reasserts its importance. Refusing to be drawn back into A-flat minor, it replaces the E♭ in i^6 in order to convert it into VI$_4^6$ (bars 28–29), thus initiating a modulation to its own key, spelled for convenience as E♮. This time it is the turn of the E♭ to assume the subsidiary role. Spelled now as D♯, it must resolve as a leading tone to E♮. The extension required to produce a convincing cadence results in the first violation of the eight-measure pattern, a phrase with one additional bar: 2 + 2 + 5. But that is not all. The final E is extended as a pedal in the bass, over which a new three-bar cadence is twice stated. The melodic and rhythmic flexibility that has gradually insinuated itself into the preceding phrases is now at its most ingratiating—by virtue not only of the three-bar format itself, but also of the triplet upbeat, the embellishing grace notes, and the chromaticism of the sinuously introduced and cancelled A♯ (bars 34–35). The melody, by completing an octave descent from the original E♮ (bars 29–33), leads into a richly sonorous lower register. The restrained, carefully measured satisfactions of the opening have been gradually transformed by the development into the more sensuous delights of a berceuse.

The return to the original key is simple: the major chord on E, by the addition of a seventh, reverts to its status as an augmented sixth on F♭ (bar 41). At the same time, the move suggests a slight uneasiness with respect to the cadence on E: was it as firm as it seemed? Was it not perhaps usurping a tonicization to which it had no right? It is significant that the key was never clinched by a clear reference to some form of subdominant. There was an obvious opportunity for a ii⁶ in bar 32 (as in ex. 1), but the offer was spurned: the retention of B in the bass converted the chord into a dominant ninth. Moreover, in bar 41, only the momentary doubling of G♯ (A♭) keeps it from being heard as a leading tone, and the entire measure as V$^{8-7}$ on E preparing for a cadence on A, with a continuation in that key (as in ex. 2). That temptation is resisted, however. The chord is interpreted as an Italian sixth, which initiates the return to A♭. At the same time, a recall of the original

Example 1

Example 2

suspension motive induces a reversion to the binary bar pattern. After two four-bar phrases (bars 40–47), the third, on a climactic *forte*, is extended to six bars by a carefully written out diminuendo-ritardando merging without cadence into the two-bar motive that inaugurates the reprise. Thus the irregularities of the development section have yielded to a version of the original pattern: 4 + 4 + 8 bars (bars 40–55) that overlap the returning 2 + 2 + 4 (bars 54–61), much as the motives of the development overlap those of the opening.

That is perhaps one reason why the reprise does not begin immediately after the arrival of the tonic in bars 46–47. There is another reason, equally important, in the F-minor harmony that introduces the transitional progression $vi^6 - vii^7 - V^{6-6}_5$ (bars 47–53). For here at last is the long-postponed discharge of the responsibilities of E♮ as a leading tone. True, the F minor is not tonicized, nor is its bass assigned to a root in the lower register; but there are significant indications of the connection nevertheless. The doublings are heavy. The *subito forte* recalls that of bars 10–12. The line, leading from F down to B♭, and forecasting an ultimate A♭, is a reinterpretation of the original descent of bars 11–16. To hear the long-range connection I am trying to establish, play the following in unbroken succession: bars $7_3 - 9_2$,[9] bars $10_3 - 12_2$, and then bars $47_3 - 53_2$ (ex. 3).

At last, then, the promise of E♮ as a leading tone has been kept. Yet how close the music came to forestalling the fulfillment! That can be demonstrated very simply by a performance that omits the passage comprising bars $47_3 - 53_2$. The result, superficially at least, is acceptable. And is there not perhaps a touch of irony in the insinuation of the problematic note once again into the descending line of bars 51–53, immediately after the emphatic proclamation of F minor? To be sure, the note now seems docile, forming a passing and passive diminished seventh instead of a recalcitrant applied dominant. At the same time, it can be taken as a signal that the road to the final cadence is not quite clear, despite the unusually felicitous re-establishment of the tonic major.

There remain two other troubling points as well. One is the nagging doubt left by the E-major cadence in bar 33: was it a completely satisfactory tonic, or did it exude a faint dominant flavor? Did the development, in giving E to its own head, perhaps encourage it to incur still further obligations? The other point looks forward to the course of the recapitulation: now that the V/vi has been satisfactorily resolved, how can it return? If it cannot, what will replace it?

What does occur, as Elizabeth Bowen says of the action of a well-constructed novel, is unforeseen in prospect yet inevitable in retrospect.[10] The first phrase of the reprise is regular; it differs from its model only in a cadence that is *f* rather than *fp*. That modification permits a *forte* consequent that retains the lower bass register and its octave doubling—a type of instrumentation appropriate to a crucial chord: an alteration of the original IV⁷ into the most painful dissonance of the entire piece. For the E♮ has returned once more, now as an F♭ that replaces the F (bar 62). This F♭, in turn, twice forces the suspended C to pass through C♭ on the way to its resolution on B♭—thereby filling in the one element missing in the chromatic descent of

Example 3

bars 51–55, and at the same time reversing the situation of bars 10–12, where it was the B♮ that had called forth the E♮.

The new combination of F♭ and C♭ is too strong to be resisted. The *fortissimo* continuation of the phrase brings them both back with a new bass, E♭♭, here spelt as D♮. That, of course, is none other than the dissonant tone of the old German sixth of bars 16–17. This time, however, it is in the powerful bass position; and this time the chord insists on being treated as a dominant, thus confirming our earlier suspicions.

The result is an expansion of the consequent phrase that is terrifying in its intensity. The phrase is, as it were, broken wide open by reiterations of the new V_2 and its resolution to a tonicized Neapolitan. A first attempt to return to the true tonic fails, interrupted again by an echo of the Neapolitan interpolation. The effect of that interpolation lingers even when the return to the tonic at last succeeds. The approach is made each time through the minor; and it is the minor color that remains in the ear, even though the final resolution is on a starkly ambiguous octave A♭. The harmonic material of the development, then, has infiltrated the reprise with devastating effect. In the same way, the rhythmic irregularity, experienced in the development as an agreeable loosening of the tight proportions of the opening, has now almost destroyed the original balance. Eight bars, 2 + 2 + 4, are answered by sixteen, but not 4 + 4 + 8: they are 2 + 2 + 5 + 7!

The final empty octave is a neat tactical device. A return to major would have produced a sudden jar after the minor i_4^6; moreover, it would have been immediately canceled by the conventional repetition of the entire section. But a minor chord would not have led into the Trio, which, construing the final A♭ as a dominant, plunges immediately into D-flat as a new tonic.

About the Trio I shall point out only that it too plays with the chromatic neighbors to the fifth degree (now G♮ and B♭♭), but in an innocuous way, as befits the unproblematical lyricism of the interlude. (In fact, even the minor third is safe here. It is heard only once—bar 97—and then enharmonically as a passing E♮, not as a true F♭). The only moment of ambiguity occurs during the little digression, when the E♭♭ and its embracing diminished seventh are given a new interpretation (bar 101) in a passage that occasions the only exception to the regularity of the phrase structure (six bars instead of the prevailing four). The following reprise can now dispense with the B♭♭ altogether, basing its consequent phrase on the unalloyed major scale.

The subdominant tonality of the Trio as a whole can be heard as the expansion of a function embedded in the opening motive of the entire piece. That initial progression, before its second chord resolves as a suspension, sounds like I–IV⁷. The impression is even stronger when the first bars, returning after the close of the Trio, echo the V–I of the D♭ cadence. Song form and Trio are bound together by the A♭–D♭ bass that introduces the Trio and that governs its departure.

The foregoing partial analysis of the structure of the *Moment musical* has also been an analysis of its congeneric meaning, for those terms are simply two ways of characterizing the same body of information. Congeneric meaning—or structural content, as I prefer to call it, stressing that identity—is precise and specific, for it is uniquely defined by a single composition. But possible extrageneric meaning—or what I call expressive content—seems to depend on choices from a bewildering array of admissible interpretations. I have coined the phrase "expressive potential" to signify this "wide but not unrestricted range of possible expression."[11] The range is wide because (*pace* those who subscribe to the more rigid versions of *Affektenlehre*) there is no rule or code by which we can translate musical gestures into exact expressive equivalents—certainly not in the sense that we can translate words into concepts, or images into objects. At the same time it must be stressed that the range is not unrestricted; for the expressive content—the human activity or state of mind adduced as an interpretation of the music—must be congruous with the structural content—the musical action itself. In other words, "we subconsciously ascribe to the music a content based on the correspondence between musical gestures and their patterns on the one hand, and isomorphically analogous experiences, inner or outer, on the other."[12] What all such experiences have in common constitutes what I call the expressive potential.

What, then is the expressive potential of *Moment musical* no. 6? What kinds of human situations present themselves as congruous with its structure? An astute reader will have noticed that my analysis has not been wholly objective. I have insinuated a few leading phrases to suggest to him the kind of expression I find in the work, and to encourage him to hear it in the same way. As I apprehend the work, it dramatizes the injection of a strange, unsettling element into an otherwise peaceful situation. At first ignored or suppressed, that element persistently returns. It not only makes itself at home but even takes over the direction of events in order to reveal unsuspected possibilities. When the normal state of affairs eventually returns, the originally foreign element seems to have been completely assimilated. But that appearance is deceptive. The element has not been tamed; it bursts out with even greater force, revealing itself as basically inimical to its surroundings, which it proceeds to demolish.

That is an account, in as general terms as possible, of the expressive potential I find in the principal song form of the *Moment musical*. When I try to relate this abstraction to a more specific situation by adducing an "isomorphically analogous experience" (always, of course, with Mendelssohn's reservation in mind), I assume the arrival of the "foreign element" to be symbolic of the occurrence of a disquieting thought to one of a tranquil, easygoing nature. Disquieting, but at the same time exciting, for it suggests unusual and interesting courses of action. As an old teacher of mine used to say (probably quoting one of the church fathers), "the first step in yielding to a temptation is to investigate it." That is what happens here. One can imagine the protagonist becoming more and more fascinated by his discoveries, letting them assume control of his life as they reveal hitherto unknown and possibly forbidden sources of pleasure. When he is recalled to duty, he tries to put these experiences behind him and to sublimate the thoughts that led to them. At first he seems successful, but the past cannot remain hidden. What was repressed eventually returns and rises in the end to overwhelm him.

The Trio, of course, tries to forget the catastrophe—just as one might try to comfort oneself in the enjoyment of art, or natural beauty, or the company of friends. The identification of the new D-flat tonic with the subdominant of the opening phrase might even be taken as symbolizing the attempted recovery of a past innocence. No matter: the Trio is doomed to failure. The memory of the original course of events is bound to recur, and the *da capo* leads inevitably to the same tragic conclusion. (Formal repetitions are often best interpreted as representations of events rehearsed in memory. A dramatic action can never be exactly duplicated; yet, as the *Moment musical* illustrates more than once, we must frequently accept literal repetitions of sections of music usually considered to be highly dramatic.)

This, then, is the personal contact I make with the psychic pattern embodied in the musical structure of the *Moment musical*. It is an example of what I have called *context*: "not the content . . . [but] the necessary vehicle of the content." For I believe that "the content of instrumental music is revealed to each listener by the relation between the music and the personal context he brings to it." [13] I can go further and suggest a more specific interpretation of that context: it can be taken as a model of the effect of vice on a sensitive personality. A vice, as I see it, begins as a novel and fascinating suggestion, not necessarily dangerous though often disturbing. It becomes dangerous, however, as its increasing attractiveness encourages investigation and experimentation, leading to possible obsession and eventual addiction. If one now apparently recovers self-control, believing that the vice has been mastered, it is often too late: either the habit returns to exert its domination in some fearful form, or the effects of the early indulgence have left their indelible and painful marks on the personality—and frequently, of course, on the body as well.

I stress this interpretation, not for any moralistic reason, but because of its bearing on the final step in my investigation. That consists in an attempt to answer what is possibly a forbidden question. What context might the composer himself have adduced? What personal experiences might Schubert have considered relevant to the expressive significance of his own composition?

In dealing with the relation of music to its composer's own emotional life, I realize that I can put forward only the most tentative of hypotheses. But I am encouraged to do so in this case by the memory of an illuminating passage from Edmund Wilson's essay on Oscar Wilde. In a discussion of the effects of the writer's syphilitic infection on his life and work, he wrote:

> Read *The Picture of Dorian Gray*, or even the best of the fairy tales, *The Birthday of the Infanta*, with the *Spirochaeta pallida* in mind. In such stories, the tragic heroes are shown in the peculiar position of suffering from organic maladies . . . without, up to a point, being forced to experience the evils entailed by them. . . . But in the end, in both cases, the horror breaks out: the afflicted one must recognize himself and be recognized by other people as the odious creature he is, and his disease or disability will kill him.[14]

It is now virtually certain that Schubert, too, suffered from syphilis.[15] The disease was probably contracted late in 1822; and although it was temporarily ameliorated by treatment, or perhaps just by time, it was, of course, in those days incurable. Did Schubert's realization of that fact, and of its implications, induce, or at least intensify, the sense of desolation, even dread, that penetrates much of his music from then on? (Our *Moment musical* dates from 1824.)[16] To be sure, a rapidly increasing emotional maturity was already in evidence—witness the contrast between the so-called "Tragic" Symphony of 1816 and the "Unfinished" (although that doom-laden score of fall 1822 may already reflect the composer's early awareness, or suspicion, of his condition). Later on a cold wind seems to blow through even some of his sunniest or most placid movements. Listen, for example, to the Andante of the String Quartet in G, to the Adagio of the String Quintet, to the Andante molto that introduces and interrupts the finale of the Octet.

Listen, above all, to the *Moment musical* no. 6. Here, if anywhere, "the horror breaks out." As Shakespeare's Edgar puts it:

> The gods are just, and of our pleasant vices
> Make instruments to plague us.

Is it too fanciful to hear a similar reaction musically embodied in the tonal structure of the *Moment musical*?

Notes

1. E.g., Leonard B. Meyer, *Emotion and Meaning in Music* (Chicago: University of Chicago Press, 1956); Deryck Cooke, *The Language of Music* (London: Oxford University Press, 1959); Donald N. Ferguson, *Music and Metaphor* (Minneapolis: University of Minnesota Press, 1960); Terence McLaughlin, *Music and Communication* (New York: St. Martin's, 1970); Wilson Coker, *Music and Meaning* (New York: Free Press, 1972); Peter Kivy, *The Corded Shell* (Princeton: Princeton University Press, 1980).

2. Coker, *Music and Meaning*, p. 61.

3. Ibid., p. 172.

4. Letter to Marc-André Souchay of 15 October 1842, repr. in *Composers on Music*, ed. Sam Morgenstern (New York: Pantheon, 1956), p. 140.

5. For further discussion of this analogy, see my "Music, a View from Delft," in *Perspectives on Contemporary Music Theory*, ed. Benjamin Boretz and Edward T. Cone (New York: Norton, 1972), pp. 57–71.

6. Coker, *Music and Meaning*, pp. 174–75.

7. It has been suggested to me (by my student Kenneth Hull) that the view expounded here is at odds with the one I defended in "Beyond Analysis" (in *Perspectives on Contemporary Music Theory* [see n. 5], pp. 72–90). There is certainly a difference in emphasis, but I consider the two as complementary rather than contradictory. True, the earlier essay was somewhat polemical, celebrating the role of "concrete" as opposed to "analytical" values. But even there I insisted that "artistic expression must involve both concrete and analytical values" (p. 85), just as here I shall illustrate, by specific example, my earlier contention that "expression, by its very definition, implies a relationship between the work of art and something else" (p. 85).

8. The Phrygian cadence that serves as a slow movement for the Third Brandenburg Concerto is a revealing exception. Whatever this progression may represent in the way of improvised cadenza or other elaboration, its isolation and rhythmic weight are sufficient to ensure the promissory status of its concluding V/vi, for which there has obviously been no opportunity of advance payment. Satisfaction comes with the first modulation in the second section of the binary finale, which introduces an extended passage in vi, punctuated by an authentic cadence (bar 16) that explicitly recalls and resolves the dominant previously left hanging. A standard developmental progression is thus imbued with wider significance.

9. I.e., from the third beat of bar 7 through the second beat of bar 9.

10. "Story involves action. Action towards an end not to be foreseen (by the reader), but also toward an end which, having *been* reached, must be seen to have been from the start inevitable." Elizabeth Bowen, *Pictures and Conversations* (New York: Knopf, 1974), p. 170.

11. Edward T. Cone, *The Composer's Voice* (Berkeley and Los Angeles: University of California Press, 1974), p. 166.

12. Ibid., p. 169.

13. Ibid., p. 171.

14. Edmund Wilson, "Oscar Wilde: 'One Must Always Seek What Is

Most Tragic,'" in *Classics and Commercials* (New York: Farrar, Straus, & Giroux, 1950), p. 341.

15. See Eric Sams, "Schubert's Illness Re-examined," *Musical Times* 121 (1980):15–22.

16. It first appeared in an *Album musical* published by Sauer and Leidesdorf in December of that year. Gary Wittlich has called my attention to the suggestive title it bore in that collection, *Les Plaintes d'un troubadour*. Perhaps the title was the publishers' invention; but one who believes it was really the composer's may well wonder whether he was not his own troubadour. See O. E. Deutsch, *The Schubert Reader*, trans. Eric Blom (New York: Norton, 1947), pp. 387–88.

Dance Music as High Art:
Schubert's Twelve Ländler, op. 171 (D. 790)

◆

DAVID BRODBECK

In December 1863 Brahms set out to have printed some un-published dances by Schubert that he had recently acquired. "I could give you a beautiful collection of 'waltzes,'" he wrote to his publisher Rieter-Biedermann. "(I would ask 50 fl., which I paid for the manuscripts.) The best of all are 12 'waltzes,' which stand in rank and file on a leaf, with quite the loveliest faces."[1] Brahms's added note that one entire dance and part of another had already seen print identifies these pieces as the Twelve Ländler, D. 790. The autograph, inscribed "Deutsches Tempo," is dated May 1823; the second dance and a transposed version of part of the eighth dance had been published in Janu-ary 1825 as op. 33, nos. 1 and 10b.[2] Henceforth I shall refer to this source as B. 47, after its registration in Maurice J. E. Brown's inventory of Schubert's dance autographs.[3]

Although Rieter agreed to Brahms's proposal, he met op-position from a Viennese competitor, C. A. Spina. The latter publisher eventually triumphed and in the summer of 1864 re-leased the dances under the title *12 Ländler (componirt im Jahre 1823) für das Pianoforte von Franz Schubert. Op. 171. Nachgelasse-nes Werk.*[4] Brahms served—anonymously—as editor. His ef-forts did not go unnoticed, however; the *Allgemeine musikalische Zeitung* not only disclosed that it was Brahms who saved the manuscript from oblivion, but also made a pointed reference to his editing, which, the journal reported, "was scrupulously limited to [producing] an accurate copy of the manuscript."[5]

That Brahms respected the integrity of B. 47 is worthy of

note. For most, if not all previous editions were compilations of dances drawn from an assortment of manuscripts.[6] Brahms was cognizant of this earlier practice and did not object to it in principle; on the contrary, in 1869 he compiled just such a collection himself, issued by J. P. Gotthard as *20 Ländler für Pianoforte . . . von Franz Schubert (Nachgelassenes Werk)*.[7] Why, then, did he take the extraordinary step five years earlier of basing an edition on a single intact manuscript? The answer, not surprisingly, reflects an apparent accord between the music in B. 47 and the editor's own aesthetic sensibilities. In brief, Brahms seems to have judged the dances in the manuscript small-scale masterpieces, which when played together make up a satisfying whole.

Rather than address the merits and flaws of Brahms's edition (the latter of which are surprisingly numerous), here I shall be concerned with the dances themselves—with the creative work of Schubert, not the redactional work of Brahms. Yet from this examination, it is hoped, will come an accounting for both the editor's high estimation of the Ländler and his decision to print them together.

I

Maurice Brown described Schubert's dance autographs as "journals" or "notebooks" in which the composer was able to try out—often during casual evenings spent improvising at the piano—new ideas and techniques that might later be developed in more substantial pieces.[8] Dance as sketch: it is a fascinating concept, but one whose outlines Brown himself only adumbrated. This is not the place to elaborate his idea, or to dispute it. The subject arises here only because Brown's solitary example concerns D. 790, no. 6, which he paired with the scherzo of the "Death and the Maiden" String Quartet. To be sure, the dance, written in May 1823, and the scherzo, composed ten months later, are in very different keys (G-sharp minor and D minor). Yet long stretches of the pieces are otherwise identical (cf. bars 1–8 and 9–16 of the dance, and bars 9–16 and 23–30 of the quartet).

Brown probably did not intend the term "sketch" to be

taken literally, for, as he must have seen, the Ländler is a fully achieved work. In it, for example, Schubert skillfully restricts the statement (but not the strong implication) of tonic harmony, and throughout the piece he employs poignant, frequently unprepared dissonances. Thus the opening chords, iv–V–V/iv–iv, are colored respectively by a 7–6 suspension, a 4–3 suspension, a minor ninth, and a double appoggiatura (ex. 1a). In the analogous passage in the second part of the dance, this delicate material is transformed to display a contrary character (ex. 1b). Most obvious is Schubert's replacing of the quiet dynamics, legato touch, and restricted compass with loud dynamics, detached mode of performance, and wide range. More subtle is his reworking of earlier motivic materials. The "circling" motive, appearing at the outset in the inner parts and set sharply there against the bass line, recurs in varied form in part 2, where it appears in the lowest voice and actually incorporates all but the first note of the old bass line (cf. the lower analytical staves in exx. 1a and b). Similarly, the melody and remaining voice in the right-hand part of bars 1–4 reappear in a different disposition in the later passage. Strikingly enough, this variation is accomplished by invertible counterpoint at the octave (cf. the upper analytical staves in ex. 1). Likewise, the harmony is redefined. The ninth bar corresponds to the first but is a tonic $^6_4$ chord, not a first-inversion subdominant chord. Here the D♯, which was a suspended dissonance in bar 1, is a harmonic tone, and the C♯, once the note of resolution, is a neighbor note. By the same token, bar 12, corresponding to the fourth bar, unfolds not a root-position IV chord, but an applied dominant chord that functions sequentially.

Even the form of the dance—unique, so far as I know—demonstrates Schubert's studied use of dramatic reinterpretation. Part 1 comprises two four-measure units (a + b = A), each of which is doubled in length in part 2 to produce a sixteen-bar period (a′ + b′ = A′). Most of Schubert's dances, by contrast, are in more usual binary or rounded binary forms and present melodies set above simple accompaniments in stereotypical dance rhythms. In several respects, therefore, the dance at hand can be looked upon as representing an "advance" in Schubert's style. It is more daring even than the scherzo later

*Example 1 (a) D. 790, no. 6, bars 1–4; (b) D. 790, no. 6, bars 9–12; (c)
D-Minor String Quartet (D. 810), Scherzo, bars 1–12.*

modeled on it (ex. 1c). Although the remarkable opening measures of the piano piece were taken over into bars 9–12 of the quartet, they are preceded there by a passage that establishes the tonic in the most patent way and thereby robs the borrowed material of much of its original mystery. The dance, in short, is a miniature masterpiece wherein Schubert's ambitions were consummately realized.

The two parts of the eleventh Ländler are also related as statement and varied restatement. Here, however, Schubert's revision is more extreme, cutting to the harmonic core: chords that arose as products of contrapuntal elaboration in the first part reappear beneath melodic structural tones in the second. Example 2 illustrates this rather complex state of affairs. In the original statement of the material, the nonstructural e♮″ and d♮″ are supported by the dyads c′–e♮′ and b♮′–d♮′, which merely act as neighbor chords to the structural harmonies (ex. 2a). Both these tones and their supporting dyads recur in analogous positions within the restatement, but now the melodic tones are structural and the dyads components in applied harmonies (ex. 2b).

The transformation of nonstructural tones into structural ones is but part of the tale of Schubert's revision. Actually, the dissimilar surfaces of the melodies in bars 1–4 and 9–12 result from different unfoldings of the same set of tones (e♭″–e♮″– f″–d♮″–e♭″). Here again the notes e♮″ and d♮″ are conspicuous. Originally chromatic neighbor notes, in part 2 they first occur as consonances (bars 9 and 11); yet in bars 10 and 12 they revert to their original form, becoming dissonant and, as before, leading respectively to f″ and e♭″.

Example 2   D. 790, no. 11, harmonic sketch: (a) bars 1–4; (b) bars 9–12.

Example 3   D. 790, no. 11, motivic-rhythmic analysis.

Of equal importance to this imaginative application of what might be called "structural variation" is Schubert's use of what Schoenberg termed "developing variation," whereby a theme is built by subjecting a small number of motives to continual modification. In the first phrase each of the note pairs e♮″–f″ and d♮″–e♭″ coheres in a trochaic motive that becomes the basis of subsequent material (ex. 3, motive a). The figure recurs in varied form in bars 5–8 (b), where the melodic direction is reversed; now it embraces three different tones and, most important, begins on the weak beat and is iambic. The motivic evolution reaches its final stage in the second half of the dance, nearly all of whose melody derives from the two versions of the figure in the first period (c).

One new development is the acciaccatura that precedes each statement, another the slurring of the three notes; both contribute to the impression that the downbeat in the right hand has shifted to the middle of the measure—a displacement first hinted at when the motive began on the second beat in bar 5. Significantly, this melody binds salient features of both earlier versions of the motive: the rhythm is trochaic (as in bars 1 and 3), but the pattern begins on the middle beat (as in bars 5–8). The accompaniment, however, persists in presenting the meter directly, and right-hand and left-hand parts are thus out of phase, a touch that Brahms would surely have savored.

II

The charm and graciousness of numbers 6 and 11 are very much in keeping with Schubert's style. What is not typical about them is also what is most striking: their complexity and refinement of detail. Why this qualitative difference between the Twelve Ländler and other collections? Probably it derives from a dissimilarity in compositional circumstances. By and large Schubert's dances—more than 400 in number—were occasional pieces, created spontaneously at parties for the enjoyment of friends. In the words of Josef von Spaun, Schubert "from time to time . . . surprised us dancing enthusiasts with the most beautiful *Deutsche Tänze* and *Écossaises*, which were the fashion at that time." And from Leopold von Sonnleithner we learn that the composer "was always willing to sit down at the piano, where for hours he improvised the most beautiful waltzes; those he liked he repeated, in order to remember them and write them out afterwards."[9]

The by-products of these evenings were hundreds of engaging "written-out improvisations." But it is difficult to believe that the pieces in B. 47 are fruits of that kind. In the first place, the subtle manner of the dances implies that Schubert spared no time and none of his abilities. Moreover, the state of the autograph suggests that the dances were more soberly conceived and executed than those in other manuscripts. If, as seems probable, one sign of the casual origin of many of Schubert's dance autographs is their lack of title, date, and signature, then the inscriptions at the head of B. 47 ("Deutsches Tempo[.] Mai 1823 [.] Frz. Schubertmpia"), before its first dance ("Pianoforte"), and after its last dance ("Fine") might indicate a more formal origin. At all events, the layout of the manuscript—a bifolium with a single inserted leaf, all of which is filled—implies that Schubert knew beforehand how much space he would be likely to need; it shows, that is, a measure of planning.

This planning is also reflected in the order of the dances,

Table 1   *Twelve Ländler, D. 790*

		Tonal Groups			Form	
	Key	D	B and A♭/G♯		Scheme[a]	Length[b] (bars)
1	D	I			$\|{:}16_A^{\,V}\,20_B^{\,I}{:}\|$	72
2	A	V			$\|{:}8_A^{\,vi}\,16_B^{\,I}{:}\|$	48
3	D	I			$\|{:}8_A^{\,I}\,8_B^{\,I}{:}\|$	32
4	D	I			$\|{:}8_A^{\,I}\,8_B^{\,I}{:}\|$	32
5	b/B	vi/VI	i/I	iii/III	$\|{:}8_A^{\,III}\,16_{BA'}^{\,I}{:}\|$	48
6	g♯		vi	i	$\|{:}8_A^{\,V}\,16_{A'}^{\,i}{:}\|$	48
7	A♭		VI	I	$\|{:}8_A^{\,I}+8_{A'}^{\,VI}\,16_{BA''}^{\,I}{:}\|$	48
8	a♭		vi	i	$\|{:}8_A^{\,i}\,16_{BA'}^{\,'i}{:}\|$	48
9	B		I	III	$\|{:}8_A^{\,V}\,8_B^{\,I}{:}\|$	32
10	B		I	III	$\|{:}8_A^{\,vi}\,8_B^{\,I}{:}\|$	32
11	A♭		VI		$\|{:}8_A^{\,I}\,8_B^{\,I}{:}\|$	32
12	E			I	$\|{:}8_A^{\,I}\,14_B^{\,I}{:}\|$	44

a. The Arabic numerals indicate the number of measures in the period; the Roman numerals indicate the cadential goal of the period.

b. Including repetitions.

which is by no means arbitrary (table 1). Schubert flanked numbers 2–11, each of which has the orthodox length of thirty-two or forty-eight bars, with two formally anomalous dances. Discussion of the last dance will be put off until later, but at this point we might briefly consider the opening number. Because of its comparatively large dimensions—at seventy-two bars it is the second most extensive dance in Schubert's *oeuvre*— as well as the unusual phrase lengths of its second period (ten bars + ten bars), this dance does much to establish the composer's high aspirations. But the long-range role of the dance becomes apparent only as the succeeding ones unfold. When we ultimately learn that pieces with more common and ordinary dimensions typify the collection, we understand in retrospect that the first number stands apart, at least with respect to form. In a sense, then, this piece, aptly described elsewhere as an "Invitation to the Dance," sets the stage for the main event—a series of pieces in more modest dance forms.[10]

In view of this hierarchic principle, it is not suprising that B. 47 displays a high degree of tonal coherence. Numbers 1–4 form a rounded tonal group in D, numbers 5–11 a group focused on the keys of B and A-flat (see table 1).[11] The first dance tonicizes the dominant at the end of the first period, thus anticipating the key of number 2. This relationship is, of course, common enough; more unusual, and therefore unexpected, is the tonicization of the submediant G-sharp minor in number 10, which prefigures the key of the eleventh dance (in A-flat) and underscores the importance of the axis between B and A-flat/G-sharp. The fifth dance, significantly, couples the two groups. The tonic of its first period, B minor, is the relative key of the preceding dance; the tonic of its last period, B major, is the relative key of the following one. This number also strengthens the tie between the tonal groups in another way: the mediant (D)—the key of numbers 1, 3, and 4—is tonicized at the end of part 1.

The first eleven dances display motivic coherence as well. Numbers 3 and 4, for example, constitute an "organic" pairing. Both are formed out of two eight-measure periods, each of which culminates in a tonic cadence, and both contain prominent chromatic sequences and applied diminished-seventh chords. In addition to these shared traits—which are admit-

Example 4   (a) D. 790, no. 3, bars 15–16; (b) D. 790, no. 4, bars 1–2.

tedly stylistic commonplaces—there is a more significant relation. The melody at the outset of number 4 is a retrograde version of that ending number 3, the last three notes of the one
dance being turned around to form the first three of the other
(ex. 4). The eighth-note motive in the penultimate measure of
the third number is similarly echoed in the second measure
of number 4. The later dance thus seems to grow directly out
of its predecessor.

On the matter of motivic relationships we might let the
editor himself speak, through a remark made in a letter to
Adolf Schubring in June 1865. Apparently, Schubring had
asked whether Brahms knew that the second parts of D. 790,
no. 8, and op. 33, no. 10, were identical but for their keys
(A-flat minor and A minor). Brahms exclaimed: "Something
by Schubert to have escaped me! And that I should not have
known the beautiful A-minor waltz in the German dances [op.
33, no. 10]! But this new first part [in my edition] is exactly
what is of interest." [12]

What was meant by this remark? For one thing, given the
predilection for motivic connections demonstrated by Brahms
the composer, we can presume that as editor he found gratify-
ing the relation between the patterns of structural tones in the
first part of the eighth dance in B. 47 and its immediate predecessor (ex. 5). (The structural tones in op. 33, nos. 9 and 10,
significantly, bear no relation to one another.) Brahms would
also have appreciated the tonal bond between the seventh and
eighth dances in B. 47 (A-flat/A-flat minor). In other words,
he probably preferred the A-flat-minor version of the dance
largely because of its tonal and motivic echoes of the dance that
immediately precedes it.

Example 5 Melodic-structural tones: (a) D. 790, no. 7, bars 1–4; (b) D. 790, no. 8, bars 1–4.

Example 6 (a) D. 790, no. 8, bars 1–4; (b) D. 790, no. 8, bars 17–18; (c) op. 33, no. 10, bars 1–4; (d) op. 33, no. 10, bars 17–18.

But the editor would have had additional reasons for his choice. The version in B. 47 is superior to the earlier published version both in its dissonance treatment and its internal motivic connections. Prominent neighbor notes, which characterize the melodies in both versions, are given expressive harmonic support only in B. 47 (ex. 6a and c). Thus in the A-flat-minor setting d♮″ is harmonized with a French-sixth chord, and g♮″ forms part of a diminished-seventh chord sounded over a tonal pedal point; by contrast, in op. 33 similar melodic dissonances merely clash against tonic and dominant chords.

A closer relation between sections is also noticeable in B. 47. The French-sixth chord, heard in the opening phrase as a neighbor chord, recurs in part 2, now as a true chromatic preparation for the dominant (bars 11 and 15). Furthermore, in B. 47 (but not in op. 33) the first phrase of the dance is recast to form the final phrase (cf. ex. 6a–b with ex. 6c–d). In other words, the two parts of D. 790, no. 8, are comparatively more cohesive than those of op. 33, no. 10. In B. 47 Schubert maximized coherence at once within the dance and between it and its neighbor.

To point out the various tonal and motivic connections between dances is not necessarily to demonstrate the "unity" of the collection. Although the dances follow one another agreeably, they do not imply a specific conclusion; one piece, or ten pieces, or some other number, could conceivably follow the eleventh dance. Accordingly, if the last dance, number 12, secures closure, it does so not by realizing any long-range implication, but by being saturated, so to speak, with numerous features having closural force. Put in different terms, should the final dance be markedly closed, it would bring the entire set to a satisfactory conclusion.[13]

The anomalous tonal center of number 12 (E) obviously checks the prevailing implication of numbers 5–11 that the key of each dance will be B or A-flat (or the parallel mode of either key). Yet that says nothing about the direction that the cycle might take. This new course soon becomes apparent, however. Unlike the other dances, number 12 begins with an archetypal cadence, thus signaling not continuation but closure (ex. 7a); and as the dance progresses the impression of having reached the end of the series is reinforced. The opening cadence is, extraordinarily, the source of almost all subsequent material. In

Example 7   D. 790, no. 12: (a) bars 1–2; (b) bars 19–22.

part 1 it is repeated in bars 3–4, varied slightly in bars 5–6, and sounded again in bars 7–8; the material in part 2 is similar. The unusual disjunct melody of the dance also contributes substantially to the growing sense of finality. Instead of a real tune, Schubert merely provides an arpeggiated animation of the upper three voices of the cadential harmonies. This melody thus has no long-range goals; its motion is only local and is played out against the static background of the reiterated V–I cadences.

As a concomitant of this integrated melodic-harmonic pattern, the tonal vocabulary of the dance is unusually diatonic. This simplified stock of pitches also suggests impending termination, as do two other "natural" signs of closure: the quiet dynamics (*pp*) and uniformly thin, uncomplicated texture. Closure, finally, is enhanced—settled, actually—in the last four measures, wherein the original form of the opening cadence twice recurs (ex. 7b). The loud return of material signals completion; its quiet echo, rewritten to allow of a tonic chord on the final downbeat, clinches it.

Still, Schubert's decision to end in E remains something of a mystery. Of course, the composer could have achieved long-range closure by ending in the key of the opening number (D). In any event, the concatenation of closural features in number 12 leaves little doubt that the placement of it last in the manuscript was a calculated act, one intended in its own way to impart closure to the entire collection.

III

In spite of the evident relations among the dances, it might be argued that B. 47 displays in essence a paratactic, or additive, structure—that is, that its coherence does not depend upon the sequential arrangement of its components.[14] Each of the dances is an integral whole, and though the opening and closing numbers have features appropriate to their positions—number 1 is a *préambule*, number 12 provides a satisfactory conclusion—the dances *could* be interchanged or even taken out of context altogether without risking incomprehensibility. Nevertheless, the ten inner dances show traces of a sequential structure, comprising linked tonal groups and motivically related pairs. Thus to interchange dances would be to do violence to the characteristics of the set most attractive to a mind attuned to "organicism" in art.

Brahms had such a mind. And thus, it would seem, he had no will to violate the integrity of his source—no reason to omit, transpose, or reorder any of the dances, or to interpolate extrinsic ones, all of which earlier editors had done as a matter of course. Perhaps we can now understand why Brahms described the set as twelve dances "in rank and file on a leaf, with quite the loveliest faces." The subtle style of the pieces must have prompted the second half of this description. Brahms's striking metaphor of military order, by contrast, was probably induced by the "framing" quality of the outer dances, as well as by the tonal and motivic relations existing among the inner ones. For though the Ländler do not form a unified cycle of character pieces in the manner, let us say, of Schumann's *Carnaval*, they are nonetheless distinguished miniatures displaying many aesthetically significant interconnections.

Finally, let us turn our attention again to Schubert and to the eleventh dance. As Nicholas Temperley has observed, this piece begins with a striking prolongation of the dominant, comprising the voice leading $^{8-9}_{6-7}$ over a dominant pedal (i.e., a "tonic $^6_4$" without the tonic note, followed by a dominant-ninth chord without a third or fifth; see ex. 2). Temperley mentions the dance only in passing, as but one example of Schubert's use of the unusual $^8_6$ chord, which he attributes to a deep influence upon the composer of Beethoven's Seventh Symphony. Nonetheless, Temperley's pointed observation that in the Ländler the Beethovenian chord appears in a "progression . . . intensified to a point of anguish, both by the use of a $^9_7$ and by chromaticism," occasions us to take pause.[15] "Anguish"— in a dance?

One of the saddest facts of Schubert's life—his contracting of syphilis late in 1822—may explain this paradox and, at all events, dispels any notion that the dances might be the products of an evening's entertainment.[16] During the month in which the Ländler were written, May 1823, the composer suffered the throes of an early exacerbated phase of his fatal disease. It is improbable, accordingly, that Schubert made all his usual social rounds at this time; indeed, at least part of this month was spent in the hospital. Very likely, then, the dances in B. 47 were not produced casually in the cheerful company of friends, but were, on the contrary, more "normal" artistic products, thoughtfully written when the composer was, in more than one respect, very much alone. Whatever hope Schubert might have held earlier for a return to good health seems to have been dashed by his outbreak of symptoms in the spring of 1823, and on 8 May he composed "Mein Gebet," a feverish poem replete with images of inescapable doom.[17] If the excruciating tone of Schubert's verse is not matched in each of the Twelve Ländler, this contemporaneous set of dances nevertheless penetrates feelings seldom hinted at in other collections. Whence, in part, the title of this essay: D. 790 is composed not of lighthearted improvisations set down on paper, but rather of deeply felt works of high art.

Notes

1. "Ich könnte Ihnen eine schöne Sammlung 'Walzer' geben (50 fl. erbäte ich mir, die ich für die Manuskripte gab). Vor allem stehen 12 'Walzer' auf einem Blatt in Reih und Glied, die ganz allerliebste Gesichter haben." Johannes Brahms, *Briefwechsel*, vol. 14, ed. Wilhelm Altmann (Berlin: Deutsche Brahms-Gesellschaft, 1920), p. 82. Brahms's activity as an editor of Schubert's dances is discussed in my Ph.D. dissertation, "Brahms as Editor and Composer: His Two Editions of Ländler by Schubert and His First Two Cycles of Waltzes, Opera 39 and 52" (University of Pennsylvania, 1984), chapters 1, 2, 4, and 5. Parts of the present essay have been adapted from that study.

2. Brahms left this source, along with most of the rest of his collection of autographs, to the archive of the Gesellschaft der Musikfreunde (catalogue no. A 262).

3. Maurice J. E. Brown, "The Dance-Music Manuscripts," in his *Essays on Schubert* (New York: St. Martin's Press, 1966), p. 238.

4. Brahms's correspondence with Rieter from the winter of 1863–64 (*Briefwechsel* 14:81–87) depicts the composer as an intermediary between the two publishers. Although Spina, who at that time claimed the rights to all Schubert's music, wrested control of the dances, Rieter and Brahms later collaborated in the first editions of the piano score of the Mass in E-flat (D. 950, 1865), and the *Drei Clavier-Stücke* (D. 946, 1868).

5. "Seine [Brahms's] Redactionsarbeit beschränkte sich gewissenhaft auf eine getreu Abschrift des Manuscripts." "Zwei Schubert-Novitäten aus Spina's Verlag," *Allgemeine musikalische Zeitung* 2 (1864), col. 872.

6. See Brown, "Dance-Music Manuscripts," p. 219. Schubert's role in his own editions is uncertain. In preparation for the first published set, which A. Diabelli and Co. released in late 1821 as the *Original Tänze*, op. 9, the

composer set down the incipits of nine dances on the back of the arietta *La pastorella al prato* (D. 528, B. 20), and wrote out the melodies of six others on the back of the part song *Ruhe* (D. 635, B. 31). But only some of the fifteen dances in these "memoranda" were printed, and most of those in a different version. By the same token, many of the dances in the autographs containing complete pieces found in op. 9 were held back from the edition. Some appeared in 1823 in Diabelli's next set, op. 18, but others were left unpublished in Schubert's lifetime altogether.

Op. 18 occasioned a dispute between Schubert and Diabelli, which led the composer to seek other publishers. Thus the next edition, op. 33, appeared in 1825 with Cappi and Co. The change in publishers did not alter editorial policy, however; the dances in this set were likewise drawn from many sources, including, as we have seen, B. 47. Although Schubert might have supervised the organization of opp. 9, 18, and 33, it is doubtful that he played any role whatsoever in the next three sets, opp. 49, 50, and 67; for these appeared in 1825 and 1826 with Diabelli, with whom Schubert no longer had any dealings. Since the only dated source for these prints (B. 45) was written in February 1823, just before Schubert left Diabelli, it is reasonable to assume that the manuscripts upon which the publisher based his editions were acquired in earlier years, and that in all likelihood Schubert had nothing to do with the prints.

Much less can be inferred about opp. 77 and 91, published by Haslinger in 1827 and 1828; no handwritten sources or any other documents that might shed light on the question of Schubert's involvement have been preserved. For a somewhat elliptical discussion of Schubert's approach to grouping dances, made confusing by its failure always to distinguish between the composer's and his publishers' sets, see Paul Mies, "Der zyklische Charakter der Klaviertänze bei Franz Schubert," in *Bericht über den Internationalen musikwissenschaftlichen Kongress, Wien, Mozartjahr 1956*, ed. Erich Schenk (Graz: H. Böhlaus Nachf., 1958), pp. 408–11; Mies's conclusion that the editions published in Schubert's lifetime were not coherent cycles, it seems to me, is surely correct.

7. On the Twenty Ländler, see Brodbeck, "Brahms as Editor and Composer," chapters 4 and 5, and idem, "Brahms's Edition of Twenty Schubert Ländler: An Essay in Criticism," in *Brahms Studies: Papers Delivered at the International Brahms Conference, The Library of Congress, Washington, D.C., 5–8 May 1983*, ed. George S. Bozarth (London: Oxford University Press, forthcoming).

8. Maurice J. E. Brown, *Schubert: A Critical Biography* (New York: St. Martin's Press, 1958), p. 230; and idem, "Dance-Music Manuscripts," p. 218.

9. Otto Erich Deutsch, *Schubert: Memoirs by His Friends*, trans. Rosamond Ley and John Nowell (New York: Macmillan, 1958), pp. 133 and 121.

10. Alfred Einstein, *Schubert: A Musical Portrait* (1951; repr. New York: Da Capo Press, 1981), p. 216. Schumann later did something similar in *Carnaval*, whose lengthy first number—entitled "Préambule"—is followed by a series of shorter character pieces.

11. The final Ländler, in E, is not a member of the two interlocking

tonal groups. This move to a "foreign" key at the end may, as we shall see, have significance for our understanding of the set as a whole.

12. "Mir soll bei Schubert etwas entgangen sein! Und ich sollte den schönen a moll-Walzer in den Deutschen Tänzen nicht wissen! Aber dieser neue erste Teil ist gerade deshalb interessant." *Briefwechsel*, vol. 8, ed. Max Kalbeck (Berlin: Deutsche Brahms-Gesellschaft, 1915), pp. 206–7. For a clarification of Kalbeck's erroneous editorial remarks concerning this passage, see Brodbeck, "Brahms as Editor and Composer," p. 91 (n. 26).

13. As Barbara Herrnstein Smith has observed, many poems are brought to an end in a comparable fashion, with a final stanza that makes reference "to any of the 'natural' stopping places of our lives and experiences—sleep, death, winter, and so forth." Such allusions "tend to give closural force when they appear as terminal features in a poem" (*Poetic Closure: A Study of How Poems End* [Chicago: University of Chicago Press, 1968], p. 102). The musical analogues to such images are "closural signs," which can involve tonal harmony and tonal pitch (e.g., the harmonic progression $I_4^6 - V^7 - I$, and the melodic motion $\hat{3} - \hat{2} - \hat{1}$), as well as elements like registral pitch, dynamics, and tempo (e.g., descending lines, decreasing dynamics, and slackening tempo). Leonard B. Meyer has termed the former "syntactic" signs, the latter "natural" signs; see "Toward a Theory of Style," in *A Concept of Style*, ed. Berel Lang (Philadelphia: University of Pennsylvania Press, 1979), pp. 3–44; see also Robert George Hopkins, "Secondary Parameters and Closure in the Symphonies of Gustav Mahler" (Ph.D. dissertation, University of Pennsylvania, 1983), pp. 1–104.

14. For discussion of paratactic and sequential poetic structures, see Smith, *Poetic Closure*, pp. 98–139.

15. Nicholas Temperley, "Schubert and Beethoven's Eight-Six Chord," *19th-Century Music* 5 (1981): 149.

16. The most thorough account of Schubert's disease is Eric Sams, "Schubert's Illness Re-examined," *Musical Times* 121 (1980): 15–22. Edward T. Cone has drawn a fascinating (and surely provocative) connection between the tonal structure of the *Moment musical*, op. 94, no. 6, and the emotional side effects of the disease ("Schubert's Promissory Note: An Exercise in Musical Hermeneutics," included in this volume). I hasten to add that nothing like Cone's specific, extrageneric analysis is intended here.

17. Schubert's poem can be found in O. E. Deutsch, *The Schubert Reader*, trans. Eric Blom (New York: Norton, 1947), p. 362.

A Romantic Detail in Schubert's *Schwanengesang*

JOSEPH KERMAN

Ihr Bild is one of two Schubert songs to which Heinrich Schenker devoted an entire essay. Schenker was evidently fascinated by the gigantic simplicity of the piece, of the first two notes:

Two measures serve as introduction:

Certainly one should not already discern a motif here; so the question arises: what other goal do these notes have to fulfill? Do they simply lead into the tonality, or perhaps prefigure the opening note in the voice, or both? However this may be, and in any case, one has to ask further why the Master sounded the same note *twice*, when it would have been perfectly possible to have simply held it through two bars. As a matter of fact, it is only the answer to this question that brings us to the solution of the puzzle. To repeat each note in slow tempo, and what is more to re-peat it in this manner after a rest, amounts to "staring" at it, as it were; and in doing this, we feel ourselves wonder-fully transported to the side of the unhappy lover, who stands "in dark dreams" staring at the picture of his be-loved. With him, we too stare at the picture. A simple de-vice, is it not, this placement of a repetition, separated by a rest, for a note held through two bars. Yet it takes a genius—it is only granted to a genius—to grasp the difference between such possibilities, as also (above all) to plunge himself into the very midst of the spiritual experience with a force that can yield a device of this kind. Thus with his very first stroke Schubert shows himself the true magician who binds a secret thread around the exterior situation (here, the staring at a picture), around the soul of the unhappy lover, and around us—a thread that invests the experience with an eternal prospect full of ever-new immediacy, over and above the single manifestation.[1]

Schenker's leap from the two B♭s to the notion of "staring" is a breathtaking one, which many readers will find hard to follow, even if they consider possible cognate meanings in *starren*, *stare*, *stern*, and *stark*. Nevertheless, the fanciful paragraph was worth writing, and it is worth reading both for what it suggests about Schubert and for what it tells about its author. When a musical analyst senses that his regular tools will work no further, it is better for him to stammer out some of his instinctive response to the music, rather than to decree that such talk is "literally meaningless" and leave the passage unglossed. The two B♭s are remarkable and evocative; clearly Schenker was on to something. Clearly, he did not get to the bottom of it. Perhaps this is a case where the analyst's insight can be helped along by comparative information, from outside the single piece itself.

More is involved, certainly, than establishment of the tonic. That function we might call the lowest common denominator of the piano introduction in all but a handful of Schubert's songs.[2] In his later work—let us say the 250-odd songs written after 1819—Schubert almost invariably established and articulated the tonic by means of a full anticipatory phrase. What is anticipated is the piano figuration to come, and something of the initial melodic outline, and in many cases also some later events in the song, generally of a harmonic nature. This norm includes all but one of the *Winterreise* songs, for instance. But it does not stretch very comfortably to include *Ihr Bild*, nor several of its companions among the songs of Schubert's last year.

Earlier, Schubert had often done without a piano introduction altogether—an economy that he lived to avoid studiously, and to regret; after 1821, on the few occasions when he published an old song lacking a piano introduction, Schubert would compose one anew.[3] Or sometimes he had written a small stretch of piano figuration all on the tonic, amounting to something less than a phrase. (*Gretchen am Spinnrade* is the famous example; the only late ones are *Willkommen und Abschied* [D. 767], *Wohin?* [from *Die schöne Müllerin*], *Der blinde Knabe* [D. 833], and *Hippolits Lied* [D. 890].) Or else he had merely struck a tonic chord or two. This seems a poor excuse for an introduction, though occasionally it may be granted some poetic justification in the suggestion of chords strummed by way of intonation, before the harpist embarks upon his lay. Is *Ihr Bild* some kind of sophisticated throwback to this type of introduction—which indeed "simply leads into the tonality"? Among the mature songs are a few—a very few—instances of such throwbacks (see ex. 1). Here one would speak just barely of figuration anticipated, or at least of motion begun; and one would have to reckon on the air of assumed simplicity that informs the entire *Schöne Müllerin* cycle. Nothing of the kind characterizes *Ihr Bild*.

A distant but more revealing precedent for *Ihr Bild* may be found in *Gondelfahrer* (D. 808), an unassuming but deft little song written in March 1824. The piece is not well known—it does not appear in the seven volumes of the Peters edition— but it has its modest anecdotal fame as the last song set to words by Mayrhofer. During 1818–20, when they roomed together, and even before, the gloomy poet had played a major role in Schubert's development as an artist; now Schubert was drawing away.

As always, this piano introduction (ex. 2) establishes the tonic—but with a little more than a chord, and less than a phrase. A single harmony moves to the tonic, and the progres-

Example 1   *(a)* Trockne Blumen; *(b)* Der Müller und der Bach

Example 2   Gondelfahrer

sion is repeated exactly (a pattern that may be diagrammed T—x-T—x-T̂). Technically, "x" may be thought of as a type of plagal cadence, or as an appoggiatura chord, or as a stressed auxiliary chord, resolving to the tonic. The heart of the matter, however, seems to be the sensuous quality of the particular progression. The concept is fully Romantic, the intent "poetic": indeed, Schubert's impetus was not purely musical but illustrative in a very simple way. The poem runs as follows (italics mine):

> Es tanzen Mond und Sterne
> Den flücht'gen Geisterreih'n;
> Wer wird von Erdensorgen
> Befangen immer sein!
>   Du kannst in Mondesstrahlen
> Nun, meine Barke, wallen,
> Und aller Schranken los
> Wiegt dich des Meeres Schooss.
>   *Vom Markusthurme tönte*
> *Der Spruch der Mitternacht;*
> Sie schlummern friedlich Alle,
> Und nur der Schiffer wacht.

> [The moon and the stars are dancing the fleeting round dance of the spirits. Who will ever be possessed by earthly cares?
>   My boat, you can now float in moonbeams; and free of all bonds, you will be cradled by the lap of the sea.
>   From the tower of St. Mark's chimed the knell of midnight. Everyone is sleeping peacefully, and only the boatsman is wakeful.]

After the introduction Schubert avoided A♭ (or anything at all on the flat side) up to the ninth line, where he abruptly brought in A-flat triads again, *ppp* and *arpeggiando*, dutifully echoing out twelve times to mark the midnight hour. In the autograph, Schubert actually numbered the A♭s from 1 to 12.[4] This is a Venice quite in E. T. A. Hoffmann's spirit, with deep, veiled, Romantic chimes sounding across the canals to Mayrhofer's meditative gondolier. The same device, in the same key, but without the forecasting introduction, occurs in Schubert's contemporary setting of the poem for male quartet (D. 809).

For four years and nearly a hundred songs, Schubert did not write another piano introduction according to this pattern. In 1828, however, he returned to the idea with a much broader insight into its expressive applicability. The Heine song recalled most directly by *Gondelfahrer* is *Am Meer* (ex. 3). The key is the same, the scheme (x—т—x—т̂) very similar, with a dissonant augmented-sixth chord at "x" richer than the ♭VI of the earlier song. In mood, Schubert had refined the rather obvious *misterioso* of the midnight bell to an unforgettable, enigmatic solemnity, which seems to plumb infinite marine and spiritual depths. What is most interesting, and most unusual, is the independence of the introduction here. It does not signal ahead to a later event in the song, nor does it anticipate figuration or melody. It simply recurs; the song begins and ends with an oracle framing or glossing the poetic statement, rather than playing in to it. From the Classical point of view, the introduction is nonfunctional; it illuminates nothing. But from the Romantic point of view it suggests everything—everything in the world that is inward, sentient, and arcane. It might stand as a prototype for those "unconsummated sym-

Example 3   Am Meer

Example 4   Die Stadt

bols" that Susanne Langer has urged us to comprehend in music.

A third song of water, once again in C, develops the same kind of introduction in a striking variant. Heine's *Die Stadt* begins as in example 4. The scheme is т—x——î; if Schubert meant the dissonant harmony to sound all the way through, his pedaling indication leaves much to be desired. As will be suggested in a moment, he would have appreciated the ambiguity of the bare low C. "x," here a diminished-seventh chord, strikes quite a different note of mystery, but again one that "plunges into the very midst of the spiritual experience," as Schenker puts it. Presently the grisly arpeggio is revealed as illustration of the chill wind rocking the poet's boat, and it rustles away with almost expressionistic fixity during the entire center stanza of the song. The whole picture, of course, with its gray waters, expresses the poet's frame of mind:

> Am fernen Horizonte
> Erscheint, wie ein Nebelbild,
> Die Stadt mit ihren Türmen
> In Abenddämmrung gehüllt.
>
> Ein feuchter Windzug kräuselt
> Die graue Wasserbahn;
> Mit traurigem Takte rudert
> Der Schiffer in meinem Kahn . . .

> [On the distant horizon, like a misty apparition, appears the city, its towers enveloped in the dusk.
> A damp gust of wind ruffles the gray surface of the water; with mournful strokes the boatsman rows in my skiff . . .]

Schubert in 1828 was no longer thinking like Goethe. But perhaps Heine's verse woke in him a final intense response to that impressive mystical incantation of Goethe's:

> Seele des Menschen, wie gleichst du dem Wasser!
> Schicksal des Menschen, wie gleichst du dem Wind!

> [Soul of mankind, how you resemble the water! Destiny
> of mankind, how you resemble the wind!]

The lines form the conclusion of the "Gesang der Geister über den Wassern," a poem that must have haunted Schubert, for he set it as many as five times.

The piano introduction to another Goethe setting, *Geistes-gruss* (D. 142),[5] evokes another, more amiable ghost, though his harmonic vocabulary closely approximates that of *Die Stadt*. These measures (ex. 5) show how far Schubert interested himself in this introduction pattern in 1828: the song dates from 1815, but the measures in question were added when the piece was rewritten for publication, in July 1828. As a matter of fact, all the revisions on this occasion are extraordinarily instructive. Though few changes were made in the notes pure and simple, *Geistes-gruss* was transformed as few works ever were in their revisions. Originally the first half of the song had employed the barest recitative (ex. 6). Since he now found recitative stiff, Schubert rewrote it in tempo. To make it more impressive, he slowed it down and punctuated it with broad, contemplative rests. Since he cared less now for songs that

Example 5   Geistes-gruss

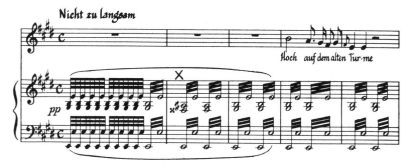

Example 6 Geistes-gruss *(earlier version)*

change style brusquely in the middle, he specifically directed that the second half (a sort of arioso) is to proceed "im ersten Zeitmass." The most striking improvement came through the addition of pictorial immediacy to the song by means of the tremolo. As usual, Schubert seized on a single, central poetic image to translate into music: water once again, water that carries man's ship of fate, as in *Die Stadt*—an image suggested so faintly by the poet that Schubert had scarcely noticed it in 1815:

> Hoch auf dem alten Turme steht
> Des Helden edler Geist,
> Der, wie das Schiff vorübergeht,
> Es wohl zu fahren heisst.
> "Sieh, diese Senne war so stark,
> Dies Herz so fest und wild,
> Die Knochen voll von Rittermark,
> Der Becher angefüllt;
> Mein halbes Leben stürmt' ich fort,
> Verdehnt' die Hälft' in Ruh,
> Und du, du Menschen-Schifflein dort,
> Fahr' immer, immer zu!"

> [High upon the old tower stands the hero's noble ghost; as the ship passes by, he bids it a safe journey.
> "Behold, these sinews were so strong, this heart so firm and fierce, these bones full of knightly marrow, the goblet always filled up.
> For half my life I tossed like a storm; I let the other half go by in peace. And you, you little shipload of humanity there, travel ever onward!"]

And since in 1828 Schubert considered some kind of piano introduction obligatory, he added three measures according to his latest pattern (T—X—T). The opening auxiliary chord progression, and the *quasi recitativo* in tempo over the hushed Romantic tremolo, both recall *Am Meer* immediately.

There are two sides to the coin of harmonic experimentation in the early Romantic period. On the one hand, composers concentrated on certain rich chords and interesting progressions, deriving new expressive force by means of novel spacing, texture, instrumental color, tempo, and context. This is manifest in all the song introductions that we have discussed. On the other hand, composers grew fascinated by possibilities of ambiguity to be gained by stripping away harmony and texture: by dealing in paradoxical single notes, unison passages, melodic fragments open to various harmonizations, parallel and hollow sounds of all descriptions. This side of the coin, also, shows up very clearly in the *Schwanengesang*; the admirable low C in *Die Stadt* is only one of many such experiments, which date back to the *Winterreise* and even before. (One need only think of *Der Leiermann, Gefrorne Tränen,* and *Die Wetterfahne.*) A Rellstab song from the *Schwanengesang, In der Ferne,* capitalizes on bare octaves in its piano introduction (D—x—D̂; ex. 7).

An introduction all on the dominant (D), incidentally, is a great rarity in Schubert. Besides the present song, the only other late example is the quite extraordinary *Letzte Hoffnung,* from *Winterreise.* In *In der Ferne,* the semitone step and the suggestion of parallels prefigure *inter alia* the grating juxtaposition of B-minor and B-flat-major root-position triads later in the song, which so exacerbated a contemporary critic cited by Richard Capell:

> If such unseemliness, such insolently placed harmonic distortions, could find, in defiance of all common sense,

Example 7   In der Ferne

their impudent swindlers who would foist them as sur-
plus originality upon patient admirers of extravagance,
we should—supposing that the egregious thing should
succeed—soon be removed into the most blissful of all
states, a state of anarchy similar to that of the days of the
interregnum.[6]

As often happens with music critics, this man has indulged his
tendency to overwrite so far as to obscure a tolerably good
point.

Stark octaves bring us back to *Ihr Bild*, whose introduction can now be regarded as a condensation of the pattern that
we have been tracing, or as a skeleton of it, an exoskeleton.
Things become explicit only when the two B♭s recur later in
the song, just before stanza 3 (ex. 8)—a progression that recalls the beginning of *Am Meer* (but notice the empty fifth).
Schenker, who remarks that the staring is resumed at this
point, for some reason fails to relate the passage back to the
opening in technical terms. But retrospectively, at least, this
passage helps construe the duality of the notes at the start: by
now, the first B♭ is made to resolve into the other (x—т). The
new passage is bodied out motivically as well as harmonically,
deriving its motif from an earlier vocal cadence echoed by a
piano interlude (ex. 9). This piano interlude on the dominant,

Example 8   Ihr Bild

Example 9   Ihr Bild

with its augmented fourth, sounds very like the introduction figure itself, in its second, unambiguous manifestation.

Here the reader may be inclined to observe with some asperity that this long sequence has got him no closer than Schenker's paragraph to the mysterious intensity and "rightness" of *Ihr Bild*, to the "magician's secret thread." Perhaps not; and perhaps certain artistic magic will not be very far "explained" by any course of analysis. But something is gained by recognizing echoes of the two B♭s later in the song; and something is gained by seeing a context for them outside the song itself. The context, furthermore, is subject to analysis in terms of a progression, one that is characteristic of Schubert, and perhaps of music more widely.

The seed of the idea was literary, nonmusical, even onomatopoeic. Actual chimings are echoed, in the piano introduction to *Gondelfahrer*. Yet of course the bells of San Marco have their distinctive Romantic coloring, which already seems to be the main point of the introduction, in spite of the fact that this also functions as a signal ahead toward the end of the song. A similar function occurs in *Die Stadt*, where again the introduction illustrates a detail in the poem, directly and now much more powerfully. In *Geistes-gruss* and *Am Meer* the illustration is just as clear, though markedly less specific in reference; and in these works the harmonic cell has so caught Schubert's imagination that it no longer bears an integral relation to the song proper—as though the spirit has freed itself from the song, and hovers above it, rapt in its own sibylline evocation. With *In der Ferne* and *Ihr Bild* a significant process of abstraction sets in. Technically, the "x" pulls in to bare octaves, and the repetition disappears; formally, the introduction is made to grow rather subtly within the song; and poetically, there is really now *no direct pictorial reference*. In the final analysis, then, Schenker's effort to link the introduction of *Ihr Bild* to staring or any other concept from the poem misses the point. This introduction is more purely musical than any others of the same type.

A device that begins frankly as a reflection of a literary idea and ends up as a purely musical resource: how often we see this principle working itself out in the course of music history. In the century from Schubert to Schoenberg and Debussy—not to speak of earlier times—ideas acted constantly as a stimulus in this sense to "absolute music." With Schubert, finally, the tendency of his introduction pattern toward abstraction and intellectualization can be followed in one or two of the last instrumental works.[7]

Many writers on Schubert have pointed out illuminating vocal derivatives in the instrumental music. On the basis of such derivatives, indeed, Harry Goldschmidt has concluded that Schubert's remarkable stylistic development in 1828 owed its impetus directly to the Heine songs.[8] Hans Költzsch, in his study of the piano sonatas, noted that the rumbling trill in the B-flat Sonata of 1828 (ex. 10) has a parallel in the piano interlude of *Ihr Bild* (cf. ex. 9).[9]

The mood is analogous, as is the function, a muffled repeated half cadence after the first melodic segment; the chord is almost the same augmented sixth, in practically the same spacing, with the same A♭ in the offing; in both pieces ♭VI serves to prepare the first modulation. The key is the same (it is the key of Beethoven's "Archduke" Trio, which must have inspired Schubert's lyric first subject). Writing a sonata, Schubert was determined to carry the trill figure on, notably in his retransition section. But the figure does not develop, certainly not in any Beethovenian sense. The passage, so handsomely treated by Tovey, is superb, but the figure remains essentially what it was at the beginning: a mysterious, impressive, cryptic, Romantic gesture.

The C-Major Quintet of 1828 opens with a similar gesture (ex. 11). Since Schubert was writing not a song introduction but a theme, he found a need to add a four-bar consequent, less colorful and more businesslike than the pregnant harmonic cell. How was such a manifest hybrid of a theme to be manipu-

Example 10   Sonata in B-flat Major

Example 11   Quintet in C Major

Example 12   Quintet in C Major

Example 13   Die Allmacht

lated? Once he had started his great structure moving by repeating the theme in sequence, Schubert employed it very sparingly indeed, and in ways that are more akin to thematic transformation than to Classical development. In the transition, the theme appears as a vigorous *fortissimo* in the bass. In the recapitulation, the theme sprouts ecstatic arpeggios. In the coda, it is violently racked (ex. 12). Here, as the diminished seventh at "x" explains itself away to the tonic $^6_4$, we may perhaps think of the somewhat gross apocalyptic sounds that introduce *Die Allmacht* (C major once again; ex. 13).[10]

Example 14   Quartet in G Major

Actually, the most impressive theme of this kind had been composed two years earlier, for the G-Major Quartet of 1826 (ex. 14). Like the quintet theme, but more concisely, this one comprises a startling harmonic cell followed by more active material, the whole designed for sequential repetition. The cell, though not cut in the same pattern as those of 1828, has strong points of contact with them. However, its great power lies in its ambiguity—ambiguity more far-reaching than that of the hollow octaves and the bare low Cs mentioned above. Schubert interpreted the cell in several different ways; alternation of major and minor triads is only the most obvious way. On account of its simplicity, perhaps, this is the function that recurs in the finale, and that emerges in the coda of the first movement, which has been markedly unstable and tense, and now receives a splendid firm resolution. But at the start, as quoted above, the G-minor triad seems to act as a stressed nonharmonic chord, a passing harmony leading by spasms from G major to its dominant. As though to force this interpretation, much is made of the melodic step B♭–A (which is at once repeated, bar 5, then echoed on other degrees, bars 10, 11, 12–13, 13–14). At the recapitulation, where the chords are reversed so that G minor comes first, the G-minor triad seems to resolve up into the major tonic. In this transformation, then, the second, accented chord of the theme is treated as something functional, rather than as a willfully stressed passing chord: a fact that contributes with many others to the serenity of this famous passage. The passing note has been transformed out of existence. The progression B–B♭–A is gone and even the residual B♮–A is hidden by new emphasis, in the first violin, on the descending fifth E–A.

No other work, perhaps, hints more excitingly at what Schubert would have made of thematic transformation, had he lived into the age of Chopin, Berlioz, Liszt, and Wagner. The proleptic technique of the well-known "Wanderer" Fantasy, composed in 1822, seems by comparison elementary.

His Romantic orientation, in the last years, stands out clearly if the first themes of the G-Major Quartet and the quintet are viewed in the light of earlier compositions such as the "Trout" Quintet and the Sixth Symphony (ex. 15). These themes, too, make a phrase out of an auxiliary diminished seventh plus blander continuations. But Schubert saw nothing special in the chord: the themes are merely trite, strongly reminiscent of a Rossini cliché, and perfectly serviceable for development later on. In the quintet, Schubert reinterpreted this kind of theme in a thoroughly new light, investing the auxiliary progression with color, mystery, and emotion. Such themes will not develop in any Classical spirit. They have been crossed with the brooding introductory sounds of Heine's poems of the sea.

Der Freischütz and Euryanthe played in Vienna in 1821 and 1823: the very heralds of German musical Romanticism. The town fell into camps, one upholding the reigning star of European opera, Rossini, another supporting the composer of the Wolf's Glen scene. The Schubert circle was on the whole less

Example 15   (a) "Trout" Quintet; (b) Symphony No. 6

than enthusiastic about Weber, and Bauernfeld tells a well-known story about Schubert's own coolness.[11] One is reminded of his equivocal, disturbed statements about Beethoven. Toward a less challenging figure, Rossini, Schubert had once been quick in praise:

> You cannot deny him extraordinary genius. The orchestration is most original at times. . . . (Schubert to A. Hüttenbrenner, 1819)
> Schubert has so much praise for Rossini's *Otello*; talk with him about it. . . . (Holzapfel to Stadler, 1819)[12]

But to set Schubert's C-Major Symphony of 1818 next to his C-Major Quintet of 1828 is to see how emphatically, and how magnificently, his allegiance shifted.

Notes

1. Heinrich Schenker, *Der Tonwille* 1 (1921):46.

2. The piano introduction in Schubert's songs is well treated by Edith Schnapper, *Die Gesänge des jungen Schubert* (Bern: P. Haupt, 1937), pp. 137–51.

3. The best-known example, *Die Forelle*, is incorrectly printed in the Schirmer, Ditson, and Peters editions, following Diabelli's edition of 1829: the first bar of their six-bar introduction is spurious. See O. E. Deutsch, *Franz Schubert: Thematisches Verzeichnis seiner Werke in chronologischer Folge*, rev. W. Dürr, A. Feil, etc. (Kassel: Bärenreiter, 1978), pp. 319–20.

4. Walther Vetter, who points this out in *Der Klassiker Schubert* (Leipzig: Deutscher Verlag für Musik, 1953), takes the sonority as evidence of Schubert's realism: "Der Komponist hat den Glockenklang genau studiert. . . . Schlagton, Unterton und Obertone sind . . . deutlich vernehmbar" (p. 373). I have not been able to consult Paul Mies's article "Zwei Kompositionen zum Gedicht *Der Gondelfahrer* von J. Mayrhofer," in *Deutschen Sängerbundes Zeitung* 19 (1927):614–15; it is mentioned in his *Schubert der Meister des Liedes* (Berlin: Max Hesse, 1928), p. 379n.

5. There are in all five earlier versions of the song; see Deutsch, *Schubert Verzeichnis*, pp. 99–100. Three are given in the old collected edition as nos. 174 a, b, and c. No documentary authority exists for the date of the final, published version—the autograph is lost—but the internal and circumstantial evidence seems decisive.

6. Cited in Richard Capell, *Schubert Songs* (London: E. Benn, 1928), p. 251 n. Actually the B♭ triad functions as a passing harmony between i and ♭iii (B minor and D minor), an extreme relationship of a kind much favored by Schubert at this time: see also *Kriegers Ahnung, Aufenthalt, Der Atlas*, and (best of all) *Der Doppelgänger*.

7. A survey of Schubert's song production reveals at least three other introductions bearing a technical affinity to those that have been discussed. Each in its own way differs in spirit so far from the main class that to treat any of them with that class would be tendentious; but they are interesting enough to deserve a note.

The reader may have thought of *Der Atlas* in this connection: as in *Gondelfahrer*, the introduction runs T—X-T—X-T—T. The distinction, of course, comes in the rigorous motivic organization of *Der Atlas*. It is the powerful motive that creates the appoggiatura "x," and thereafter it controls the song measure by measure until the end.

Heimliches Leben (D. 922), another late song (from 1827), opens with an introductory phrase of the kind used in the C-Major Quintet, which will be discussed presently. A stressed auxiliary diminished seventh is followed by more neutral material. Far from foreshadowing the quality of the quintet, the auxiliary as articulated melodically here turns out to be one of Schubert's tawdrier creations. The poem was a little warm for Schubert.

Ihr Grab (D. 736; ?1822) begins D—X—D—X—D, where "D" is the dominant of vi (C minor), not of the tonic (E-flat major). This anomaly relates back to a whole set of harmonic experiments among the songs of 1817–18. What seems to be involved in this introduction is the establishment of the step G–A♭, both in the top line and in the dissonance "x." Then the important motive that begins the song proper ("Dort ist ihr Grab": E♭–B♭–G) pivots around G by moving from I⁶ (G in the bass) to vi (G in the voice), and leads via another bass G to the key of A-flat. Harmonic ambiguity is reduced prior to the final stanza of the song, where the rather delicate dissonance at "x" is replaced by something closer to the introduction of *In der Ferne*. While A♭–G is still in evidence, the emphasis shifts to another semitone, C♭–B♭, which is harmonically direct. This "clearing up" recalls the elucidation of the ambiguous hollow octaves in *Ihr Bild*, but the situations are too far apart to throw much light on one another.

If *Ihr Grab* remains a cold song, in spite of its mawkish poem, and in spite of its very great harmonic interest, one reason may be its lack of any binding musico-poetic image. Even the dissonance "x" is for once promoted contrapuntally, not coloristically.

8. See Harry Goldschmidt, "Zu einer Neubewertung von Schuberts letzter Schaffenszeit (1828)," in *Bericht über den siebenten internationalen musikwissenschaftlichen Kongress, Köln 1958* (Kassel: Bärenreiter, 1959), pp. 118–20.

9. See Hans Költzsch, *Franz Schubert in seinen Klaviersonaten* (Leipzig: Breitkopf und Härtel, 1927), p. 131.

10. Compare also the Fantasy for Violin and Piano of 1827 (D. 934), still in the key of C.

11. O. E. Deutsch, *The Schubert Reader,* trans. Eric Blom (New York: Norton, 1947), pp. 892, 294.

12. Deutsch, *Schubert Reader,* pp. 117, 120.

Schubert's Tragic Perspective

◆

WILLIAM KINDERMAN
for Eva

I

In his article "Prinzipien des Schubert-Liedes," Hans Heinrich Eggebrecht wrote that "in Schubert's songs major and minor are often juxtaposed with one another as the illusory world of beautiful, bright dreams to the real world of banal, wretched, naked reality. . . ."[1] This suggestive analogy points toward a much larger issue in Schubert's music: the relationship between overt musical contrast and the dichotomy of external and internal experience—perception and imagination—that so preoccupied the Romantic poets set by Schubert in his Lieder. Contrast between the vision of the imagination and a bleak or threatening reality occurs frequently in the works of Goethe, Wilhelm Müller, and Heine, and this aspect of the poetry is almost invariably seized upon by Schubert. His familiar predilection for moving between major and minor, his techniques of modulation, his use of heightened thematic contrast—all contribute to a duality of perspective rooted in the poetry but expressed even more vividly in the music.

The first outstanding instances of this dual perspective among Schubert's songs are the two early masterpieces to poetic texts by Goethe, *Gretchen am Spinnrade* and *Erlkönig*. In the former, a realistic, ostensibly "external" piano accompaniment, suggesting the spinning of the wheel as background, serves also to depict Gretchen's distraught ecstasy: at the climax, the activity of her accompaniment breaks off, and is resumed only with difficulty. In *Erlkönig*, on the other hand, an internal viewpoint, only hinted at in *Gretchen*, provides the central dramatic perspective of the song. As Tovey pointed out, the seductive vision of the *Erlkönig* presented by Schubert is that of the child, not that of the father.[2] The psychological depth of the setting is made possible by a sudden shift of perspective expressed in the music, which enables Schubert to do justice to both the pictorial dimension of the poem and the inner experience of the boy.

The turbulent background of the scene, suggesting the horse's hooves and rushing wind, is expressed by the repeated octaves and marked rhythmic motives in the piano accompaniment. The tonality is prevailingly minor; the major mode is reserved for the Erlking, whose music stands in sharp contrast to the rest of the song. He addresses the boy in beautiful, coaxing melodies; only here does the stormy background of the song recede. Juxtaposed with this seductive melodic idiom is the terrified response of the boy, expressed each time by the grating dissonance of a minor ninth between the voice and piano. Schubert's tonal scheme, utilizing his favorite device of abrupt modulation, enhances this effect of a shift in perspective, from hallucination to harsh reality (see fig. 1).

Schubert's distinctive treatment of the Erlking's first two passages permits him to alter this pattern with powerful effect in the third and final one (see ex. 1). Here the rapidly repeated chords of the accompaniment finally invade the music of the Erlking. The playful melodic shape and major mode, both still present in the first phrase ("Ich liebe dich . . ."), give way to a measured declamation, and the Neapolitan E-flat drops to a cadence in D minor. Moments later, a similar but even more emphatic cadence in the tonic G minor frames the boy's last words as he dies: the inward vision expires, and with it the life of the child.

The achievement of *Erlkönig* provided a model for the coordination of music with the duality of subjective and objective experience. Years later, Schubert returned to this musical procedure in a number of important songs. Most of these songs, beginning with the setting of Friedrich Rückert's *Dass sie hier gewesen* of 1823, are concerned with tragic reminiscence, with joy remembered but lost. Here, the joy of love is recalled

Figure 1   Erlkönig: *The Tonal Plan*

STANZA

1	Introduction: Narrator	G minor – B-flat major – G minor
2	Father	C minor
	Son	C minor → F major
	Father	→ B-flat major
3	Erlking	B-flat major, lyrical melody
4	Son	V/G minor; modulates to B minor
	Father	→ G major, as V/C
5	Erlking	C major, lyrical melody
6	Son	V/A minor; modulates to C-sharp minor
	Father	→D minor
7	Erlking	E-flat major; cadence in D minor on "Gewalt"
	Son	V/B-flat minor; cadence in G minor on "gethan"
8	Postlude: Narrator	G minor

NOTE: Thematic juxtaposition is shown by boxes.

as a flashback, as the memory of something that no longer exists in reality.

Dass sie hier gewesen captures both the sense of unreality of the reminiscence and its subjective force: the song remains poised between the perspectives of external and internal experience. The external scene is suggested by the first two lines of the text, "Dass der Ostwind Düfte/hauchet in die Lüfte" (That the east wind/breathes scents into the air) (see ex. 2). The first twelve bars assume an eerie, mysterious quality through the soft appoggiatura chords in the high register, the effective use of silence, the unsettled tonality, and the narrow range

Example 1   Erlkönig

of the melody—especially its persistent emphasis on the interval E–D.

An extraordinary feature of this setting is that the revelation of the tonic key, C major, is delayed until the reminiscence of the beloved at the words "dass du hier gewesen" (that you were here). These words reflect the internal, subjective per-

Example 2   Dass sie hier gewesen

spective of the song, which is embodied by a melodic fragment of two bars in the clearest C major, employing only tonic and dominant chords. The simplicity of this phrase is underscored by its immediate repetition. The first half of the phrase, comprising the descending fourth C–G, is then repeated once more in the piano before it is abruptly broken off in a bar of silence (bar 18). The simplicity and repetitive character of this phrase make it sound insubstantial, despite its tonal stability— an impression confirmed by the dissolution into silence in the middle of the phrase. The return of the soft appoggiatura chords mark the resumption of the external perspective at the words "Dass hier Tränen rinnen" (that here tears are running).

The musical substance of the entire song is built of these two contrasting phrases, one associated with the external scene, the other with the reminiscence of the beloved. The song remains delicately balanced between the two perspectives and ends in C major, with a final repetition in the piano of the musical phrase for "dass sie hier gewesen." Unlike in *Erlkönig*, a tragic end is forestalled here: the consolation of memory, even if illusory, compensates for the sense of loss. The song is poised on this expressive ambiguity derived from the text.

In 1827 Schubert wrote the second of his song cycles to texts by Wilhelm Müller, *Winterreise*, whose subject matter is the quintessentially Romantic theme of the wanderer. *Winterreise* is a particularly grim example: the quest of the disillusioned wanderer leads ultimately to madness and oblivion. As in *Dass sie hier gewesen*, Müller's wanderer seeks emotional sustenance in dreams and memories; but here every illusion is shattered, leaving no escape from the desolate reality that confronts him.

Several of Schubert's *Winterreise* songs exploit the tragic pathos latent in illusion, but perhaps none more effectively than *Frühlingstraum* (no. 11) and *Täuschung* (no. 19). The first stanza of *Frühlingstraum*, which describes dreams of spring, is set by Schubert as a gently swinging tune in $\frac{6}{8}$ meter, in the bright key of A major. The first words of the second stanza dispel the illusion, as the traveler awakes to the crowing of the cock, and to bitter cold and darkness. At the same time, the music shifts into the minor mode, and the melody disappears, replaced by rhythmic declamation in the voice and dissonant, syncopated appoggiaturas in the piano. *Täuschung*, placed much later in the cycle, employs the same general musical idiom as *Frühlingstraum* in the same poetic context.[3] It is also in $\frac{6}{8}$ meter and in A major and even employs some of the same turns of phrase, particularly at the cadences. Unlike *Frühlingstraum*, however, it remains within the major mode—and hence the sphere of illusion—until the end of the song. In this instance, the confrontation with grim reality is postponed until the next song, *Der Wegweiser.*

Duple meter and steady movement in eighth notes give *Der Wegweiser* a processional character. In this respect it is reminiscent of *Gute Nacht,* the opening song in the cycle. But whereas *Gute Nacht* launches the winter's journey, *Der Wegweiser* points to its end: it is a procession to oblivion. Its persistent rhythm and darkness of key—G minor after the A major of *Täuschung*—contribute to its overwhelming immediacy of effect. The climax of the song, heightened by a chromatically ascending bass, occurs on the words "eine Strasse muss ich gehen/die noch keiner ging zurück" (a path must I follow/from which no one has ever returned).

The suggestion of physical movement in *Wegweiser* allies itself with a spatial, or external perspective, while pure lyricism, as in *Täuschung,* can be identified with the internal and nonspatial realm of imagination or illusion. Not infrequently, the evocation of the pictorial in Schubert is associated with such rhythmic movement, in particular a steady processional movement. This is true not only of the songs but of instrumental works—a striking example is the Andante of the "Great" C-Major Symphony, composed in 1825–26. After the composition of *Winterreise* Schubert's processional movements tend to assume a more fateful, and even tragic, character, as in the slow movement of the E-flat Piano Trio or the Fantasy in F Minor for piano duet. This reflects a shift in emphasis in the last two years in Schubert's life from the somewhat naïve nature worship of *Die schöne Müllerin* to a more deeply introspective world, which is embodied above all in the six Heine songs of 1828.

The second of the Heine songs, *Ihr Bild,* contains one of the most sensitive and powerful examples of tragic reminiscence in all of Schubert's Lieder. In a sense, the basic idea of this song is the reinterpretation of the single note, B♭, which acts as a focal point for the voice throughout (see ex. 3). The song opens enigmatically, with a twofold repetition of an octave B♭ in the piano. After the entry of the voice, the stability of the B♭ is undermined. In bar 4, it descends to A, in a strong rhythmic position; similarly, the G♭ in bar 5 descends to F in the following measure. In the next two-bar phrase in the piano,

Example 3   Ihr Bild, *first strophe*

the Bb and Gb are heard as unequivocally dissonant, as a double appoggiatura to an F-major triad. The interpretation of the Bb here as a dissonance, and in the following passage as a consonance, as well as a change in mode from minor to major, embody the shift from an external to an internal perspective, from emotional desolation to the consolation of the imagination, the memory of the beloved. The harmonic basis for the opening bars is the resolution of the major third B♭–G♭ to A–F, while the simultaneous resolution of both semitones to an F-major triad is presented by the echo of the second phrase in the piano. Until the piano echo, in fact, the entire passage consists of bare octaves; the austere setting embodies the sense of disconsolate staring at the picture in Heine's poem.[4]

Then, secretly, the picture—and the music—come to life. The voice returns to the same B♭ that began the song, now treated as a consonance and harmonized in B-flat major. The words "Heimlich zu leben begann" are set to a full authentic cadence, echoed a moment later in the piano. The crux of Schubert's musical setting is his suppression of the major mode, and of any vertical sonority, in the opening phrases. After this, the straightforward tonal progression beginning in bar 9 has the effect of an awakening of the imagination—its consonant harmonies embody the warmth of feeling expressed in the words. The most subtle aspect of this musical setting is that it seems to make the major mode dependent for its existence on the fragile mood implied in the poem. For the beloved is lost. The emotional consolation of this memory is transitory, and is dispelled before the end of the song.

The second of the three stanzas in Heine's poem continues the reminiscence about the beloved, now set in G-flat major, another harmonization of the crucial opening pitch, B♭. Then the third and final strophe breaks the mood of illusion, bringing a recapitulation of the music of the first strophe. This time, however, the musical shift from minor to the harmonized major tonic accommodates a very different sentiment in the text (see ex. 4). In this final strophe, the warmth embodied by the harmonized major tonality returns, in spite of a consciousness of the loss of the beloved. There is no need to read an ironic intention into this passage; such an interpretation actually misses the most profound aspect of the song.[5] For while the "awakening" of the picture was illusory, the feelings of consolation and happiness were real; the return of the feeling in the music of the last stanza speaks to the universal human capacity to experience happiness despite the pain of loss. The deeply poignant quality of this setting is intensified, moreover, by the shift into minor in the piano postlude, which restores the tragic perspective of the song at the last possible moment.

Example 4 Ihr Bild, *last strophe*

Ihr Bild represents the last Schubert song to explore the distinction between external perception and internal imagination, the territory brilliantly opened up by *Erlkönig* thirteen years earlier. It is the most concentrated and unified of these songs, for in it any direct sense of the pictorial dimension is withdrawn.[6] The sound of the cryptic B♭ is carried through the entire song, and the changing harmonic interpretation of this note embodies the change in feeling, or state of being, suggested in Heine's poem. The unity of *Ihr Bild* is like the unity of the self—that residue of consciousness which registers the inconstancy of experience against its own constant being.

II

As we have seen in several examples from Schubert's songs, contrast between major and minor may represent one aspect of a more profound thematic juxtaposition suggesting the dichotomy of inward imagination and external perception. This interpretation is strongly supported by the poetic text. Even in the absence of a text, however, certain of Schubert's late instrumental works employ an analogous musical treatment based on the exploitation of thematic, tonal, and modal contrast. Our final example is the great Fantasy in F Minor for piano duet, composed early in 1828. While clearly indebted to the model of the songs, this composition goes far beyond them in exploring the structural and expressive possibilities inherent in the controlled juxtaposition of strongly contrasting themes.

Like the earlier "Wanderer" Fantasy, the F-Minor Fantasy consists of four interconnected movements performed without a break. In both works, an opening allegro is followed by a slow movement, scherzo, and final movement employing fugue. The thematic treatment in the F-Minor Fantasy, however, has no parallel in the earlier work.

The lyrical opening theme of the Fantasy bears some affinity to the processional themes of pieces like the Andante of the C-Major Symphony, and *Gute Nacht* and *Wegweiser* from *Winterreise*. Its processional character derives from a regularity of rhythmic pulse in duple meter and the steady octaves in the bass, repeated twice per measure (see ex. 5). As Eric Sams has pointed out, the melody itself has an insistent conversational character, suggesting the rhythm and intonation of speech.[7] The overall quality of the theme is narrative; it seems to evoke the landscape of ceaseless wandering familiar from the two Müller song cycles.

After the repetition of the initial thematic statement, the music shifts into A-flat major, and the lyrical melody passes to the bass. This section represents the middle part of a ternary

thematic construction. The opening theme returns, however, in F major, and the brighter sound of the major mode is enhanced by richer harmonies in the bass and the emphasis on A♮ in the melody (see ex. 6). Schubert also exploits the high upper register of the piano in the last phrases before the melody cadences in the tonic.

That cadence brings a shock—a contrasting second theme in F minor, which is utterly opposed to the opening theme in affective character. The menacing character of the new theme is due to its stress on D♭, the dissonant minor second above the dominant note, its pointed accents, and its funereal rhythm. This rhythm, first announced in the bass, consists of the pattern ♩. ♪ ♩ ♩, representing a related but more energetic form of the rhythm associated by Schubert with death in the song *Der Tod und das Mädchen*, ♩ ♩ ♩.

By analogy with Schubert's songs, the statement of the first lyrical theme in major assumes an air of unreality, of illusion. The illusion is rudely shattered by the plunge into minor and the threatening second theme. This drastic thematic juxtaposition then serves as the structural basis for the rest of the first movement. After the initial statement of the second theme, the lyrical theme returns in D-flat minor, closing with a cadence in A minor, where it is once again juxtaposed with the

Example 6   Fantasy in F Minor

theme in funereal rhythm. A last statement of the opening
theme in F minor completes the series of modulations through
a circle of descending major thirds, F–D♭–A–F. This appearance too is juxtaposed with the second theme, which, in a reversal of roles, now appears transformed—*pianissimo, legato,*
and in major. The statement of the second theme in major has a
resolving effect, serving to round off the first movement before
the dramatic opening of the Largo in F-sharp minor. The tonal
and thematic plan of the first movement is shown in figure 2.

Figure 2   Fantasy in F Minor, first movement: The Tonal Plan

Lyrical theme	F minor
Melody passes to bass	A-flat major, modulates to V/F minor

Lyrical theme restated	F major
Second theme, funereal rhythm	F minor, modulates to

Lyrical theme	D-flat minor, modulates to
Second theme, funereal rhythm	A minor, modulates to

Lyrical theme	F minor
Second theme, funereal rhythm	F major (leads to second movement)

NOTE: Thematic juxtaposition is shown by boxes.

The tonal relations and thematic juxtaposition in the first movement of the Fantasy are similar to those in *Erlkönig*: in each, material of strongly melodic character is pitted against more dramatic, turbulent material in minor, and the contrast is heightened by means of abrupt modulation (cf. fig. 1). In the Fantasy, however, this dual perspective reaches its culmination only in the final bars of the work. The last movement represents a recapitulation and development of the first movement.[8] After a sudden modulation from the key of the scherzo, F-sharp minor, the lyrical theme returns in F minor. The entire opening section is then restated, in somewhat condensed form, up to the crucial passage in which the lyrical theme appears in the major mode. From this point, the work takes a new course.

The dark-hued second subject now becomes the basis for an extended fugue. In the latter part of the fugue, the principal rhythmic motive undergoes a series of canonic imitations, while its free inversion is worked into the rhythmic accompaniment as triplets in the bass. The music then builds toward a tonic cadence in F minor, which is twice avoided before it appears at the final statement of the fugal theme in the lowest register. Again the music comes to a climax on a series of diminished-seventh chords, with the expectation of a cadence in the tonic. This time, however, the cadence is denied: the fugue simply breaks off on the dominant (see ex. 7). (This passage is reminiscent of the climax of the Andante of the C-Major Symphony, where an analogous passage leads to a diminished-seventh chord, followed by a dramatic silence, and a melancholy transformation of the principal theme of the movement [bars 241–66]. The impact of the climax causes, as it were, the subsequent transformation of the main theme.)

The conclusion of the Fantasy after this dramatic silence is one of the most extraordinary passages in Schubert's works, and merits detailed analysis (see ex. 7). It begins by recalling the plaintive lyrical theme from the outset of the work; but the reminiscence lasts only a few bars. The last bars, rising in sequence, already pick up the darker coloring of the second theme; then, ten bars before the close, Schubert steps from one theme into the other through a subtle transformation of his material. The melodic continuation of the reminiscence is related to the second theme, particularly to the rhythmic pattern at the climax of the fugue, three bars before it is broken off. At the same time, the bass stresses the crucial semitone D♭–C, and a version of the funereal rhythm returns in the treble in the bar before the cadence in F minor (see bars 562–63). The closing eight-bar statement is a further development of the second theme, employing not only the funereal rhythm, but the melodic stress on D♭; the descending triplets in the bass are derived from the fugue. In these final measures, the dark-hued second theme supersedes the lyrical theme to provide the cadence and resolution of the entire work.

Since the relationship and expressive conflict between these themes have been key elements in the Fantasy, their juxtaposition in the coda seems to sum up the whole piece in a single gesture. Yet the appearance of the themes here goes beyond any earlier passage in the work; it achieves a new synthesis. This final statement is laden with tragic overtones. In context, directly following the forceful, almost orchestral impact of the fugue, the lyrical opening theme sounds fragile, insubstantial. This impression is confirmed in the last bars of Schubert's coda, a passage that Maurice Brown has described as "the most remarkable cadence in the whole of Schubert's work."[9]

Example 7   Fantasy in F Minor

This cadence owes much of its power to the fact that it serves as the true conclusion of the fugue, after the abrupt interruption and the reminiscence of the lyrical theme. The actual cadential progression refers back to several cadential passages in the fugue, in which the dotted rhythmic motive of the subject is extended by a series of quarter notes. This time the progression is strengthened by the presence of a descending chromatic line, doubled in octaves, that highlights the dissonant semitone D♭–C in the last two chords. The chromatic line, beginning on F, passes through E♮, E♭, and D♮, reaching D♭ in the penultimate chord, which is emphasized dynamically.

This penultimate sonority may be regarded as a subdominant minor triad with added sixth, or as a first inversion seventh chord on the supertonic. In either role it might be expected to resolve to the dominant—as in fact happened at an earlier point in the Fantasy, at the end of the transition from the scherzo to the last movement. Schubert's omission of the dominant chord at this cadence illustrates a cardinal principle in the evolution of nineteenth-century harmony from Beethoven to Wagner: since the dominant is so clearly implied in the context, its actual appearance would be neutral and inexpressive. Its absence therefore greatly strengthens the expressive force of the cadence. The result is a kind of enhanced subdominant cadence, which combines two crucial motivic elements of the work: the D♭–C semitone relationship in the treble, and the fourth in the bass, the thematic hallmark of the opening theme.

Critics have frequently pointed to a looseness of organization in Schubert's work; Theodor W. Adorno even wrote of a "potpourri," in which themes follow one another without being organically related on classical lines.[10] The case of the F-Minor Fantasy reveals that his claim misses the point, for thematic conflict actually becomes a structural device. Transitional passages characteristic of the Classical style are absent here; indeed, the dramatic power of the work derives in large measure from abrupt thematic juxtaposition. The first and last movements of the piece, themselves interrelated, systematically exploit the juxtaposition of the two contrasting themes. Furthermore, there is progress in the relationship of these themes in the course of the Fantasy. In the coda of the last movement, the lyrical theme, recalled in a final brief reminiscence, is obliterated by the funereal theme, which dominates the entire closing section of the work, just as the lyrical theme had dominated the beginning.

The overall scheme based on the relationship of these two evocative themes suggests a latent symbolism analogous to that of *Winterreise*. Like the song cycle, the F-Minor Fantasy is haunted by a sense of progress toward an inescapable destiny, an idea tied to the universal human theme of mortality. In a sense, the very structure of the Fantasy is posited on this appropriation of poetic content from the world of Schubert's Lieder. In this remarkable composition, the expressive content of the wanderer's tragic journey is transformed, as it were, into a purely musical structure, absorbed into the sphere of instrumental music.

Notes

1. "Prinzipien des Schubert-Liedes," *Archiv für Musikwissenschaft* 27 (1970):96.

2. "Franz Schubert," in *Essays and Lectures on Music* (London: Oxford University Press, 1949), p. 109.

3. As Maurice Brown has pointed out, the melody of *Täuschung* was drawn from Troila's song at the beginning of act II of *Alfonso und Estrella*, from 1822. See Brown, "Schubert's Operas," *Monthly Musical Record* 79 (1949):126.

4. Heinrich Schenker related the stark octaves of the piano introduction to the notion of "staring" in his essay in *Der Tonwille* 1 (1921):46. A translation of the passage is provided by Joseph Kerman in "A Romantic Detail in Schubert's *Schwanengesang*," elsewhere in this volume, pp. 48–49.

5. For an interpretation of this passage as ironic, see Charles Brauner, "Irony in the Heine Lieder of Schubert and Schumann," *Musical Quarterly* 67 (1981):277–80. For another recent discussion of this issue, see Gernot Gruber, "Romantische Ironie in den Heine-Liedern?" *Schubert-Kongress Wien 1978*, ed. Otto Brusatti (Graz: Akademische Druck- u. Verlagsanstalt, 1979), pp. 321–32. Gruber distinguishes Heine's sarcastic, self-distancing irony from Schubert's "Romantic irony," yet in *Ihr Bild* the source of apparent irony— the discrepancy between the words and music of the last stanza—is resolved on a plane of experience combining subjective feeling with an awareness of external reality.

6. See Kerman, "A Romantic Detail," p. 58.

7. "Schubert's Piano Duets," *Musical Times* 117 (1976):121.

8. For a discussion of the form of this work and a comparison with Schubert's earlier fantasies, see Arthur Godel, "Zum Eigengesetz der Schubertschen Fantasien," *Schubert-Kongress Wien 1978*, pp. 202–4.

9. "The Fantasia in F minor, Op. 103," in his *Essays on Schubert* (London: Macmillan, 1966), p. 96.

10. See Adorno, "Schubert," in his *Moments musicaux* (Frankfurt: Suhrkamp, 1964), pp. 18–36. This essay originally dates from 1928. See also Charles Rosen, *The Classical Style* (New York: Viking, 1971), pp. 454–59.

Lyric as Musical Structure:
Schubert's *Wandrers Nachtlied*
("Über allen Gipfeln," D. 768)

THRASYBULOS GEORGIADES
Translated by Marie Louise Göllner

More than six hundred of Schubert's Lieder have come down to us, including almost seventy on poems by Goethe. The composition of a masterpiece such as Goethe's "Wandrers Nachtlied" ("Über allen Gipfeln") raises the question—one frequently asked—whether it is possible, permissible, or worthwhile to set poems of this rank to music. To be sure, Goethe himself gave his poem the title of "Lied,"—"Wandrers Nachtlied,"— and his words of praise for Zelter's setting indicate that he was not opposed in principle to the setting of his poems to music.[1] Nonetheless we are probably justified in asking to what degree an outstanding composition—like Schubert's—is compatible with a poem that is complete in itself—like Goethe's. Or, to be more precise, in what way does the music of a Lied exhibit characteristics independent of the poem? What is the relationship of the composition to the poem? We will examine Schubert's *Wandrers Nachtlied* (D. 768) in depth, viewing it not only as an independent work of art, but also taking into consideration the questions we have just raised. In so doing we hope to clarify what transpired as a result of Schubert's Lied production, within both the history of music and history of the lyric (as a category of poetry).

We begin with Goethe's poem:

         ʹ ◡ ʹ ◡ ʹ ◡   *Rhyme*

1. Über allen Gipfeln   *a*

     ◡ ʹ

2. Ist Ruh;   *b*

     ◡ ʹ ◡ ʹ ◡

3. In allen Wipfeln   *a*

     ʹ ◡ ʹ

4. Spürest du   *b*

     ʹ ◡ ◡ ʹ

5. Kaum einen Hauch;   *c*

     ◡ ʹ ◡ ◡ ʹ ◡ ◡ ʹ ◡

6. Die Vögelein schweigen im Walde.   *d*

     ʹ ◡ ◡ ʹ ◡

7. Warte nur, balde   *d*

     ʹ ◡ ◡ ʹ

8. Ruhest du auch.   *c*

[Above all the peaks there is peace; in all the treetops you feel scarcely a breath; the little birds are silent in the wood. Only wait, soon you too shall rest.]

Although of varying length, the lines are clearly delimited by the rhymes. They are also formed in different ways: in lines 1–4 accented (ʹ) and unaccented syllables (◡) alternate; lines 5–8 each have two unaccented syllables between the accented ones. Lines 1, 4, 5, 7, and 8 begin with an accented syllable; lines 2, 3, and 6 with an unaccented one. Some of the line endings are feminine ($\overset{a}{1}, \overset{a}{3}; \overset{d}{6}, \overset{d}{7}$), others masculine ($\overset{b}{2}, \overset{b}{4}; \overset{c}{5}, \overset{c}{8}$); in the first half of the poem the succession alternates ($\overset{a}{1}, \overset{b}{3}; \overset{a}{2}, \overset{b}{4}$), but in the second half the outer lines enclose the middle ones ($\overset{c}{5}, \overset{c}{8}, \overset{d}{6}, \overset{d}{7}$). The number of accents is also variable. Line 2 contains only one accent; lines 3, 4, 5, 7, and 8 each have two. The first line can be interpreted as having either three accents (ʹ◡ʹ◡ʹ◡) or only two, preceded by two unaccented syllables (◡◡ʹ◡ʹ◡). Only line 6 is more leisurely; it has three unambiguous accents of which it takes full advantage, leaving two unaccented syllables between each. As a result, it is considerably longer than any of the other lines: the continuously unfolding triple rhythm gives it a swinging movement and the feel of a regularly built, songlike form. In this way it differs from all the other lines, which, with their contours veiled in darkness, express so emphatically the idea of night, as well as the character of the spoken as opposed to the songlike.

Line 6 also differs from all the others in its content. "Vöge-lein" and "Wald" conjure up images from the naïve, folklike sphere, making us realize how completely different in content is the rest of the poem, with its deep significance, its person-alized statement. To understand the importance of line 6 more clearly—to realize that it is only the interruption caused by the change in rhythm and conceptual direction of this single line that lends the poem its depth and its greatness—we need only attempt to leave it out. The intellectual content, the reality of the poem, is destroyed, replaced by a subjective image of mood that is not binding. The critical role of this line is not so much in the addition of a third element, the living creature, to the images of lifeless (lines 1–2) and awakening vegetative nature (lines 3–5), as in the interruption in continuity which we have just described.

This can also be illustrated in the structure of the poem. Although the succession of rhymes when taken by itself re-sults in a division into 4 + 4 lines (*abab*—*cddc*), the rhyme "Hauch"–"auch" and the poetic content lead us to interpret lines 1–5 as a unit, as an antecedent, which is then followed by the statement of the personal sphere, the inner self: *ababc*, then *ddc*. ("Ruhest du auch" is also an echo of line 2, of the *Ruh* of nature.) But this statement encompasses only the final two lines (7–8). Then what of the third line from the end, line 6? It hangs suspended between antecedent and conclusion, leading a life of its own. According to the structure of the poem (partic-ularly the rhyme "Walde"–"balde"), it seems to be separated from the first four lines and bound to the last two; but accord-ing to the content, it acts as a later and independent supple-ment to the poetic observations of lines 1–5. This sixth line functions—from whichever angle we choose to look at it—as an island within the poem.

Schubert's setting was composed in his mature period, about 1823 (the exact date is unknown), perhaps shortly before the cycle *Die schöne Müllerin*. (See the Appendix, ex. B, for en-tire song.)

The Lied encompasses a scant fourteen bars in $\frac{4}{4}$ time and remains entirely within the main tonality, B-flat major. Only the half cadence on the dominant in bar 6 is emphasized by the preceding diminished-seventh chord on the leading tone E♮. In the following diagram the numbers indicate the length of the individual phrases in units of $\frac{2}{4}$, since it is not the whole but rather the half bar that represents the basic unit of the composition. We encounter phrases of 1½ bars (in the diagram, three half bars); and the literal repetition of the passage "Warte nur . . . auch," consisting of 1½ + 1 bar (bars 9–10 + ½ = ½ + 12–13), appears to be displaced within the boundaries of the $\frac{4}{4}$ bar, although musically no metrical displacement occurs.

½-bar units:

| 2 | 2 | | 3 | | 2 | | 3 | | 2 | | 3+⌒ | | 2 | | 2 |

Bass notes:

B♭₁ F B♭₁ ‖ B♭₁ │ G F E♭ D │ E♭ E F │ f │: G F B♭₁ F₁ B♭₁ ‖ F₁ B♭₁

Structure:

A B A′ [setting of lines 3–7] B B

The two-bar introduction consists of two parts. The first bar returns, somewhat varied, when the voice enters ("Über . . . ruh"), and the second bar is identical with both the closing phrase of the song, "Ruhest du auch" (which comes twice, in bars 10 and 13), and with the single-bar coda. The setting of lines 3–7 appears, then, to be clamped firmly between the two (now separated) bars of the introduction (A and B; see diagram above). And conversely, the introduction acts as a contraction of the entire Lied. There is in fact a noticeable caesura between bars 1 and 2; the sudden entrance of the $\frac{6}{4}$ chord (bar 2) after the tonic triad is accompanied by a separate light impulse. It acts as a mild thrust that does not emerge from the continuous flow of harmony in the first bar, but rather creates a firm juncture point. For a smooth harmonic progression a different chord—for example, one from the subdominant area, as in bar 4—would have been introduced either between the triad and the $\frac{6}{4}$ chord or in place of the latter. The caesura resulting from the succession I_{3-4}^{5-6} receives even greater emphasis at the close of the voice part by the fermata that precedes the words "Ruhest du auch" each time; and the equally unexpected entrance of the coda confirms the character of this passage.[2]

The symmetrical structure of the introduction (1 + 1 bars)

is not incorporated into the main body of the song (with the exception of bars 7–8). Bars 3–6 consist of three phrases, containing respectively three, two, and three units of $\frac{2}{4}$ ("Über . . . Ruh," "In allen Wipfeln," and "Spürest . . . Hauch"). The first phrase of the vocal part represents a variation of the first bar of the introduction and is thus based on the pedal point B♭ and built around the tonic triad. Unlike the introduction, however, it adds notes of the dominant, instead of the subdominant, on the third beat of the bar and proceeds only after two quarter notes to the tonic, which now likewise fills out the space of a half note. The second phrase is constructed in an entirely different manner. The bass descends stepwise through the fourth G–D, and the upper voice follows in parallel sixths, embellished by suspensions. And in the third phrase we find yet another framework. The bass ascends chromatically, proceeding, along with the upper voice of the accompaniment which circumscribes the tone c′ (c′–d♭′–c′), from the sixth (E♭–c′) through the tension-building diminished seventh (E–d♭′) to the release provided by the dominant fifth (F–c′).

Common to the first and third phrases is their formation around a single tonal *center*. Through them the two main poles of the key, tonic and dominant, are placed in direct opposition. The second phrase, however, presents a *progression* of sonorities. Progression and center are two elementary forms of sound structure; they determine even the oldest forms of notated polyphony from the ninth century and have retained their fundamental significance ever since.[3] Their elemental meaning shines forth in its original purity from the passage we have just examined. The initial bar of the introduction also presents the tonic as a tonal center, to which the cadential formula I_4^6–V^7–I is added in bar 2. However, this does not yet result in a convincing cadential effect. Only in the further progress of the composition, through the structural establishment of the dominant (bars 5–6), its extension (bars 7–8), and the resulting cadential progression VI–V–I (bars 9–10)—during which the voice part continues to hover around the fifth, f″—only in light of these proceedings does the second bar of the introduction appear as a genuine cadence when it returns in its twofold presentation (bars 10 and 13). Only now does it assume the importance of an event, "Ruhest du auch" (You also shall rest).

The individual character of the three phrases in bars 3–6 is not, however, confined to their sonorities. The first one brings the modified pavane rhythm

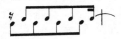

in the accompaniment, thus linking itself with the introduction. The second presents a calm movement in quarter notes, and the third a syncopated web of eighth notes:

Each phrase thus has its own distinctive structure that differentiates it essentially from the others, and this within the closely packed space of just three bars. And in spite of this the listener has an impression of unity—so much so that he has no inkling of the remarkable structure we have just described, fashioned, as it were, from individual blocks of granite. This impression of a unified flow is contingent largely upon the voice part, although even here the technique of building with separate phrases is not only present, but in fact reaches its culmination.

But Schubert's vocal setting is the musical sounding of language; it is language as music. And language is coherence as well as articulation, connection as well as separation, unity as well as distinction. That is to say, it is the sentence—and the sum of the sentences—as well as words, syllables, and sounds. Music as a *natural* phenomenon can be compared to a continuous flow; like words taken by themselves it embraces no centripetal forms that can distinguish among meanings and are themselves distinct as manifestations. And thus music as something "natural" can mirror language as unified flow—without ever penetrating more deeply to the level of language's specific distinguishing word structure. But music as the *bearer of meaning*, expressly formed by man, is capable, by adapting itself to language in different ways in the different epochs, of something more. From the fullness of its own powers, it can create a reality which contains a distinguishing principle similar to that of language—from the fullness of its own powers, and yet in the final analysis still based on the model of language as the given factor. The music of the Viennese Classical masters and Schubert's Lieder are fashioned in this manner, but at the same time they appear *as if* they were natural.

And it is thus that the impression of the unproblematic continuous flow of bars 3–6 is determined by the vocal part. It mirrors not that progress of the musical structure which articulates as distinguishing language, but rather the continuous gesture of expression, the mood invoked by the words, the atmosphere emanating from the language. It mirrors, in summary, not the specific quality of the language but only its babbling aspect. From the extremely peaceful beginning ("Über allen Gipfeln/Ist Ruh"), akin almost to psalmlike recitation, there develops with "In allen Wipfeln" a more animated gesture of intensified expression—the treetops ("Wipflen") are not as rigid as the mountain peaks ("Gipfeln"). At "Spürest du/Kaum einen Hauch" the vocal part assumes a more intimate, even melancholy (d♭″) tone, determined by the mood—one feels ("spürt"), albeit barely ("kaum"), the stirring of life—and fades away into the low register.

This unproblematic, "natural" unity, however, is like a mere shadow of another unity—this one genuine—which comes about only as an event. In this case music is active as the bearer of meaning, in which the distinguishing principle similar to language is inherent.

Let us proceed therefore from the language. Together the first two lines form a sentence. However, the verb "is" carries no weight of its own as far as the statement is concerned, but rather functions merely as a coupler, joining the two images, "Über allen Gipfeln" and "Ruh," in a single image. This is presented in an almost impressionistic fashion in the sentence; in translating the static quality of the *one* image of reality into language, however, of necessity it makes use of a succession of words. In contrast, "In allen Wipfeln" is the first genuine statement of the poem; it contains an active verb ("spürest du") and exhibits a goal-oriented, dynamic structure.

The musical setting of "Über allen Gipfeln ist Ruh" captures not only the unity of the image, but also both the formal function of "ist" as a verb and its dependent character as a coupler. Its function as a verb, that of forming a complete sentence, is expressed through the dominant sonority (second half of the bar, in place of the subdominant sonority in the first bar of the introduction), its coupling, static–impressionistic character through the pedal on B♭, which negates the dynamic-directional tendency of the dominant. And the voice part merely circumscribes the tone b♭′ with the least possible movement. The dactylic pavane rhythm, anchored firmly on the first quarter note when it appears in the introduction,

is transformed into a gently cohesive shape which underlines the unit of the sentence:

"In allen Wipfeln": after the static character of the preceding phrase, what an event now confronts us in this all-enveloping rhythmic, melodic, and harmonic gesture! The spirit of the wanderer embraces *all* of the treetops:

The same word, "allen," appeared in the first line, too. But only at this point, in the third line, can it be grasped in its specific breadth, its own weight, its unique structure of imagery. The setting of the beginning of the sentence "In allen Wipfeln" as a separate phrase is paralleled by the distinction made between the following two phrases, "Spürest du" and "Kaum einen Hauch." This renders the entrance of the first genuine verb, now even accompanied by the subject "du," musically convincing as linguistic event, as *musical* structure. This result is also contingent on three factors: (1) the new pattern of the accompaniment,

(2) the rhythmic impulse accorded to the syllable "Spü-,"

In al - len Wip - feln spü- rest du

Whereas the rhythm of "In allen Wipfeln" began with an upbeat

and unfolded as a unified, encircling gesture, "Spürest du" begins emphatically with a downbeat, is declaimed rapidly on a single tone—

instead of

analogous to "allen Wip-"—and has a concisely measuring quality. (3) the tone c'' on "Spürest du." Whereas the two preceding phrases, beginning and ending on $b\flat'$, had remained anchored on the $B\flat$ sonority, the c'' and its accompanying sonority now leave the sphere of $B\flat$ and move forward into a new area. Only a genuine verb can speak to us in this fashion. "Kaum einen Hauch" stands out as a separate phrase by virtue of the weight given to the word "Kaum" (its length, and the extension both of the c'' to $d\flat''$ and of the sixth $E\flat-c''$ to the diminished seventh $E-d\flat''$) and by virtue of the entire rhythmic structure,

Melodically, however, it stands in a unified relationship to the two preceding phrases, "In-[Wip]feln Spü[-rest]Kaum," supported by the structure of the accompaniment, which remains the same from "Spürest du" onward.

It is thus clear: musical structure is created when language is captured as something real, when it is taken "at its word." Language, understood in this way as sentence structure and verb function and the linking of images, stands not only above music, but also—and this is the crucial point—above poetry as a work of art. It appears as the primary phenomenon spending life and making art possible. Both Goethe and Schubert are confronted with the fact of language. Goethe too takes as his point of departure not mere syllables and sounds but rather preexistent language, his mother tongue. Whereas he, however, fashions from it a poem, that is lines, Schubert brings forth musical structure—based on the poetic language. Both are committed to language; both create directly out of it, the one as poet, the other as composer. Yet in the poem the distinction between linguistic and poetic structure must obviously remain hypothetical. The reality of the poem embraces both in one. Thus the musical composition mirrors the structure of the poem as well as the language. The rhyme "Gipeln"/"Wipfeln" appears as melodic correspondence,

"Spürest du" as a contraction of "Über allen Gipfeln ist Ruh,"

transposed up a major second from b♭' to c″. Similarly, the pause on the word "du" corresponds unmistakably to ("Über . . .") "Ruh," and the rhyme "Ruh"/"du" is further emphasized by the caesura after both words and by the rhythmic-melodic contrast

In the musical setting of the lines

> In allen Wipfeln [b♭′−b♭′]
> Spürest du [c″]
> Kaum einen Hauch [d♭″−f′]

linguistic and poetic structure work together hand in hand. Through musical means Schubert here establishes the coherence of the sentence while simultaneously separating the three independent linguistic images, thus condensing each line, like a crystal, into an unmistakable reality that is almost solidly constituted. The composition of this passage alone is proof of his creative rank. Its core is formed by the passage "Spürest du," anchored on the root syllable "Spü-." This entire passage, however, is brought into relief by the manner in which it is set against the plane of the unified, undifferentiated setting of the first two lines. After

> Über allen Gipfeln ist Ruh

come the separate units

> In allen Wipfeln Spürest du Kaum einen Hauch.

(Both as a rhyme and in the music "Hauch" remains open, unanswered; only the close of the final line, "auch," brings the awaited correspondence.) When musical substance is created in such a manner from language, it scarcely seems necessary to point out that the mood appropriate to the poem, the atmosphere resulting from its content, enters into the music almost of its own accord, or that the vocal part acts as if it were "natural" (see above, pp. 89–90.)

What a concentration of substance in just four bars! There now follows the folksonglike sixth line. In the composition it too forms an island (bars 7–8 fall in the exact center of the Lied: 6 + 2 + 6). Whereas up to this point the bass has been weighty, corresponding to the sixteen-foot stop in the low register, it now jumps suddenly to the upper octave, in the eight-foot register, where it sheds its weight and becomes light, playful, mobile—only to plunge back into the depths at the following line, "Warte nur, balde." Whereas bars 1–6 contained significant harmonic motion, we now find, over the intermittently sounded dominant bass, a primitive fluctuation between dominant and tonic in the nature of a guitar accompaniment. And whereas the independent formation of all the other phrases results in contours individual to each, we are here met with a symmetry, brought about by the repetition of bar 7, which emphasizes the playful character of the passage. Even the accompaniment figure, while corresponding in its rhythm

to the 1½ bars before bar 7, at the same time separates itself from them with its playfully varied inversion of the bass figure:

instead of

All of this appears suddenly in bar 7 and disappears just as abruptly after bar 8. Schubert realizes the songlike, popular character of Goethe's poetic line with *musical* means. Through repetition of the word "schweigen" he creates a musical-songlike symmetry:

This passage, then, represents the songlike sphere, achieved in the poem by linguistic-poetic means, and here as music, by those means available to the composer. We are thereby specifically made aware of the unsonglike nature of the remaining phrases of the Lied.

After this winsome dream, gravity returns; the bass is once again in the low register, phrases are again formed individually, and we again find significant harmonic movement, now supporting the Lied's statement.

The sentence formed by the final two lines of the poem

is divided, similar to lines 3–5 ("In allen Wipfeln/Spürest du/Kaum einen Hauch"), into separate images,

$$\downarrow \qquad \downarrow \qquad \downarrow— \quad \downarrow \qquad (\downarrow)$$
Warte nur—warte nur—balde—Ruhest du auch;

and these phrases, in themselves stable, are joined together as a whole. In the language, and thus likewise in the poetic form of presentation, the appropriate image emerges from the declamation of "Warte nur" (Only wait). This "Warte nur," however, is repeated by Schubert: music operates with time as a material factor; the *musical* image "Warte" takes on the form of longer duration by actually lingering. The pause on "balde" (the fermata) should be similarly understood. The fermata signifies an extension lasting approximately the duration of a quarter note, so that the passage "Warte nur, warte nur, balde" occupies the space of $3\frac{1}{2}$ bars, $\frac{2}{4} + \frac{2}{4} + \frac{3}{4}$. This variable metrical form captures the as yet undirected hovering of the line "Warte nur" and creates simultaneously the necessity of continuing to the close.

The succession ´˘˘ which characterizes the rhythm of Goethe's line "Warte nur, balde" is canceled out by the repetition of "Warte nur" and by the division into three phrases:

Wár̆te nŭr—wár̆te nŭr—bál̆de.

The rhythm of line 6 is changed in a similar manner. Instead of

Dĭe Vö́gĕlĕin schwéĭgĕn ĭm Wál̆de

Schubert gives it the rhythm

Dĭe Vö́glĕin schwéigĕn—schwéigĕn—ĭm Wál̆de.

(The succession ´˘˘, "schweigen–im," is not to be interpreted as a unit here.) The continuous succession ´˘˘´ is thus maintained in the composition only for

Káŭm eĭnĕn Háuch *and* Rúhĕst dŭ aúch,

that is, for the endings of the first and second parts. They correspond to one another as half and full cadence (dominant and tonic), a relationship further strengthened by the musical rhythm: the open-ended rhythm

♩. ♪ ♪ ♩
Kaum einen Hauch

is answered by the closing

Ruhest du auch.

On the other hand, by joining together lines 1 and 2 the musical setting of "Gipfeln/Ist Ruh" forms ◡◡◡, a succession not found in the poem. As a result, this passage too is placed in relation to "Ruhest du auch" so that—with the exception of line 6, which stands by itself even this respect—all the cadences of Schubert's setting correspond to one another:

Gip– feln ist Ruh
Kaum ei–nen Hauch
Ru– hest du auch.

In its rhythm and melodic descent,

links up with

and

"Balde" has the same rhythm, but is directed upwards melodically. The fluctuation in direction of this compound gesture, mirroring the content of the poetic lines,

warte nur–warte nur–balde,

is supported in part by the accompaniment, which moves in the opposite direction,

but in particular by the variable division into three units, as
mentioned above ($\frac{2}{4}$ + $\frac{2}{4}$ + $\frac{2}{4}$). The rhyme "Walde"/"balde" is
reflected in the rhythmic identity of the two words,

in their melodic inversion

Walde—balde,

and in the sonorous brightening from

to

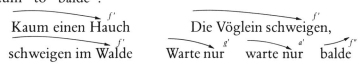

In addition, the fermata catches up the entire action from
"kaum" to "balde":

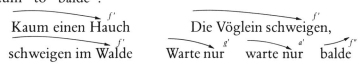

Through this inclusion of "Kaum einen Hauch" the second
section of the poem is joined to the first; and thus the entire
Lied up to the fermata on "balde" appears as a single, albeit
open-ended unit, as a single antecedent, as the meaning-laden
premise. If therefore even this structure, "Über allen Gipfeln
. . . balde," so differentiated in its parts and yet so monu-
mental, carries such weight, how heavy must be the closing
block! Yet this consists of a mere two half bars:

Now at last the closing tone b♭′ is reached—actually *reached*, whereas at the beginning of the Lied ("Über allen Gipfeln/Ist Ruh") it was merely presented. First, however, the melody descends once more to f′,

summarizes with this f′—and with the motive d″–c″–f′, which is reminiscent of

and

—the melodic activity of the entire poem, and brings it to a close with the step

The fulfillment of the poetic message, "ruhest du auch," appears as the cadential completion (I_4^6–V^7–I) of the Lied; the weight of this passage is brought to our attention by the sound of the contra-octave F, which enters here for the first time. The specific structure of this counterpositioned closing block, however, comes from the bare, undisguised entrance of the dactylic rhythm on the downbeat

which now—and only at this point in the Lied—stands all alone: the heaviest weight, the most static element possible within the rhythmic sphere. At the first "Ruhest du auch" the static quality of this rhythm is still somewhat veiled by the figure in the accompaniment

which, reminiscent of "balde," forms a transition to the repetition of the sentence, "Warte nur, balde/Ruhest du auch." In this way the statement "Ruhest du auch" becomes milder, more conciliatory; the contextual emphasis on "auch" is softly accentuated (pointing to the calm of nature: "Über allen Gipfeln ist Ruh"). Only the second "Ruhest du auch" stands completely by itself. But when the rhythm

appears in the final bar, in the coda, it is stripped bare, completely alone, absolutely at rest—like the immovable tombstone above our final resting place.

Schubert has transformed the poem into a composition by penetrating, as it were, through the poem and beyond it to the deeper level that sustains it—to the language—and by drawing directly upon this. In place of poetic form he has set *musical* structure. At the same time, however—since the linguistic and poetic layers interact with one another—his music allows the poetic work of art to shine through and illuminates it anew. To be sure, Schubert's music as a natural phenomenon reflects the continuous flow, the babbling; but as meaning captured in musical structure it has adopted a method similar to language. And precisely because the centripetal quality of the linguistic form is foreign to the nature of music, this factor is expressly singled out when it is realized in musical structure. Words (and thus also their elements, the syllables), phrases, and lines appear as substances fitted firmly together, each with its own weight. The character of being expressly joined together (com-posed) predominates.

Since a poem is also language, it contains the centripetal, distinguishing factor in its linguistic aspect. But it would be an error to assume that this factor must always be given concrete form in poetry by appearing as the determinant of structure at the level of art. Thus the songlike forms of Goethe's lyric, and the contemporary poems in general that Schubert preferred to set to music, exhibit for the most part what we might call *smooth contouring*. This finds expression in a uniformly flowing progression of lines and sentences, in a forward movement fashioned by the relationships of meaning in the language. This movement, intercepted at the end of each line by the rhymes, causes the poem as a whole to vibrate and generates its tuning, its "mood." This is the atmospheric magic in the songs of the "singer," the harpist, and Mignon in *Wilhelm Meister*. Thus we find Goethe's Lieder "musical," probably because the generation of mood is considered a specifically musical domain. And this is in fact justified—but only to the extent that music is regarded primarily as something "natural." It would be more appropriate to call such poems "musiclike" rather than "musical," not so much because their character as a whole, related as it is to the nature of music, can be easily borne "on the wings of music," but rather because in them the centripetal element of language is not advanced to a structural principle even in *poetry*. Because of this the linguistic framework is not defined in every respect, not completely established from every angle; and this allows the possibility of composition, the possibility of transforming linguistic lyric into musical structure.

There does exist, however, a poetry that takes up the centripetal element of language at the level of art and raises it to a structural determinant. Hölderlin's poetry is fashioned in this manner. By realizing this element that is latent in the language it renders the words corporeal, firmly joined together, completely determined from every angle. Precisely for this reason, however, a poem by Hölderlin cannot, in contrast to Goethe's Lieder, be composed to music. For as a poem it has been finished, as it were, down to the last detail. A procedure of this kind expresses itself in the art of poetry as *sharp contouring*; the edges of the individual patterns are sharply incised, and rhyme has no place in a poetic form of this kind. Goethe's descriptive lyric is suspended within the overall mood, is born of it. But Hölderlin's poetry is characterized by its dispassionate tone. Individual clusters of word patterns, complete in themselves, are placed next to one another, and unity results from their being joined together, "composed": the musical term now transferred to this kind of poetry and applied in its literal sense. The first strophe of Hölderlin's "Brot und Wein" is dominated by images similar to those in "Wandrers Nachtlied": rest, night, stillness, the peaks of the glade, mountain tops. But how "singing" are Goethe's lines, how warmly flowing, bathed in sentiment, and intimate;[4] and by contrast how corporeal, how mercilessly dispassionate, how *real*—and thereby still glowing—are Hölderlin's forms! They too suggest the mood in an extremely forceful way; but this happens only incidentally, as it were: "Ringsum ruhet die Stadt;/Still wird die erleuchtete Gasse."

If we attempt a recitation of "Wandrers Nachtlied," especially of lines 2–4, based on Schubert's setting—in such a way, that is, that not only the rhythm but also the reality of Schubert's Lied becomes apparent—then Goethe's lines will appear as though transformed into the language of Hölderlin: "In al-len Wipfeln Spürest du Kaum einen Hauch." Schubert's technique in *Wandrers Nachtlied* of joining together through separation is related to that of Hölderlin. The one discovers it as music, the other as poetry. Both are committed to the language, albeit in a manner different from Goethe. Schubert is related to Goethe by the warm uniform flow, the surfacing of his Lieder out of the whole of the mood: through that aspect, then, which is particularly encouraged by the "nature" of music, as we have seen.

The free verse form of "Wandrers Nachtlied," which avoids a specifically songlike character, enabled Schubert to compose it in the manner described above. He does not, however, realize the linguistic model as musical structure in the same way in all of his Lieder. It is characteristic of *Wandrers Nachtlied* that the accompaniment—with the exception of the songlike passage in bars 7–8—is not distinguished from the vocal part by means of an independent pattern: the individual phrases, their "sharp contours," originate simultaneously in the voice part and accompaniment. There are no independent accompaniment figures running parallel to the song melody, as, for example, in *Das Wandern* or *Wohin?* from the cycle *Die schöne Müllerin*. But even those Lieder with markedly songlike, usually strophic texts are only apparently artless-natural.[5]

Notes

1. See the letters of 22 April 1814, 2 May 1820, and 4 September 1831 in *Der Briefwechsel zwischen Goethe und Zelter*, ed. Max Hecker (1913; repr. Bern, Lang: 1970), vol. 1, p. 386; vol. 2, p. 57; and vol. 3, p. 470.

In Georgiades's original essay the first word of the title of Schubert's song was spelled with an "e," *Wanderers Nachtlied*, as it appeared in the first edition of 1828. In this translation the word is spelled without the initial "e," in conformity with Goethe's original poem and with more recent editions of the song, including the old *Gesamtausgabe* and the *Neue Ausgabe sämtlicher Werke* [Ed.].

2. The $^6_4$ chord, introduced as a suspension of the dominant chord immediately after the tonic triad in order to create a marked dividing point, occurs frequently in the works of the Classical masters, and subsequently in those of Schubert. (Compare, for example, Mozart's *An Chloe*, bars 3–4 and 14–15, or no. 27 from *Le nozze di Figaro*, "Giunse alfin il momento," bars 25–26, and many others.)

3. See Thrasybulos Georgiades, *Music and Language*, trans. Marie Louise Göllner (Cambridge: Cambridge University Press, 1982), pp. 34ff. (also 18ff. and 25).

4. Still more characteristic of Goethe's approach are the strophic poems, such as "Sommernacht" (from *Westöstlichen Divan*), which has a similar underlying mood.

5. The cycle *Die schöne Müllerin* is analyzed in detail from this point of view in part 2 of Georgiades's *Schubert: Musik und Lyrik*, pp. 215–381 [Ed.].

Two Analyses

◆

ARNOLD FEIL

Translated by Walter Frisch

I. *Im Dorfe*, from *Winterreise*

The principal difference between the two stanzas of Wilhelm
Müller's poem is that the first comprises an external description of a sleeping village on a winter night ("Es bellen die
Hunde . . ."), while in the second a subject steps forward and
speaks, beginning abruptly with the imperative voice ("Bellt
mich nur fort . . . !"). This person is an outcast, standing
apart from the village and its sleeping inhabitants. A wanderer,
he must continue on his way:

> Es bellen die Hunde, es rasseln die Ketten.
> Es schlafen die Menschen in ihren Betten,[1]
> Träumen sich manches, was sie nicht haben,
> Tun sich im Guten und Argen erlaben:
> Und morgen früh ist alles zerflossen.—
> Je nun, sie haben ihr Teil genossen,
> Und hoffen, was sie noch übrig liessen,
> Doch wieder zu finden auf ihren Kissen.
> Bellt mich nur fort, ihr wachen Hunde,
> Lasst mich nicht ruhn in der Schlummerstunde!
> Ich bin zu Ende mit allen Träumen—
> Was will ich unter den Schläfern säumen?

> [The dogs are barking, their chains are rattling.
> People are sleeping in their beds, dreaming of much that
> they do not have, delighting in good and evil. And to-
> morrow morning everything will have vanished. Still,

they have enjoyed their share, and hope to find once more
upon their pillows whatever remains.

Let your barking send me on my way, you wakeful
dogs; do not let me rest in the hour for sleep! I am
through with all dreaming. Why should I tarry among
sleepers?]

From the two-part poem Schubert fashions a three-part
song, of which the third corresponds musically to the first (see
the Appendix, ex. C). The more idyllic middle part, oriented
toward the sleeping inhabitants, is set in opposition to the
outer ones. But can this contrast be described more precisely?
The middle part has many distinctive features: (1) It lies in the
subdominant, which creates a distinctly softer effect. (2) Voice
and piano relate to each other in the manner of a traditional
Lied. (3) The vocal line is divided into shorter segments, whose
brevity is reinforced by the repetition of "Je nun" and "und
hoffen." (4) But above all, the agitated sixteenth-note motion
characteristic of the piano in the outer parts is abandoned. But
is the characteristic tension of this song due solely to these
rather obvious kinds of contrast? When we describe the contrast between the middle and the outer parts, have we said
everything there is to say—or even the most important things?

The question cannot be answered until we undertake to
describe with more precision what happens musically in all
three parts—until we examine compositional technique and
poetic content. Only then can it be determined whether the
opposition we have remarked was important to the composer
himself. Indeed, Schubert might have intended to set another
element in relief, for example the atmosphere of the winter's
night, with the sleeping village and the barking dogs. Analyses
of this song always suggest that the sixteenth-note figure of the
piano accompaniment is inspired by the rattling of the chains,
or even the barking of the dogs—thus by an element of the
poem's atmosphere. I repeat: is that really important? There is
little doubt that the sixteenth-note figure is significant. But we
must consider further whether its primary function is to capture the atmosphere of the poem.

Listening to the piano prelude in relation to the whole
song, we discover that it is not a conventional, dispensable
piano introduction, placed at the beginning merely to pro-

vide a starting point, or to prepare the entrance of the singer. Schubert eliminates the distinction between "prelude" and "song" proper. Whether we can legitimately say that the prelude runs into the song remains to be seen. At any rate, what we hear is a compact succession of repeated chords, with an almost trill-like figure in the bass, flowing into the same chord in open position. At this point the music breaks off abruptly, and there is a long pause before the succession of repeated chords reappears in the second bar. Only in the following measures does the harmony become active; its goal is to move from the dominant degree to the tonic, thereby leading back at bar 7 to a repetition of the opening measures. The harmony, however, is less striking than the persistence, indeed the obstinacy, of the repeated pattern: agitated chords–long pause/agitated chords–long pause. Again we must ask what it is we really hear, what stands out.

To express this with words requires the help of musical notation, and of the appropriate description of that notation. Let us note first Schubert's tempo indication, *Etwas langsam*, which was in fact originally *langsam*. *Etwas* was added later by Schubert: apparently *langsam* was too slow. What does *Etwas langsam* really connote? What is it that really goes "somewhat slowly" in this piano part? Even at a slow tempo the chords, thus the eighth notes of the $\frac{12}{8}$ measure, follow each other swiftly, the sixteenth notes still faster. In rehearsing and performing the song, one comes to understand that *langsam* implies only a regular ebb and flow within the overall motion; the unit of breath, so to speak, is the half bar, not the twelve individual eighth notes. If we attempted to conduct this, the result would be a gentle motion in half bars, swinging between downward and upward strokes; a strong attack comes on each down stroke—thus on the downbeat. (By placing accent marks on the chord in the middle of the bar in bars 1–4, Schubert sought to bring into relief both the tiny melodic motion in the upper voice and the change of chord from close, root, to open, inverted position; but by no means did he want to introduce a pattern of accents different from that implied by the notated meter.)

The motion pushes off from the downbeat, from the first

Example 1

Example 2

beat of the bar. The upbeat arises out of the long pause in the second half of the bar, then sinks down again on the first beat of the next bar, onto the disquieting, agitated chords that present the sharpest possible contrast to the basically tranquil pulse of the piece. This contrast between surface rhythm and underlying pulse is of deeper significance than the one observed earlier between the three parts of the song.

An experiment reveals still another dimension of contrast. If we play the prelude (either on the piano or on a recording) without looking at the notes, and then attempt to bring in the voice part, our natural tendency will be to follow the rhythmic structure of the prelude: we will, I think, perform as in example 1. Should we continue to sing and play naturally, our

Figure 1

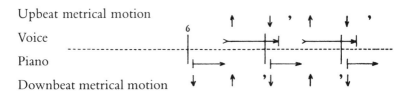

error will become apparent only at "träumen sich manches," where voice and piano no longer fit one another.

What do we learn from this experiment? Schubert brings in the voice where the listener neither expects it nor finds it natural; it enters *not* as the "prelude" implies, but as in example 2. Schubert's intention will become clear to anyone who attempts to begin in a "naturally" incorrect manner. Indeed, it is very difficult to sing correctly, to make the proper attack, for there is a very real opposition built into the musical structure. The piano prelude suggests a downbeat orientation by the almost stereotyped repetition of its down-and-up motion; we expect the entrance of the voice to continue this pattern. But when the singer does *not* conform—and Schubert wants it so—the voice establishes a tendency of motion in direct opposition to that of the piano. We can represent the musical experience graphically as in figure 1 and verbally as follows: although united by the restful *Etwas langsam* of the music, voice and piano articulate this motion in different, contradictory fashions. Thus arises the impression of distinct levels of motion, in which one kind of rhythmic structure runs in opposition to another.

The whole first section of the song is dominated by the opposition between a voice part that enters continually on an upbeat (and an upbeat half a bar long!) and a piano part that insists on the downbeats. The contradiction is not resolved but gives in to compromise, so to speak, in bars 17–18, where the right hand creates from the sixteenth-note figure (now lying in the upper part) a melodic closing figure that appears to accommodate the voice.

As a consequence of this compromise, a certain rhythmic

tranquillity prevails in bars 18–19, which lead from the first to the second part of the song. Both the underlying motion and its surface divisions appear to be reduced to a rhythmic zero point—if such an extreme image may be permitted. The sixteenth notes in the first of the two bars and the eighth notes in the second flow unarticulated, in a vacuum, as it were. Thereby emerges the possibility of introducing a new articulation, and of allowing it to be perceived as really new. A new key, G major, blossoms forth suddenly in bars 18–19 from the pedal tone D, the tonic of the first part. In a similar way a $^6_8$ measure emerges from the compromise between piano and voice (who now seem reconciled). Although no change of meter is notated— it would not have been customary in Schubert's time—it is clearly felt. In this short-winded $^6_8$ measure (as against the long $^{12}_8$ of the first part) the voice seems to be cradled within the melody. The piano, having now given up its resistance, likewise revels in the simple accompaniment. In more technical terms, this moment signifies a change in the relationship between piano and voice: the obbligato accompaniment of the first part gives way to a homophonic texture, in which the "accompaniment" has merely to fill out the harmonies implied by the voice.

We have already remarked on the three-part form of this song, a design that *Formenlehre* customarily identifies with the formula A B A′. Had a closer examination of the A and B parts established nothing more than the fact that they are different, we could expect that the third part would be a simple reprise of the first, possibly with a few deviations. But the distinction we have observed affects the musical structure so profoundly that no repetition—not even a varied one—is possible at the conclusion. What is required is a careful musical working out and resolution of the problems. If we are to take seriously the experience of listening and our analysis of the results, the characteristic tension between voice and piano, which are related to one another as obbligati, cannot be resolved as easily as in the "compromise" of bar 17. The contrast of the middle part is less one of atmosphere than of technique: its powerful effect is based on a different texture (Liedlike accompaniment of a tuneful vocal part), a different quality of motion ($^6_8$ instead of

$\frac{12}{8}$), and a different structure (abandonment of the division into different "levels"). Moreover, at the beginning of the third part tension once again permeates the music, the same tension we encountered in the first part. The listener asks himself—no matter whether consciously or unconsciously—how a piece of music like this could really reach a conciliatory conclusion.

Although the poet avoids such an ending, Schubert attempts to resolve the conflict by uniting the different elements. He wants to—indeed, he must, to assure the *musical* unity of the composition—bring into agreement the opposing types of motion represented in figure 1. He must therefore bring about the result by a decisive act of will, as it were. Schubert achieves his goal in this way: in bar 37, at the first "was will ich unter den Schläfern säumen," the voice enters unexpectedly at the tenth eighth note in the bar and in the middle of the upbeat. Neither voice nor piano has hitherto begun at this point or with this rhythmic pattern. It is as if the wanderer has torn himself free from the picture, as if by contemplating the sleeping village he has realized his situation, and now wants suddenly to change it. For the first time (except in the middle part) the piano does not insist on its stereotyped sixteenth-note figure; for the first time it is subordinate to the voice; for the first time voice and piano are united within the obbligato accompaniment, and indeed, within a common, broad gesture of motion. This moment arrives so suddenly—deviating so forcibly from the unity that has prevailed until this point—that it suspends the metrical arrangement and disrupts the rhythmic continuity. Schubert not only renounces the subdivision of the bar into eighth notes; he changes the even arrangement of pulses into an uneven one, by replacing the $\frac{12}{8}$ bar, which is divided structurally into eighth notes, with an uneven $\frac{18}{8}$ bar, whose unit value is the dotted quarter. The *Etwas langsam* motion is thus changed from 2 ♩. ($\frac{12}{8}$) to 3 ♩. ($\frac{18}{8}$) (see ex. 3).

A digression is necessary in order to answer a question that has no doubt occurred to some readers: "Change of meter? No change is notated in my edition!" In Schubert's time the law of regular recurrence of stressed beats was still in effect. For example, in a succession heavy–light/heavy–light (downbeat–upbeat/downbeat–upbeat), thus in a $\frac{2}{4}$ meter (or in our slow $\frac{12}{8}$ as well, in which the half bar provides the unit of pulse—there

Example 3

is no question here of an uneven bar, or of a four-pulse bar), the downbeats succeed each other at constant intervals; between the strong "ones" there is always a weak "two." This fundamental law of musical meter developed to full strictness in the eighteenth century. Schubert was among the first composers to call it into question, as our Lied demonstrates. But notational practice could not easily accommodate changes of meter. In order to realize a certain unconventional rhythmic configuration within the notated meter, Schubert would have had somehow to ignore the immovable barline and make the new meter apparent by other means. (For it is the barline that stands as the visual representation of the metrical pattern of stresses.)

In order to indicate stresses that do not coincide with the notated meter, Schubert uses either an accent mark or the dynamics *fp* or *fz*, or both together, prepared by a hairpin or a written crescendo. So far so good. But neither every accent nor every *fp* preceded by a crescendo suggests a change of meter, though admittedly many serve to highlight a particular rhythmic configuration that still remains entirely within the notated meter. In published versions of Schubert songs (even in contemporary prints) Schubert's accent mark—his favorite sign, which appears thousands of times—is normally represented as a decrescendo hairpin, which suggests a swelling and subsiding of the dynamics. Nevertheless, Schubert's intentions should become apparent, especially to those who observe and listen carefully. What he had in mind was a particular rhythmic phenomenon transcending the notated meter.

The crescendo hairpin in the piano at the end of bars 37 and 42 (accompanying the word "was") is by itself meaningless: it appears beneath an eighth note followed by rests. But in connection with the corresponding signs of the next bar, it becomes an indication of a metrical shift; the rhythmic structure of this passage thus becomes clear despite the fixed barline. When other such places in Schubert raise some question about whether the printed decrescendo hairpin is to be read as an accent mark or as a real decrescendo, the performer should let himself be guided by the music into passive conducting motions, simple motions that reflect visibly what is being heard or sung.[2] The composer's intention will then immediately become apparent. In our example, correct declamation is impossible within the notated meter:

↑ | ↓   ↑ | ↓   ↑— | ↓
was| will ich unter den |Schläfern säu—|men?

If we disregard the barlines, however, and observe instead Schubert's accent marks, there emerges another meter, one that contradicts the barline but yields a proper declamation:

↑ | ↓   →   ↑ | ↓ | ↓
was| will ich unter den Schläfern |säu—|men?

The second "säumen" (bars 44–46) is, of course, surprising; and in order to understand it we must return to our discussion of the song.

All the rhythmic levels or surfaces intersect in the upbeat-like 3 ♩. motion at "was will ich unter den Schläfern säumen?" The union of the different levels, which contradicts the prevailing metrical design, makes this a crucial moment in the overall structure of the song.

To reinforce its importance, Schubert repeats the segment, but not without further clarifying its original purpose. The first time around, in the second 3 ♩. bar (bar 40), the stereotyped sixteenth-note figure breaks in, bringing with it the earlier metrical arrangement, as well as the conflict between rhythmic levels (see ex. 4). It is as if the action has not been bold enough, its power insufficient to resolve the painful opposition—as if the wanderer's determination to tear himself away has not been decisive enough. After the downbeat, the 3 ♩. motion is broken off abruptly by a new downbeat, a new

Example 4

first beat, which appears in place of the proper upbeat or second beat. With one stroke Schubert brings back the former
metrical/rhythmic structure and cancels out the anomalous
segment (bars 37–39). The force of this reversal is enhanced
by the juxtaposition of two downbeats, violating the law of
musical meter, which prescribes regular alternation between
stressed and unstressed events. The listener experiences this as
the intrusion of a free, essentially nonmusical rhythmic element into the prevailing articulation of musical time. This moment reveals to us both the individual strands of the rhythmic
fabric and the larger structure that binds them. The listener can
thereby experience the musical process as a physical reality, as
musical motion.

We are made vividly aware that the conflict has failed to be
resolved, and that another, more forceful action is necessary to
bring about resolution.

The second time, the broader gesture of *two* complete 3 ♩.
bars (beginning with the notated bar 43 and the repeated "was
will ich") fuses the disparate elements, cancels out the conflict,
and brings about resolution. The wanderer has at last broken
free (ex. 5).

In order to create such a decisive moment, the composer
draws on all the means at his disposal—including, of course,
melody and harmony. We experience all dimensions of the passage, even if it is analyzed from only one viewpoint—specifically from that of rhythm, or, more precisely, motion. We hear
the entire work even if our perception sometimes singles out

Example 5

one element from the others. Thus, we would already have heard the melodic change between bars 37 and 42, from G to G♯ (on the upbeat, "was"), as an expression of the most painful anguish. The sensation becomes so intense that it not only yearns for resolution, but appears literally to bring it about by its expressive power. Nor will we have escaped the effect of the color contrast between the B-flat/G minor of bar 37 and the D major of the following bar, where "will ich" seems to be flooded with bright light.

Indeed, there are few places in the literature of Classical music like bars 43–46, in which the listener can *feel* a full cadence as both a resolution of long-range tension and as a complete harmonic closure. In this cadence even the suspensions are savored, as it were. To be sure, this effect presupposes that we have already heard the cadence once, in bars 38–40, where, although harmonically complete, it was abruptly broken off. We should also be aware that in the first part of the song and in the portion of the third part corresponding to the first, the harmony changes only with each bar, and thus scarcely makes apparent any progression. But here a succession of chords leads swiftly to a cadence within only two bars: harmonic motion comes all at once, and the progression sets in relief the rhythm we have already examined. We can truly say that "harmonic rhythm" determines the musical structure.

Tranquillity prevails at last. The rhythmic motion seems to have slowed down, especially in the second cadence with the 3 ♩. bars, where the voice sustains an infinitely long A (actually lasting a *complete* 3 ♩. bar). All compositional elements seem now to reflect this deceleration. For the first time the root of the D-major chord is in the top of the right hand (bar 46); for the first time the chord remains in the same position for the second half of the bar. The stereotyped sixteenth-note figure of the left hand has lost all its restless agitation. The F♯ in the bass on the tenth beat of bar 47 seems only a pleasant reminiscence of the upbeat articulation that had created such a discrepancy in rhythmic structure.

Let us return to our starting point and to the problem of song composition in general. *Im Dorfe* is not a strophic song. But is it through-composed? Goethe disapproved of "so-called through-composing" because it "completely destroys the general lyrical character, and it necessitates and encourages a false preoccupation with individual elements." According to these criteria, our Lied is *not* through-composed, since a preoccupation with many different details—which is clearly what Goethe had in mind—is neither encouraged nor necessitated. Rather, the whole song appears to be composed from a single viewpoint.

The wanderer, at once fettered to and ostracized from the village, finds his way out of the conflict by tearing himself away. Schubert's song is constructed from this viewpoint; it culminates in the moment of tearing away, that is, in an actual event. The song is based on the musical realization of an occurrence (in the sense of an act rather than an action), on the compositional techniques that correspond to the singularity of the wanderer's deed. The "general lyrical character" is of significance insofar as it gives rise to the conflict we have described between voice and piano; this presses toward decisive resolution in the act. To be sure, Schubert sees this tension not as a prevailing condition; he composes it as a musical occurrence. That is, he does not depict a "general lyrical character"; nor does he "necessitate or encourage preoccupation with individual elements"; nor does he paint any specific "atmosphere" or frame of mind. Rather, he develops the tension as an event in the music, as reality in a narrower sense, by means of compositional structure.

When Schubert realizes a lyric as a musical structure, he interprets the poem from a definite point of view. But this is something different from the "focal point" described by E. T. A. Hoffmann in connection with Goethe's "general lyrical character": "Inspired by a poem's fundamental meaning, the composer must capture all its emotional elements as if in a focal point, from which the melody radiates forth ["melody" here is synonymous with composition]. The tones become the external symbol of all the different aspects of the inner emotions contained in the poem."[3]

As a poet, E. T. A. Hoffmann is thinking about the general atmosphere in which the musician must bathe the whole: the medium of music realizes what lies behind the words of the poem. The basic mood must be developed to physical perceptibility by the composer.

Such settings are rarer among Schubert's Lieder than we might expect. Indeed, by these standards we might admit that other composers—perhaps Robert Schumann and Johannes Brahms, and later Hugo Wolf and Richard Strauss—wrote much more beautiful songs. But our actual musical experience makes us ask: More beautiful? Now that is a different matter! Consider Schumann's *Mondnacht* (op. 39, no. 5 [1840]; to a poem by Eichendorff) or Strauss's *Traum durch die Dämmerung* (op. 29, no. 1 [1894–95]; to a poem by Otto Julius Bierbaum), whose texts are comparable to that of *Im Dorfe*. These songs are more concerned than Schubert's with depicting a nocturnal atmosphere and the attuning of a soul. They are more coloristic, and the musical procedure is thus entirely different. That these Lieder differ in this way from Schubert's is clear; that they are thereby more beautiful no one would seriously consider. Schubert had a different goal from Schumann and Strauss: therein lies the distinction. He was inspired neither by Goethe's "general lyrical character" nor by Hoffmann's "focal point," which contains "all the aspects of the inner emotions" and from which the Lieder of Schumann and Strauss "radiate forth." Schubert, however, seeks to transform the lyrical element into musical motion, to compose it as musical structure.

II. *Moment musical* in F Minor, op. 94, no. 3 (D. 780)

As a composer for the piano, Schubert "had his final say in the short pieces of his last years. . . . It is their deeper, Schubertian originality that distinguishes these pieces." Alfred Einstein, who accords the Impromptus, op. 90 (D. 899), and the *Moments musicaux*, op. 94 (D. 780), such significance, believes at the same time that "it is easy to understand why they are his 'last word.' For he was an inventive spirit, a composer of the spontaneous, striking inspiration, and not one, like Haydn or Beethoven, who could fashion something great out of a trivial idea."[4] Yet if we accept this latter statement, the first one will seem strange. Is it really easy to understand just how these pieces achieve greatness? Are they in fact distinguished above all by spontaneous, striking inspiration? Of what might this consist? We shall investigate this question with regard to the *Moment musical* in F Minor, that "musical epigram, or 'Divertissement in miniature,'" as Einstein called it. This work appeared as "Air russe für das Pianoforte" in an *Album musical* published by Sauer and Leidesdorf in December 1823; early in 1828 it was reissued by the same firm, together with other short pieces, under the title *Moment musical*. (See the Appendix, ex. D, for entire piece. In the following discussion, all bar references will be to the score as printed in ex. D.)

In his investigation of meter and motive, Jammers has emphasized that a strong beat must be accented perceptibly at the beginning of a composition so that a listener can learn how to measure the passage of time. "His attention must be drawn primarily to the meaning of the musical event. And the question of meaning leads us to the matter of motive."[5] At the beginning of our *Moment musical* no part of the bar stands out strongly; nor at first is there any motive to provide temporal articulation. The left hand begins alone, presenting an accompaniment in which a quarter-note pulse is articulated by eighth notes, a pattern encountered frequently in movements marked *Allegro moderato*. At this point the listener can discern neither mode nor meter: he awaits the entrance of an upper voice to clarify the indeterminate harmony and divide up the continuous rhythmic motion.

The key of F minor and a $\frac{2}{4}$ meter are established only in bar 3, when the upper voice begins on the third of the triad with a rhythmic figure that defines the bar. A grace note distinguishes the first eighth note from the third as the strong beat; the second eighth note is defined as weak by a melodic

Example 6

division into sixteenth notes, the fourth by a dominant harmony. Although projected unambiguously in the third bar, the
$\frac{2}{4}$ meter becomes obscured in the fourth. Here the two quarter
notes are rhythmically, melodically, and harmonically identical; and the accent marks on both prevent any dynamic differentiation. Because of the accent marks, the stress that falls
naturally on the first of the two quarter notes must fall likewise
upon the second. Thus, while the third bar conforms to the
down-up motion of a $\frac{2}{4}$ meter, the fourth does not, because neither of its quarter notes can be subordinated to the other. Nor
does the accompaniment pattern delineate a $\frac{2}{4}$ metrical scheme.
Even if we were to represent the metrical stresses as in example
6a (where downward arrows indicate perceived downbeats, upward arrows upbeats), we would scarcely capture the musical
gesture, because the two quarter-note downbeats are different
in kind from the downbeat of the normal $\frac{2}{4}$ bar that follows: the
two quarter notes of bar 4 are at once peculiarly rigid yet elastic.
Although they exhibit a remarkable precision of gesture and
movement, they do not join together to form any standard
metrical pattern. It seems as though they attain their identity
only as part of a two-bar group, which thereby establishes itself as the smallest unit of musical meaning.

More clearly than is commonly the case, the upper voice
is organized in distinct two-bar units; until bar 62, these are

organized into groups of four. Yet these groupings do not join to form eight-bar units; rather, the groups of two function so independently that the larger grouping appears neither as an integral building block nor as a musical unity of a higher kind, but actually as the sum of smaller discrete segments. The eight-bar groupings maintain a certain degree of closure solely because of the repetitions that are indicated for the first three.

At first we are inclined to interpret the small two-bar unit as a motive. But this label is evidently inadequate. For, as Riemann says, a motive is the individual *gesture* of musical expression;[6] and our two-bar group comprises two different gestures. According to the criterion of expression Riemann adduces in defining motive, we would scarcely be tempted to give each bar its own meaning; but according to the criterion of gesture or motion, we would. The two gestures within a two-bar group are essentially distinct in movement: that of the two quarter notes is fundamentally different from that of the rhythmically subdivided bar. Moreover, the gesture of what we may call the "quarter-note bar" appears to remain more or less unaltered throughout the piece, while that of the bar with different rhythmic values undergoes changes. Nevertheless— or perhaps precisely on that account—we have the impression that the two gestures complement each other, that the two bars inevitably belong together. We tend to "hear" both gestures together, if not as a motivic unit, then as a coherent figure of motion, because the element of motion is so prominent. One gesture seems to determine the other, just as a motion in one direction creates a corresponding countermotion, and as one step in a dance figure determines a second one corresponding in space.

The whole first period of the *Moment musical* follows this pattern. Indeed, although the two-bar unit is continually varied, one can scarcely speak of motivic development. The compositional procedure is that of a series of units, or rather, a series of different shapes derived from a single unit. Thus, despite the element of variation, the repetitions continually fuse the quarter-note bar and the rhythmically differentiated bar into a single figure. The repetition of the first two bars of the melody (3–4) in bars 5–6, with scarcely a change in melody and rhythm, emphasizes that they belong together. So does the following two-bar group (7–8), which is the only one to vary the quarter-note bar—thereby confirming its particular character. The cadential motion in bar 9, as well as the rhythmic activity, which imparts the quality of an upbeat, similarly link bars 9 and 10, and at the same time all the corresponding two-bar groups that preceded.

The piece is constructed entirely from two-bar groups that behave like the first two bars of the melody. The quarter-note bar gives each group its characteristic motion. The gesture, the direction of motion, differs depending on whether the quarter-note bar comes first or second within the two-bar group (see exx. 6a and b). One figure can even function as the inverse of the other, particularly when harmony and melody vary or reinforce the direction of the movement (compare bars 3–4 with 9–10 and 61–62). The different forms of the two-bar unit, which are suspended along the thread of the continuous quarter-note pulse of the left hand, function as a succession of figures of motion: in the figures of bars 3–10, the second bar contains the quarter note; in bars 35–40, it is the first bar. Each segment thereby retains a definite, pronounced tendency of motion (ex. 7). Their juxtaposition creates the effect of an abrupt shift, a change in movement—as, for example, in bars 18–19, where for the first time two quarter-note bars are placed side by side (ex. 8), or in bars 39–42, where the succession of

Example 7

Example 8

Example 9

Example 10

units beginning with a quarter-note bar is concluded by a unit with the quarter-note bar in second position (ex. 9). Furthermore, when figures with different directional tendencies are joined together, something new develops: in the second part of the melody (bars 19–34), "opposed" two-bar figures are linked together to form four-bar ones (ex. 10).

The result is a kind of game played on many levels with musical-rhythmic figures; from this arises the dancelike quality of motion in the piece. If we were to realize the quarter-note bar in dance as emphatically stamped, and the other bar as dissolved in movement, we would understand the particular quality of motion in both the individual figures and the whole composition: although the gestures change, equilibrium is maintained by the larger flow.

The composition thus appears to be constructed so that both the bar and rhythmic-motivic development are superseded as indicators of temporal articulation by a third factor: the bar group, which divides up the continuous quarter-note pulse of the rhythmic background and thereby cancels the individual bar as the unit of time and as the principle of articulation at the lowest rhythmic level. It is the group that binds these segments into musical-rhythmic figures. The constructive element of the bar group thus fulfills simultaneously a time-measuring and a time-articulating function. Because of the compound gesture and because of the way it is transformed, the bar group has a distinct character of motion as a rhythmic-musical figure in the piece. Thus the structure of the composition seems to be determined in a particular fashion by the elements of motion, and the musical rhythm by the rhythm of motion.

This aspect becomes especially apparent toward the end. In the coda (bars 59ff.), Schubert avoids linking the more active bar to the quarter-note bar. He repeats the first bar by itself; that is, he repeats in isolation the gesture which up to now was completed by a second one. As great as is our expectation of the closing gesture, still greater—when it in fact arrives—is our impression of how different the two gestures are and, at the same time, how they belong together in a single figure. Bars 65–68 appear neither as a single four-bar unit nor as two-plus-two; rather, they consist—one can actually hear this taking shape—of a single bar repeated three times, plus an additional bar necessary for completion. This reveals that both bars are "single." But that they nevertheless, indeed necessarily, belong together is shown by the subsequent repetitions of the two-bar group they form together in bars 69–70, 71–72, 73–74, and 75–76. The composition then concludes with the second, answering gesture: now that our ears have had a sufficient demonstration of both independence and interdependence, the second gesture is also detached and repeated (bar 77). This leads back again, as it were, to the easily flowing, undifferentiated pulse of the beginning, which had established the rhythmic foundation.

We have seen that the most immediately striking aspect of inspiration in this composition is to be sought more in its qualities of motion, in its gestural dimension, than in the realm of melody and rhythm, where the word "inspiration" is usually applied. To be sure, the individual gesture is also rhythmically and melodically significant; but more important are its element of motion, its terseness and plasticity, and an insistence that yields an almost physical effect. This effect apparently presupposes the composer's division of the rhythmic dimension into different levels, since in that way it is possible for one kind of motion genuinely to stand out against the others. Thus Schubert begins by laying a rhythmic foundation: the left hand commits itself to neither a clear meter nor a definite kind of motion. One might say that the broken quarter notes have the quality of pure process; the basic rhythm is so severely limited that its uninterrupted pulsation is not actually perceived as a basic "motion" at all. The continuous pattern in the left hand, avoiding any rhythmic profile and articulation, as well as any distinct quality of motion, thereby constitutes a thread running through the composition, a "filo," along which the component phrases appear to be strung.

Until the means of analyzing musical structure are refined, it seems appropriate to restrict oneself to works of simpler design, and to adduce complicated structures only if a particular characteristic can be easily perceived. The experience gained through simpler works can later—though still with great caution—be applied to larger ones. Nevertheless, let us risk casting a glance from our *Moment musical* to the *Andante con moto* of the "Great" C-Major Symphony (D. 944). Although the structure is incomparably more complicated here, we can still see an affinity between certain elements. The remarkable "introduction," the quarter-note bars that permeate the melodic-rhythmic structure, and Schubert's way of using bar groups as building blocks—all clearly show (despite the higher level of formal organization and the difference in genre and status) that the two pieces share premises of phrase construction and presentation. Although they differ in tempo, the works correspond in their manner of motion. As Grove remarked in his renowned dictionary article on Schubert, "the symphony was written as an absolute *impromptu*."[7]

Notes

1. Müller's original line 2 reads, "Die Menschen schnarchen in ihren Betten."

2. Such experiments, in which one learns how a piece "goes" by using motions like those of conducting, were proposed by the great pedagogue Leopold Mozart as early as 1756 (the year of his son's birth): "Therefore no pains must be spared when teaching a beginner to make him understand time thoroughly. For this purpose it will be advisable for the teacher constantly to guide the pupil's hand according to the beat, and also to play to him several pieces of different meters and varied speeds, allowing him to beat time himself, in order to prove whether he understands the division, the equality, and finally the changes of speed" (*A Treatise on the Fundamental Principles of Violin Playing*, trans. Editha Knocker, 2d ed. [London: Oxford University Press, 1951], p. 33). Similar advice comes from the important eighteenth-century theorist Johann Philipp Kirnberger: "Therefore the inexperienced composer is advised first to sing or play the melody that he has in his head and wants to write down, and to beat the time with his hand or his foot. In this way he will not miss the principal notes that fall on the downbeat, provided that the melody is metric" (*The Art of Strict Musical Composition* [1776], trans. David Beach and Jurgen Thym [New Haven: Yale University Press, 1982], pp. 388–89). See also my *Studien zu Schuberts Rhythmik* (Munich: Fink, 1966), pp. 17–21.

3. In a review from 1814. See E. T. A. Hoffmann, *Schriften zur Musik*, ed. Friedrich Schnapp (Munich: Winkler, 1963), p. 238.

4. Alfred Einstein, *Schubert: A Musical Portrait* (London and New York: Oxford University Press, 1951), pp. 288–89.

5. Ewald Jammers, "Takt und Motiv: zur neuzeitlichen musikalischen Rhythmik," *Archiv für Musikwissenschaft* 20 (1963): 199.

6. See Hugo Riemann, *System der musikalischen Rhythmik und Metrik* (Leipzig: Breitkopf und Härtel, 1903), pp. viii and 13–18.

7. George Grove, "Schubert," in *Grove's Dictionary of Music and Musicians*, 3rd ed., ed. H. C. Colles (New York: Macmillan, 1928), vol. 4, p. 613.

Auf dem Flusse: Image and Background in a Schubert Song

DAVID LEWIN

I propose here to explore the relation of musical structure to textual imagery in Schubert's song *Auf dem Flusse*, from *Winterreise*. The exploration will have several parts. Section I develops a general critical stance toward the relation of music and text in Schubert's songs, a stance that will underlie the subsequent critical and analytic discourse. Section II offers a reading of the text for this specific song. According to this reading—which I am of course claiming to be Schubert's, on the basis of his setting—the text is in a sense "about" the creation and evaluation of a poetic image; the essential point is to take the two concluding questions, "Mein Herz, in diesem Bache/Erkennst du nun dein Bild?" and "Ob's unter seiner Rinde/Wohl auch so reissend schwillt?", as undecided, not rhetorical. The climactic musical events over the second half of the song, which sets those questions, reflect and project the tensions experienced by the singer as he contemplates the answers.

Section III examines some of the ways in which various aspects of the musical texture combine to suggest and elaborate the reading of section II. From a theoretical view, the aspects touched on are of a traditional sort: the length of musical sections vis-à-vis text sections, tonality, modality, the relations of the vocal line to the soprano and bass lines of its accompaniment, and motivic rhythms. Novel, perhaps, is the consideration of such matters in connection with the critical stance of section I, and the sort of reading asserted in section II.

Section IV goes systematically deeper into the tonal and

rhythmic structure of the music. This exploration gives rise to reductive sketches which present in themselves striking images, images that appear to relate forcefully to the imagery of the text and the questions concerning it. The relation of my reduction technique to Schenkerian theory, and of my results to Schenker's published sketch for this song, are taken up in an appendix. Section V attempts a consistent and dramatically cogent interpretation of the images and questions raised by the sketches of section IV, as relating to the images and questions of the text.

I. A Critical Stance:
The Composer as Actor

Whatever filled the poet's breast Schubert faithfully represented and transfigured in each of his songs, as none has done before him. Every one of his song compositions is in reality a poem on the poem he set to music.[1]

Josef von Spaun's eulogy of 1829 fairly represents the critical style of Schubert's sympathetic contemporaries. Today we feel more comfortable with critical discourse of a kind that points to networks of specific events in specific compositions. Still, it would be a mistake to dismiss Spaun's prose as unsubstantial and unhelpful. If we read it closely, we will find him asserting propositions that bear directly on the methodology of analysis and criticism.

One might put these propositions as follows. A Schubert song takes as structural premises not only musical syntax, as it was understood at the time, but also the structure of the individual text at hand. The world of the song, then, is not simply a musical world. On the other hand, it is also not simply the textual world translated into music: it not only "represents" this world, says Spaun, but also "transfigures" it. So, if we have as text a poem on X, we should not consider the song to be another, related poem on X. Rather, the song should be considered a poem on the poem-on-X.

Hence we can understand the song as a poetic "reading" of the poem-on-X that is its text, a reading that employs a particular mimesis of X as a representational means. From this point of view, I find it suggestive to conceive the relations of composer, text, and song as analogous to the relations of actor, script, and dramatic reading.[2]

To exemplify the utility of this analogy, consider the famous pause in *Die Post*. The opening text reads: "Von der Strasse her ein Posthorn klingt./Was hat es, dass es so hoch aufspringt,/Mein Herz?/Die Post bringt keinen Brief für dich." Schubert extends the second sentence by repetitions of the text, going through a substantial harmonic excursion and return, using an ostinato springing rhythm throughout. There then follows an abrupt silence for one bar, before the song continues, "Die Post bringt keinen Brief," in minor and with the springing rhythm gone. These gestures involve a mimetic reading of the text by the composer, a reading that is far from a simple musical translation or mere "representation," as Spaun puts it. Imagine an actor performing the text in question as a script. According to Schubert's reading, the actor would elaborate and extend the action associated with the second sentence. He might pace back and forth, rush to the window and back, and so on. Then, as the postman approaches the door or the mailbox, the actor would stop moving during Schubert's pause, tensely cocking an ear to listen for the sound of the letter dropping. He would relax his features in dejection as the postman leaves, and continue the recitation: "Die Post bringt keinen Brief."

Contrast this performance with that of another actor, who is seated at a desk on stage, immersed in reading, writing, or composing. He looks up, momentarily distracted, and notes, "Von der Strasse her ein Posthorn klingt." He resumes his activity for a while, then breaks off in ironic amusement and says to himself, in one phrase, "Was hat es, dass es so hoch aufspringt, mein Herz?—Die Post bringt keinen Brief für *dich*." This second reading of the text is surely as plausible as the first. In fact, it would not be difficult to argue that Schubert's setting involves reading into the text a good deal more than the second actor has to.[3]

So while it would be accurate enough to say that Schubert's reading "represents" the text, one cannot go very far critically until one investigates how this particular representation, from among a number of plausible readings, interacts with musical structure to project an overall poetic conception of the poem that is the text. In this regard, for instance, one thinks of the rhythmic complexity of Schubert's composition, with its contrasts of expansion and contraction, of regularity and irregularity, of ostinato clock time, musical-phrase time, and textline time. One notes the importance of exact rhythmic and metric proportion in the effect of the first actor's scene: his "internal clock," representing his heart in the text, enters into complex relationships with external clocks of the actor's outer world—that is, the postman's springing horse, his rounds, etc. The second actor's scene has much less of an exact mensural character; it could be delivered much more "in its own time."

In the view I have just proposed, the relation between Müller's poem and Schubert's setting is formally analogous to that, say, between Shakespeare's *Hamlet* and Henry Irving's *Hamlet*. One could not sensibly analyze or criticize Irving's *Hamlet* without referring to Shakespeare's, but it is important not to identify or confuse the distinct artworks.

II. Schubert's Reading of the Text

The text of *Auf dem Flusse* follows the poet's creation of a central image, and his reaction to it. One can fairly say, as I put it in my preliminary remarks, that Schubert's reading is in a sense actually "about" the poet as image maker and image questioner. A condensed synopsis of the poem will help clarify the point. The text of the poem can be found in table 1, on pp. 132–33. The song is printed as example E in the Appendix.

In stanzas 1 and 2, the poet observes that the stream, which used to rush in a wild bright torrent, has become still, cold, and rigid, with a hard stiff cover ("Rinde"). In stanzas 3 and 4 the poet, as if idly, scratches upon the ice the name of his lost beloved, along with the dates of their first meeting and their final separation. He circumscribes the whole with a broken ring.

In stanza 5 the poet is struck by the image he has "inadvertently" created and investigates its pertinence by posing two questions, which might be taken rhetorically. The first question, insofar as it can be taken rhetorically, points out in the picture of the broken ring, guarding within it the name and the dates, the image of the poet's broken heart. The second question, insofar as it can be taken rhetorically, points out a further and potentially optimistic aspect of the image. Just as the vernal torrent of stanzas 1–2 is still rushing on beneath the icy surface of the stream, so the poet's heart is still swelling tumultuously beneath its frozen crust.

I contend, however, that Schubert's reading takes the two questions at face value, rather than rhetorically. The first question asks, "Mein Herz, in diesem Bache / Erkennst du nun dein Bild?" Read rhetorically, this does indeed assert the pertinence of the image; taken at face value, however, it *questions* the pertinence of the image. *Is* the inscribed stream truly the image of my heart? Taken at face value, the question also calls into issue the poet's capacity to judge the propriety of the image. Does my heart recognize and credit the image, perceiving or judging it as apt? (These nuances can fairly be read into "Erkennst du nun." N.B.: *Erkenne dich!* = "Know thyself.")

The second question asks, "Ob's unter seiner Rinde / Wohl auch so reissend schwillt?" An attempt to take this question on face value seems at first ridiculous: the poet, presumably a student of natural science in the spirit of Goethe, must know that rivers flow beneath their ice in wintertime. Perhaps the stream is small enough to cast the issue in doubt. But this is beside the point. It is clear that neither the geological structure of the stream nor the biological structure of the heart is essentially at issue.

Having said that, one becomes struck by the use of the word "Rinde." The word is in fact a common biological term, used to denote the cortex of the heart. So it is the use of "Rinde" in connection with the stream, not the heart, that is metaphorical. Through this metaphor, the relation of subject and image is inverted. In the first question, the stream was the putative image of the heart; now the heart with its "Rinde" is the putative image of the stream. This device was prepared by the earlier, more descriptive, reference to the "Rinde" of the stream in stanza 2.

At that time, the stream was "du"; the very opening of the poem, in fact, calls attention to the stream in the—as a—second person. By the time we get to the first question in stanza 5, however, there has been a transformation of persons:

the heart has become the second person. When we get to the second question, we have just heard "Erkennst du nun dein Bild?" addressed to the heart. Then, since the *Rinde*, in literal usage, belongs to that second-person heart, it is properly "deiner" *Rinde*, not "seiner." From this point of view we can regard the inversion of subject and image, discussed earlier, as a means of transforming and hence avoiding the implicit question, "Ob's unter *deiner* Rinde/Wohl auch so reissend schwillt?" The transformation of second and third persons over the poem also abets this interpenetration of subject and image.

In Schubert's reading, then, I say that the second question is taken to ask: Is there any capacity for flowing torrential warmth left under the frozen exterior of the heart? Or is it frozen solid, through and through? A question not to be asked! (And it is not asked . . . yet it is.) The stream will melt next spring, returning to the state described in the opening line of the poem. The subglacial flow of the stream, if existent, is a portent linking its future with its past. But will the poet's heart ever thaw, returning to a state "des ersten Grüsses"? Is there some subglacial flow within it that portends such an eventual thaw? And thus, picking up the first question again, *is* the stream, which will thaw next spring, a true image of the heart?

It is the tensions underlying this reading of the questions that, as I suggested earlier, force the expansion of the setting of stanza 5 over the entire second half of the song. In this connection, it is interesting to note that Müller's text contracts at this point rather than expands. Stanzas 1 and 2 are paired by their subject matter, and so are stanzas 3 and 4; stanza 5, however, which ends the poem, has no partner. Instead it asks two questions. The pair of questions thus substitutes, as it were, for a pair of stanzas; this contracts the time involved by a factor of two. One might say that Müller's text ends with an unresolved systole, for which Schubert's song substitutes an enormous diastole.

III. The Song: Mimetic Techniques

This diastole can be observed in table 1, which plots some of the easily perceivable aspects of the musical setting against the coextensive text. In clock time, the crucial point at bar 41

Table 1

Bar	Text	Stanza Number	Strophe Number
5	Der du so lustig rauschtest, du heller, wilder Fluss, wie still bist du geworden, giebst keinen Scheidegruss!	1	1
14	Mit harter, starrer Rinde hast du dich überdeckt, liegst kalt und unbeweglich im Sande ausgestreckt.	2	2
23	In deine Decke grab'ich mit einem spitzen Stein den Namen meiner Liebsten und Stund' und Tag hinein:	3	3
31	Den Tag des ersten Grusses, den Tag, an dem ich ging: um Nam' und Zahlen windet sich ein zerbroch'ner Ring.	4	4
41	Mein Herz, in diesem Bache erkennst du nun dein Bild?	5	5
48	Ob's unter seiner Rinde wohl auch so reissend schwillt?	(5)	6
54	Mein Herz, etc.	(5)	7
62	Ob's unter seiner Rinde, etc.	(5)	8

comes more than halfway through the song. But in strophic time, the four strophes that set stanza 5 after this point are equivalent to the four strophes setting stanzas 1–4 before it. In a sense, this musical diastole is consistent with Müller's textual systole. For one can say that the music expands with respect

Duration	Key	Relation of Voice to Piano	Right-hand Rhythmic Motive
9 bars	E minor	Voice doubles bass (low E).	𝄾 ♪ 𝄾 ♪
9 bars			
8 bars	E major	Voice (G♯) takes over from RH (G♮); now RH doubles voice.	𝄾 ♪ ♬♬
10 bars (8 + 2)			𝄾 ♪ ♬♬ [sic]
7 bars	E minor	Voice (B) rises above both hands.	𝄾 ♪ 𝄾 ♪
6 bars	G-sharp minor		𝄾 ♬♬ 𝄾 ♬♬ [sic]
8 bars	E minor	Voice reaches high E; continues in highest register, above both hands.	𝄾 ♪ 𝄾 ♪
8 bars			𝄾 ♬♬ 𝄾 ♬♬

to the text it sets or, taking a relativistic view, one can say that the text contracts with respect to the amount of music that sets it. The latter formulation is consistent with the reading of section II, which had stanza 5 contracted with respect to its emotional and structural implications.

In any case, Schubert, as he approaches the crucial text questions, makes use of temporal contraction in another way. I am referring to the rhythmic scheme that governs the durations of successive strophes. As appears from the "duration" column in table 1, the process of contraction leads directly and unambiguously to strophe 6, the climactically compressed strophe that first sets the climactic final question of our reading. (The two-measure extension of strophe 4, as the *maggiore* ends, does not disturb the sense of the rhythmic scheme.) Strophe 6, as goal of the contraction process, is consistent with what I have asserted to be Schubert's literal, rather than rhetorical, reading of the text questions.

Strophe 6 takes another kind of strong accent because of the key of its opening. In this sort of loose chaconne/passacaglia/variation structure, strophe 6 is the unique strophe that does not begin with a strong downbeat on E minor or E major. It begins with the usual strong downbeat, but in a foreign key. The relation of G-sharp minor to E major is clear enough: the G-sharp harmony represents iii of E major and as we shall see later, the G♯ in the bass at bar 48 can fit very convincingly into a structural arpeggiation of the E-major (!) triad over the bass line of the song as a whole. These functions put strophe 6 into the realm of E major, the key associated with happy memories of earlier times, perhaps springtime, in stanzas 3–4. This tonal function for G-sharp minor thus supports a potentially optimistic answer for the concomitant second text question. If indeed a secret E-major deep structure lies *unter der Rinde* of the E-minor surface structure, then the poet's heart does indeed preserve its capacity for warmth and the return of a vernal state.

Of course, the song is not in the major mode, which is to say that the optimistic answer to the questions is ultimately untenable in Schubert's reading. Though, as we shall see presently, it is not so easy to show convincingly *why* the song is not in fact in the major mode once one begins to examine its deeper tonal structure, which hinges not only on the bass G♯ of bar 48, but also on the powerful vocal G♯ at bar 23. To answer that "why," we shall have to explore what is wrong with the image the poet has constructed, what militates against the E-major image suggested by the deep-level structure.

But we must defer this study until sections IV and V. Here we can note that while the G♯ does indeed put the second question into the realm of the happy, warm E-major memories, the tonal material of strophe 6 also, and ambivalently, refers back to the icy, immobile E-minor world of the opening strophes. The G-sharp minor world of the sixth strophe specifically recalls the icy harmonies of bars 9–12 and 18–21. Those measures encompass a most desolate part of the E-minor world; the coextensive text includes the words *still . . . geworden, kalt,* and *unbeweglich.* Here (in bars 9–12) the tones A♯ and D♯ are locally diatonic, as they also are in bars 48–51. So, as it were, we have been warned that those locally diatonic tones can very easily elaborate and return to E minor in this song. With a bit of stimulation, in fact, one can hear how the melodic structure of the bass line in strophe 1 is transformed into the melodic structure of the vocal line in strophes 5 and 6. Figure 1 provides the stimulus. The reader should not be distracted by the harmonic notation, which will be discussed soon. The main point of the figure is to suggest the *melodic* transformation of the reduced bass line, bars 5–14, into the reduced vocal line, bars 41–54.

From this point of view, the bass G♯ of strophe 6 does not function as a root representing the major third degree of E. Rather, it functions as a means of providing consonant support for the structural tones B and D♯ in the vocal line. And figure 1 makes it clear that B and D♯ strongly project the dominant function in E minor. Riemann's notion of "dominant parallel"—"$(D^+)_p$,"—furnishes a good label for the G-sharp chord in this connection, as figure 1 shows.

The $(D^+)_p$ analysis of the harmony, in asserting dominant function, implicitly rejects an alternate Riemann analysis of the harmony as $\overline{\mathfrak{T}}^+$, an analysis that would assign the harmony

Figure 1

e: T   D⁺   D⁺ T   T D⁺   (D⁺)ₚ   D⁺   T

tonic function. The rejected analysis would be the way to assert in Riemannian terms the idea that the bass G♯ represents the third of a structurally prior E-major tonic. Instead, the $(D^+)_p$ analysis asserts for the bass G♯ a function as the under-fifth of the voice's D♯, the tone that is in fact the Riemann root of the harmony. And that root D♯ of the asserted $(D^+)_p$ functions as the third of a structurally prior B-major harmony, a harmony that is in turn the major dominant of a structurally prior E-minor tonic—understanding "E minor" in our sense now, not Riemann's.

The use of G-sharp minor in strophe 6 is strongly qualified, then, not only by a potential optimistic E-major arpeggiation lying *unter der Rinde* of E-minor surface events, but also by the recollection of the icy D♯ and its ultimate root B that lay, *kalt* and *unbeweglich, unter der Rinde* of the right hand, during the E-minor events of strophe 1. In this way, Schubert projects and reinforces his ambivalent reading of the second text question: What *does* lie *unter deiner Rinde*—the E-major world of strophes 3–4 or the E-minor world of strophes 1–2? The use of tonal and modal ambiguity here, as well as the progressive contraction of strophe lengths, makes it impossible to read the text questions rhetorically. In this connection, note how the *forte* dynamic at bar 48 bursts out from a song that had been *pianissimo* and *pianississimo* up to bar 41, and had risen only to *piano* at that point. One does not sing such a *forte* rhetorically.

We have so far observed that strophe 6 is a climactic goal for a number of musical processes. We have observed in this connection its ambivalence in referring both to the E-major and E-minor worlds, and we have associated this ambivalence with a structural indecision as regards optimistic or pessimistic answers to the questions of the text.

These views of strophe 6 are further confirmed by the development of the right-hand rhythmic motive, which is summarized in the last column of table 1. Once again, strophe 6 is the climactic goal of a process. And, as with the G-sharp tonality, the motive form of strophe 6 has ambivalent references to the two worlds of the song. On the one hand, the thirty-second notes pick up and continue the process of quickening that began with the sixteenths of strophe 3 and continued with the sixteenth triplets of strophe 4; hence we could read the motive form of strophe 6 as even more torrentially flowing, be-fitting an optimistic answer to the question. On the other hand, the thirty-second notes are interrupted by a syncopating rest on the third eighth of the motive: in this respect the mo-tive form resembles the shuddering forms of the pessimistic strophes 1 and 2, just recalled in strophe 5, rather than the smoother, more flowing forms of strophes 3 and 4. The poet's heart is certainly pumping furiously over strophe 6, even faster than it was during its warm beating over strophes 3 and 4; yet the heartbeat here is perhaps more a raging palpitation than a swelling flow.[4] The return of the thirty-second notes in the final strophe seems to confirm a pessimistic reading for the motive form, though this outcome is, of course, as yet unheard during strophe 6.

Finally, it is illuminating in this context to examine the doubling relations of voice, right hand, and bass line. These relations are sketched in the penultimate column of table 1. During strophes 1 and 2, the right hand incessantly reiterates 3–2 in E minor, *kalt und unbeweglich*. Meanwhile, the voice doubles the bass line, which avoids prominent third degrees. The singer seems to be saying, "I am, at this point, only a bass line, *unter der Rinde*; I have nothing to do with that terrible minor *Kopfton* in the right hand."

Consistent with that attitude, the singer thereupon takes a sharp stone and scratches a G♯ on the icy surface of the right hand, at bar 23. Using that G♯, he substitutes a reiterated major 3–2 for the earlier minor 3–2 over the next two variations of the strophe. The right hand, transformed by the image-making activity of the poet, momentarily follows him along, abandoning its own preferred minor *Kopfton* while, so to speak, the G♯ image is warm. (It will freeze over again presently.) The singer has insisted on G♯, not G♮, as the structural *Kopfton* for the melody, a feature that all the doubling relations so far em-phasize. (While the melodic activity of the third and fourth strophes is more florid than the unadorned G–F♯ gestures of strophes 1 and 2, it is not hard to hear the underlying G♯–F♯ gestures that form the basis for that activity. The underlying 3–2 will be made clear in the reductions of section IV.)

At bar 38 the voice, detaching itself from the right-hand part, leaps up to B at the cadence, rather than settling on F♯

once more. The rising pitch, coming at the end of all this material, implies a question; it thus foreshadows the explicit questions coming up in the text. The poet silently contemplates the image he has made, as we listen to the extended fluttering of his heart in the rhythmic motive of the piano. Then everything, even the heart itself, is silent for one measure.

Despite the tremendous musical climaxes later on, bar 40 can be taken as the dramatic climax of the composition. When E minor returns at bar 41, with the right-hand motive of the opening, one senses a tragic catastrophe ahead. It is as if the singer, during the silence in bar 40, had already asked himself the questions and answered them negatively. This sense is made all the stronger by the fact that, while the left hand begins to sing like a cello *unter der Rinde* of the right hand at bar 41, the singer himself temporarily remains silent. He is *still geworden* and *unbeweglich*; he cannot double *this* bass line, as it flows warmly on beneath the icy surface of the right hand. His heart ("mein Herz") is *not* like the riverbed flowing on beneath.

A Schenkerian approach to the large-scale tonal activity hereabouts is revealing. If at bar 41 the singer were indeed to double the bass—for example, by singing "mein Herz" on low B and E across the barline of that measure—then the tonic degree E could be heard as closing a Schenkerian *Ursatz*, and furthermore closing that structure in the major mode. Each strophe so far has elaborated the essential melodic gesture 3−2, in minor or major, with tonic-dominant support. A vocal E, then, at the barline of bar 41 after the vocal G♯−F♯ gestures of strophes 3 and 4, would provide a structural melodic first degree with tonic support; the *Urlinie* and a concomitant *Ursatz* would essentially close. Given the relations of the voice to the right hand, and to the modal character of the music, such a closure would make musical sense only in the major mode here. This would certainly provide a conclusive and optimistic answer for the questions of the text and the subtext as we have discussed it, questions that in fact are only starting to be presented at bar 41. This situation would indeed render the questions purely rhetorical.

This Schenkerian view, then, gives valuable insight here into the tragic structure of the song, in particular into the inability of the voice to double the bass line at bar 41. Still, the singer, while unable to double the bass, does refuse to submit to the right hand's ominous G♮. Rather than double the G♮, abandoning his major *Kopfton*, he continues his quest for a tenable position in the context. He thus sings neither E nor G♮; rather, he holds onto the questioning B of bar 38 as the one melodic tone that is available for him to take into bars 41–42—the B that sets both the broken ring and his heart. That questioning B, in fact, will sound on after the cataclysm of strophe 8 has passed. It sounds in the piano at bar 74, the very last event of the piece, as the poet moves on and away, taking his heart and his questions with him.

From the vocal B of bars 41–42 to the end of the singing—that is, over the entire questioning half of the song—bass, right-hand melody, and vocal line are essentially distinct, despite some partial doublings. In this respect the situation resembles neither strophes 1–2 nor 3–4. Instead a new mode of relationship develops: beginning at the crucial B of "mein Herz," the voice rises above both the other lines, dissociating itself from both the earlier couplings.

Such behavior is not consistent with a supposition that the poet is confirming rhetorically the validity of an image that has been well established. Rather, it supports again, and in a new way, the notion that he is examining, questioning, and criticizing the image he constructed during strophes 3 and 4. Just as he can be imagined getting up from the ice, rising up physically from his position at surface level to stand above the entire accompaniment, surface as well as bass. The rising tessitura of the vocal line, in fact, is a feature that persists continuously throughout the entire song from its beginning, not just from bar 41 on. Expanding our interpretation of the rising B as a question mark, at bar 38 and following, we can then interpret this continuous rise in the vocal line, up to the final climax, as the mimesis of a giant structural qestion mark. And this suits very well the reading of the text that I proposed above, in section II.

IV. Deeper Structure

In section III, we investigated a number of musical gestures by which Schubert, in the words of Spaun, "represented and transfigured" the images and questions of the text. Some of these matters involved phenomena progressing over considerable spans of time and bearing strongly on the central aesthetic content of the song. We were able to discuss them without invoking very deep levels of tonal structure in a technical sense. I should now like to show that such representation and transfiguration also permeate events on those deeper levels.

Some preliminary remarks are in order. It will be wise to state explicitly what I hope the analysis so far has made clear: my personal belief that the aesthetic significance of a musical phenomenon in a hierarchic tonal or metric structure should not be correlated a priori, either directly or inversely, with the depth of the structural level at which the phenomenon is manifest.

I do not want to interrupt critical discussion of the song more than is necessary to introduce the reductive sketches I shall be using. As I have already said, technical commentary on those sketches is relegated to an appendix; there, too, I discuss various differences between Schenker's diagram of the song in *Der freie Satz* and my own readings. But the reader who has not yet glanced ahead to that appendix should still be provided with a certain minimum of background information for my sketches. Each note on a sketch testifies that I hear the tone of the indicated line (voice, right hand, left hand) as an essential participant in a harmony that essentially governs the rhythmically symbolized span of the piece. The reader, while doubtless disagreeing with some of my assertions, and with some more than others, will nonetheless quickly get the sense of the method by actually performing the sketches—they are explicitly designed for performance by keyboard and possibly voice, in tempo and in the indicated meters. Within reason, some filling in of the harmony would be unobjectionable. The point is to check the harmonic, linear, and rhythmic-metric assertions of the sketches by ear, both as plausible tonal syntax in themselves and as accurate reportage of tonal and metric structuring within the piece. Time spans analyzed as expanded or contracted at a given metric level are adjusted to the asserted norm at the appropriate deeper level.

These preliminary observations out of the way, let us turn to figure 2, which brings into clearer focus a number of fea-

Figure 2

tures discussed earlier. Particularly clear is the technique of
rhythmic expansion and compression within the large hyper-
measures that demarcate the strophes. In this connection, it
is curious how the six-bar group of bars 35–41 expands a
four-bar group on one metric level (that of the half-strophe),

while the six-bar group of bars 48–54 contracts an eight-bar
group at a higher metric level (that of the entire strophe). The
bass structures of the two passages in figure 2 are remarkably
similar.

Overall, the bass line of figure 2 clarifies the sense in
which the strophes constitute a loose chaconne or set of variations. The right-hand line of the figure displays clearly its
characteristic repeated 3–2 gestures at this level.

Figure 3, which reduces figure 2 one metric stage further,
also shows repeated 3–2 gestures in the right hand and varia-
tional structure among the strophes on that metric level. In addition, it begins to bring into view some curious phenomena.
Its bass line descends an octave, from the upper E at the beginning to the lower E at bar 54. The descent takes place using
degrees of the major rather than the minor mode of E. After
reaching the low E at bar 54, the bass of figure 3 does begin to

Figure 3

Figure 4

sound in the minor mode, but only to confirm a melodic goal already attained, as it were, in E major. Meanwhile the vocal line of the figure, which begins essentially by doubling the bass, rises up the octave to the high E at bar 54, in contrary motion to the bass line. This ascent also takes place "in E major"; that is, the vocal line of figure 3 sounds firmly in that key when played or sung.

This phenomenon comes into even sharper focus in figure 4, in which the reduction is carried one stage further. The reduced bass line and vocal line, in their mirror relationship, now both sound clearly in the major mode throughout. One notes the structuring force of the G♯ in the voice over strophes 3 and 4, and the G♯ in the bass at the beginning of strophe 6. The vocal G♯ that begins strophe 3, it will be recalled, "corrected" the earlier icy G♮ of the right hand in strophes 1–2. At this metric level the G♮s that occur within the bass line during strophes 7 and 8 disappear, leaving the field completely clear for the major mode as regards the overall structure of the bass line at this level. In the piano part of figure 4 one can hear very clearly the essential variation structure underlying the succession of strophes—strophe 6 being exceptional in this respect, as in so many others.

The mirror arpeggiation of voice part and bass, both projecting the major mode, is even more starkly portrayed in figure 5. In this final reduction, only the right hand of the accompaniment maintains the minor mode, with its *kalt und unbeweglich* insistence on G♮, G♮, G♮, beating on grimly and incessantly save when momentarily scratched by G♯ in strophes 3–4 and strophe 6.

What a picture! That remark indeed gets back to the point: we are dealing here precisely with the singer as a maker of images, and a critic of images. We have already noted, in section III, how the imagery and its questioning relate to matters of essential melodic structure, modality, and the relation of the vocal line to each of the hands in the piano. Now we have to confront the emergence of these matters on a very deep structural level, and interpret the image that figure 5 conveys to us.

V. Under and Over, Inside and Outside

The vocal part, right-hand part, and bass part of figure 5 can be taken to represent respectively the poet, the surface of the ice, and the warm flow beneath the ice. The poet (vocal line)

Figure 5

rises over the static, frozen surface of the ice (right hand); the riverbed (bass line), reflecting the poet mirrorwise, descends beneath that surface. Thus *unter der Rinde*, with its E-major arpeggiation downwards, is the mirror of *über der Rinde*, with its E-major arpeggiation upwards; *über der Rinde*, or even *ober der Rinde*, is the vantage from which the poet as critic hopes to exert mastery over the image he has created.

In order to interpret figure 5 in all its complexity, it will be helpful to distinguish a "false image" and a "true image" that can be read from it. The false image develops from the apparent structural priority enjoyed by the outer voices. "I am like the riverbed, which I reflect," imagines the poet. "As melodically active outer voices, we control the deep structure of the piece in our optimistic E-major mode. The static frozen G♮ of the right hand, prominent though it may be, does not affect our deep structure, where it is only a blue note—and in an inner voice, at that. *Unter der Rinde* lies the E major of the bass, which reflects me and which I reflect, latent though this secret may be in the surface structure of the piece." In this way, the singer reasserts his association with the bass line, and his contrast with the right-hand line, which we discussed earlier in connection with doubling relations. After the B of "mein Herz" the singer can no longer double the bass line, but he hits instead upon the ingenious expedient of mirroring it, a relation appropriate to his physical action—standing up—at the beginning of stanza 5.

What makes this optimistic image musically false is the implication that the E-major outer voices of figure 5 really control the deep structure of the music. If they did, we would hear the piece in E major; and since we clearly hear the piece in E minor, the image cannot be valid. What makes the image poetically false is its misplaced obsession with the categories of "over" and "under." While these categories are appropriate to characterize the relation of icy surface to riverbed, and of right hand to left hand, they are not appropriate to the cortex of the heart and its interior chambers, nor to the relation of vocal line and bass line combined to the right-hand line of figure 5.

The correct categories in both the latter cases are not "over" and "under," but rather "outside" and "inside." It is this misfit of categories that provides a negative answer for the question, "in diesem Bache erkennst du nun dein Bild?" The stream, that is, is *not* a valid image of the heart. We have just discussed some reasons why. The poet senses such reasons with tension and alarm but is unable to analyze them; presumably the analysis would be too painful.

The true image of figure 5, then, proceeds, on the basis of "outside" and "inside." The poet, by entering into relation with the stream, has coupled his vocal line with the bass line to form a hull (*Rinde*) of "outer voices," ostensibly active and in E major. But the static "inner voice" that the right hand projects as the kernel at the heart of this *Rinde* tells us better: its innermost secret is G♮, G♮, G♮, as indeed was foretold by the opening motive of the right hand in the piece. Within the elaborately constructed exterior show of motion and warmth, the poet's heart is frozen solid forever. This must be so, since it is only and preeminently the right hand line of figure 5 that can make us hear the piece with a deep structure in the minor mode.[5] Ironically enough, it is the poet's very creation of the false image for figure 5, with its pairing of outer voices against an inner voice, that enables the true image to assert itself.

Afterword

On p. 130 I discuss the word *Rinde*, saying that it "is in fact a common biological term, used to denote the cortex of the heart. So it is the use of *Rinde* in connection with the stream, not the heart, that is metaphorical." These remarks have generated some powerful and interesting criticism by a number of readers, including Anthony Newcomb, whose splendid article follow mine in the present volume. Still, I am disposed to stick to my guns on the specific point. *Rinde is* in fact a common biological term. It is used for the bark of a tree, the shell of a crustacean, the crust on a pastry or a loaf of bread, and the rind of a cheese. In addition, it is used in specifically anatomical contexts to mean the cortex of an organ: *rindenartig* and *rindig* translate as "cortical" and "corticose" in those contexts.

In all these usages, the *Rinde* has three salient features. First, it is a curved surface surrounding completely the entire volume of a three-dimensional object; it is not a flat planar surface extending over the top of a spatial region, as ice is when it covers a stream. Second, the object that is surrounded by the *Rinde* is alive, or recently alive, or at least characteristically organic. (Perhaps we should consider French cheese rather than German in this connection.) Third, the *Rinde* protects the object from injury, in the manner of armor.

In my personal dictionaries (Heath and Muret-Sanders, 1910), I find no usage for *Rinde* that is not consistent with each of the three features discussed above. In contrast, the use of *Rinde* for the ice does not fit easily with any of the features. As already noted, the ice is a flat planar surface, not a curved surface bounding an enclosed volume. The stream is not literally, but only metaphorically, alive; it was only metaphorically recently alive; it is technically organic in the sense that water is composed of the organic elements hydrogen and oxygen, but it is not characteristically organic beyond that, except metaphorically. Finally, though a stream does develop its ice as the crayfish develops its shell, we do not normally think of the ice as having a protective function, defending the stream from accident or attack. (The *American Heritage Dictionary* [New York, American Heritage, 1969], pp. 1536–37, gives *rendh-* as the Indo-European root for English "rind," and specifically brings out the issue of attack: "*rendh-*. To tear up. . . . 2. Germanic ★ *rind-* in Old English *rind(e)*, rind (< "thing torn off"): RIND." This way of regarding the *Rinde*, from the viewpoint of the aggressor, seems all too depressingly Indo-European.)

In sum, I am still very comfortable with the idea that "it is the use of *Rinde* in connection with the stream, not the heart, that is metaphorical." The word appropriate for the ice in literal discourse would be *Decke*, not *Rinde*. The *Rinde* metaphor does not lie far from common speech of a flowery sort, but that observation makes me feel the force of the metaphor all the more strongly. Here, though, I must draw back from exploring the fascinating contentions which *that* idea suggests, and point out that I really have nothing to "prove" with all my linguistic commentary, except that it would be reasonable to imagine Schubert finding in Müller's text an interpenetration of object and image over the last stanza, a relationship projecting a subtle misfit of "underneath (the ice)" with "inside (the heart)."

I am sure that Müller was sensitive to that metaphorical

dissonance; no mere adventurer, he assumed an official post as teacher and ducal librarian at Dessau in 1819, the year after he completed the *Müller-Lieder*. My belief that Schubert was also sensitive to these matters must rest upon the manner in which I read various aspects of his musical structure. I do not really care, of course, to what extent Schubert was a fine critic of Müller's text. I do care how well he "acted" that script *per musica*, and so I have only to show that the ideas about "under the surface" and "around the kernel," ideas that emerge in my musical analysis, do engage things that can be legitimately (if not necessarily) read from the text. The musical analysis itself is amply problematic.

Appendix

As mentioned in section IV, the basic method of the reductions is to proceed from one metric level to the next, setting down at each stage as few notes as possible to represent an essential harmony governing each rhythmic unit at the pertinent metric level. At each stage, I find it important to make the sketch performable, give or take a few figures and/or some continuolike harmonic realization. In general, one can usually proceed in a straightforward way from one metric level to the next.

At times, one must adjust expansions or contractions to an asserted metric norm at the next level. The technique can be inferred from the pertinent relations of figure 2 to figure 3, etc. Interpretations as to what is expanded and what is contracted, at which metric level, are not always as clear in other pieces as they are here, where the basic strophe model provides clear large downbeats and a referential rhythmic matrix.

At times, also, one must juggle several rhythmic levels at once. The systematic elimination of accessory tones, proceeding from the more detailed to the broader metric levels, will generally lead to a clear choice of essential tones at the broadest level under consideration. Figure 6 illustrates the technique, using a tricky passage of the song, bars 27–28. The harmony at the barline of bar 28 indicates that the high E is an appoggiatura to the D♮ at

Figure 6

this metric level, and not an essential constituent of the E^6 harmony on a larger level. An alternate reading, to the latter effect, might be worked out; it would lead to the same end result.

As in most reductive methods of tonal analysis, a given event may project a variety of functions with respect to a variety of nested and/or overlapping contexts in which it is embedded. One is free to read, or not to read, any a priori aesthetic value into the largest or most final of such contexts, beyond its formal status as the largest or most final. In *Auf dem Flusse*, for example, my method yields a variety of functions in a variety of contexts for the $^6_4$ chord in bars 9–10. Considering the context spanned by the B triad at the end of bar 8 and the $G\sharp^7$ chord at the beginning of bar 11, for instance, one can hear the $^6_4$ chords as passing through. This context is certainly not the most powerful one functioning over strophe 1; still, the notion that the $A\sharp$ in the bass of the $^6_4$ can pass down from B to $G\sharp$ is clearly suggestive in connection with the approach to the climactic $G\sharp$ in the bass of strophe 6. Note the disposition of registers in the bass line from bar 44 to bar 48, the latter picking up in register the $A\sharp$ from bar 45. We have earlier discussed the G-sharp harmony of bar 48 as, inter alia, a substitute for the B harmony; this consideration lends support to the idea of passing from one to the other.

An overlapping context, that of bars 9 through 12 in isolation, suggests that the $G\sharp^7$ chord is a returning neighbor to the $^6_4$ chord, which then resolves in D-sharp minor following the standard cadential formula. Figure 7 displays the analysis. In this context the $A\sharp$ of the bass is essential, not passing, and the $F\sharp$ and $D\sharp$ above are suspensions, not essential tones.

The implications of figure 7, however, disappear in a larger context that includes all of strophe 1 and the beginning of strophe 2. Here the overall harmony of the metric unit defined by bars 5–6 is clearly E minor, as is the overall harmony of bars 7–8, and that of bars 14–15. In addition, there are

Figure 7

Figure 8

Figure 9

NB: G - F# , G - F# in the RH

Figure 10

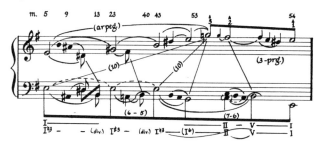

large pulses at the barlines of bars 5 and 14, along with a subordinate pulse at bar 9 and still lesser pulses at bars 7 and 12. An attempt to fit the reading of figure 7 into this larger context using my method would result in the syntactic impossibility of figure 8.

In this context, the weight of the measure-pair 12–13 must clearly be carried by the B chord, functioning as dominant of the following E, and not by the D# chord. Then the A#$^6_4$ can be heard, in *this* (!) context, to inflect the structural B chord that follows it, as in figure 9.

My methods and symbology suffer here, I think, in comparison with Schenker's. Because of the priority I assign metric hierarchies in the reduction process, I am unable (so far as I can see) to assign the D# cadence the tonal (as opposed to metric) weight I hear it bearing in the larger context. Schenker's symbology, not so strictly bound to metric hierarchies, does a much better job of demonstrating the simultaneous functioning and interpenetration of the disparate contexts portrayed in my figures 7 and 9. His sketch is reproduced as figure 10.[6]

I have already discussed in note 5 my dissatisfaction with Schenker's *Urlinie*, which begins at bar 53 and closes in bar 54. As I said there, it seems dramatically essential that an *Urlinie*, if there is to be one, should begin exactly with the opening G♮ in the right hand. (This would destroy the theoretical point of Schenker's figure, which is to exemplify arpeggiation in the structural upper voice before the onset of the *Urlinie* proper.) A *Kopfton* in bar 1 could, of course, later be transferred into the voice at bar 53. The vocal high E of bar 54 could then transfer back to the upper right hand E of bar 70, finishing the proposed *Urlinie* in the proper register (and instrument). The advantages of listening for an *Urlinie*, particularly around bar 41, have already been discussed. On the other hand, the immobile frozen G♮ projected by the right hand of my figure 5, a G♮ that does not descend, has a symbolic and dramatic value too. Figure 5 is, of course, utterly un-Schenkerian.

The other substantial divergence of my musical results from Schenker's involves the bass G♯ at bar 48, governing the beat at the onset of strophe 6. Almost all my discussion, particularly around table 1 and figure 5, has pointed to the necessity of including that G♯ in the large structure of the bass arpeggiation over the song, given my reading. Without the G♯ there is no "secret" E-major bass structure to mirror the E-major vocal structure in figure 5, and the dramatic force of the various processes converging climactically onto strophe 6 is largely dissipated.

The priority I attribute to metric hierarchies would force me in any case to write the bass G♯ at bar 48, since it carries the downbeat of its strophe. Schenker's use of the G♮ in the bass of bar 53 for his *Bassbrechung* is inconceivable in the context of my method. I think Schenker was repelled on principle by the idea of mixture in the *Bassbrechung*. He also evidently wanted good local bass support for the third degree of his *Urlinie*. Perhaps, too, he heard the G-sharp harmony very strongly as a "dominant parallel" in the sense of figure 1. Be that as it may, my methods are well suited to throwing light on the dramatic meaning of bar 48 and its environs, while Schenker's sketch jumps uncomfortably, to my critical taste, from bar 41 to bar 52.

It goes without saying that any reductive method of analysis for tonal music owes an inestimable debt to Schenker's work. I have felt, therefore, some obligation to clarify my departures both from his method and from his reading of this piece. My own method, which I have been using for some time, combines aspects of Schenkerian technique with metric considerations first suggested to me by Andrew Imbrie at Berkeley in the early 1960s. The published sketches that mine most closely resemble, I think, are those presented by Imbrie in his article "'Extra' Measures and Metrical Ambiguity in Beethoven," in *Beethoven Studies* [I], ed. Alan Tyson, (New York: Norton, 1973), pp. 45–66.

I do not consider my method worked out into a theory. It does have strong theoretical implications. I do not feel completely comfortable with all of these, nor do I always find the analytic readings produced by my harmonic-metric consistency at all levels more suggestive than alternate readings assigning more priority to higher-level voice leading. I find it important to make my sketches "performable," as opposed to conceptual, but I am not sure why I feel that way.

Important publications that bear on the theoretical assumptions I seem to be making include Edward T. Cone, *Musical Form and Musical Performance* (New York: Norton, 1968); Arthur J. Komar, *Theory of Suspensions* (Princeton: Princeton University Press, 1971); Maury Yeston, *The Stratification of*

Musical Rhythm (New Haven: Yale University Press, 1976); and Fred Lerdahl and Ray Jackendoff, *A Generative Theory of Tonal Music* (Cambridge, Mass.: MIT Press, 1983).

Notes

1. O. E. Deutsch, *The Schubert Reader*, trans. Eric Blom (New York: Norton, 1947), p. 875.

2. In making the composer a mimetic actor rather than a more general poetic reader of the text, I go beyond the stance adopted by Edward T. Cone in his heartwarming study *The Composer's Voice* (Berkeley and Los Angeles: University of California Press, 1974).

3. An acquaintance of mine once placed a telephone call and was greeted by an unfamiliar voice saying without preface, "You have the wrong number." "Yes, I do," said my friend, "but how did you know?" "Nobody ever calls *me*," said the person at the other end, and hung up.

4. It would be helpful to have some indication as to whether the thirty-second-note groups are to be played slurred, staccato, detached, or even *martellato*. The resulting effects would heighten the associations of strophe 6, more or less accordingly, with the optimistic or pessimistic worlds of the music. The autograph does not help here: its attack symbols (dots plus slurs) stop abruptly, as do those in the published scores, in bar 28. That is why I have written *sic* here and there on table 1.

5. Schenker's analysis (see appendix to this article) asserts otherwise: he hears the structural *Kopfton* for the *Urlinie* only at the vocal G♮ in bar 53. I am convinced that he errs here. The whole discussion so far indicates why I feel it is essential to attach basic structural weight to the opening G♮ in the right hand (which Schenker omits from his sketch). Figure 5 treats the G♮ as a *Kopfton*, beginning an *Urlinie* that will eventually descend and close. That hearing, the reader will recall, made excellent sense of the failure of the voice to double the bass line at the return of the *minore* at bar 41. What is at issue here is not the presence or absence of an *Urlinie*, but rather the function of the G♮ in the right hand at the opening. If there is to be an *Urlinie*, it ought to begin there.

6. Heinrich Schenker, *Free Composition*, trans. and ed. Ernst Oster (New York: Longmans, 1979), vol. 2, figure 40, 2.

Structure and Expression in a Schubert Song:
Noch einmal Auf dem Flusse *zu hören*

◆

ANTHONY NEWCOMB

I

This essay will explore the relationship between structure and expressive meaning in music. Most who have thought about this subject have realized that the expressive meaning of music cannot be translated into words. But it does not follow that musical expression should be excluded from those areas about which serious, informed words may be spoken. True, the expressive meaning of a musical work cannot be translated into words, or into anything else for that matter; no more can the expressive meaning of a painting, or a poem. To translate, in the normal sense of the word, is not the goal of expressive analysis. The goal is to interpret—not only to isolate aspects of structural function, but also to ask what it might mean that the function is fulfilled in this particular way rather than another. Clearly such an enterprise cannot set out to prove; it sets out to persuade—to enhance understanding by illuminating particular aspects of the work in a particular way.[1] Abandonment of the ideal—or the chimera—of proof does not entail abandonment of careful reasoning and of thorough factual and technical preparation. On the contrary, expressive analysis can be done with considerable precision, avoiding the loosely suggested or entirely unspecified connection between expressive interpretation and musical-technical analysis. And it benefits from a full fund of historical information.

With this in mind, I have limited myself here to one song, and one for which there is already a considerable foundation of careful recent criticism on which to build: *Auf dem Flusse* figures in recent studies by Georgiades (1967), Schwarmath (1969), Feil (1975), and Lewin (1982), and I shall refer to these below.[2] Lewin is the most recent and most detailed of my predecessors here, and the degree to which his thoughts have stimulated mine will be obvious to those who have read his essay, which precedes mine in this volume. I shall stray farther from purely structural matters than does Lewin, but I shall try to demonstrate a continuous connection between the structural and the expressive interpretation.

Like Lewin, I shall start where the composer of virtually every song has presumably started, with a reading of the poetic text. This will then lead to the interaction of music and text in the single song, then outward in turn to a consideration of the larger whole to which both belong.

II

Müller's text contains five stanzas, each with the following accent pattern and rhyme scheme (save for the first line of stanza 1, which begins , ‿ ‿):

‿ ‚ ‿ ‚ ‿ ‚ ‿	*a*
‿ ‚ ‿ ‚ ‿ ‚	*b*
‿ ‚ ‿ ‚ ‿ ‚ ‿	*c*
‿ ‚ ‿ ‚ ‿ ‚	*b*

Der du so lustig rauschtest,
Du heller, wilder Fluss,
Wie still bist du geworden,
Giebst keinen Scheidegruss.

Mit harter, starrer Rinde
Hast du dich überdeckt,
Liegst kalt und unbeweglich
Im Sande ausgestreckt.

In deine Decke grab' ich
Mit einem spitzen Stein
Den Namen meiner Liebsten
Und Stund' und Tag hinein:

Den Tag des ersten Grusses,
Den Tag, an dem ich ging,
Um Nam' und Zahlen windet
Sich ein zerbroch'ner Ring.

Mein Herz, in diesem Bache
Erkennst du nun dein Bild?
Ob's unter seiner Rinde
Wohl auch so reissend schwillt?

[You who used to ripple so happily, bright, wild stream, how still you have become: you give no parting greeting.

With a hard, stiff crust you have covered yourself. You lie cold and motionless, stretched out in the sand.

In your shell I engrave with a sharp stone the name of my beloved, and hour and day:

The day of our first greeting, the day on which I went away; around name and numbers runs an uncompleted circle.

My heart, in this brook do you now recognize your own image? Is it, underneath its shell, seething too, and near to bursting?]

In stanzas 1 and 2 the lyric protagonist addresses the stream. He does so largely as a way of giving information about the stream: it is at least frozen over, perhaps frozen through.[3] In stanzas 3 and 4 (as in the middle sections of so many of the *Winterreise* poems) he turns his glance backward in time. Here his memory is, rather exceptionally for this cycle, stimulated by a present action, which this middle section describes: with a stone he is engaged in cutting into the ice the name of his beloved, and the dates of their first and last meetings. Although when the protagonist begins the middle section he is still addressing the stream, the action and its stimulus to his memory turn his attention inward, toward his own heart. He then addresses his heart directly in the last stanza, the first one in which he makes a statement about his own present emotional condition (as opposed to observing and describing a situation from without).

He makes this statement through two rhetorical questions—that is, two questions asked not to elicit information but for other reasons, here to give information. With the first question, he directs his heart to the potential similarity between itself and the stream, perhaps including both the frozen exterior of stanzas 1 and 2, and the scratched, scarred exterior of stanzas 3 and 4. (The substitution of "erkennst du wohl" for Müller's "erkennst du nun" in the printer's clean copy and in the first edition of the song seems to emphasize the proposed affirmative answer to this first rhetorical question.) Then he uses this proposed similarity to assert that his heart, though cold and scarred outside, is still seething beneath—that he is still warm with passion for his beloved. He asserts this by asking if the stream also swells with motion beneath the surface. For the heart to recognize its image this would need to be true.

Lewin's interpretation of this last stanza especially (pp. 129–31) is quite different. It rests heavily on a double meaning of the word *Rinde*, as not only the frozen shell of the river but also the cortex of the heart. In fact, he asserts this "common biological" meaning to be the primary one here, and goes on to claim that the final question of the poem is a real, not a rhetorical one—a real one asking if the poet's heart, now frozen like the river, will warm with emotion again in the spring. But to take the appeal here to be to the biological term meaning cortex of the heart is certainly too literal. Neither the poet nor Schubert wants to call attention to the heart of biology treatises and anatomical diagrams—tubes and muscles for pumping blood.[4] Both use the conventional metaphor of a psychological not a physical heart, one that is the seat of the emotions. To insist on the cortex in this metaphor would certainly be out of place. Nor is there a mention in the poem of the idea of the river's thawing in the spring. On the contrary, the idea of an approaching spring is excluded from the expressive world of *Winterreise*.[5] It seems a questionable source for the true meaning of the climactic question of this poem.

The evident tension in the two questions of the final stanza of the poem is not the arcane one Lewin proposes, but the relatively straightforward one between, on the one hand, the mounting of internal passion excited by memory, and, on the other, the denial and repression of that passion necessitated by the external situation in which the protagonist of the poetic cycle finds himself.

III

Schubert's setting of the poem starts at a nadir of rhythmic activity. (See the Appendix, ex. E.) Georgiades has noted that the beginning of the song is unique in *Winterreise*—pure accompanimental figuration, stripped of all ornament.[6] It is in fact less a rhythm than a pulse, emitted in neutral four-bar chunks. The opening four bars of the vocal line, which circle around the tonic triad without real melodic or harmonic motion, do little to relieve this static, frozen atmosphere. The literal content of the first two lines of text—the "lustig rauschen," the "heller, wilder Fluss"—is reflected only by strong irony. While one can easily imagine using the inherent contrast in the text to build a strong musical contrast in the opening of the song, Schubert here sees only a motionless, monotone gray. With "wie still bist du geworden" comes the first distinctive movement of the song: a chilling downward slip by voice and bass in parallel octaves to an unprepared second-inversion triad on the raised seventh degree. Though violent in its unconventionality, this first move remains tiny, and even this tiny move is downward.

H. H. Eggebrecht has proposed that "numerous Schubert songs are . . . reducible to a kernel that sounds out literally at the beginning of the song, and that lies at the basis of the thematic development of the entire song."[7] This distinctive gesture at the beginning of bar 9 is such a kernel, both verbal and musical. The verbal element is, initially at least, the word "still," but it is the *still* of frozen motion—of intrinsic motion temporarily restrained—not a genuine *still* (cf. the corresponding place in stanza 2: "kalt und unbeweglich"). The ironic tension between motion and its apparent absence, intimated in the setting of the opening lines, thus continues with this musical-verbal kernel. Though as muted as everything else so far, the kernel will not remain so.

This kernel is the first of three particular features that I shall trace throughout the song, for the three together give a highly distinctive shape to a relatively conventional schematic design. The second announces itself immediately in bars 11–12, where what I have called the almost nonrhythmic pulse of the opening is animated ever so slightly by the vocal line, at the words "keinen Scheidegruss." In another instance of ironic tension between textual image and underlying musical motion, the vocal line breaks perversely out of its lethargy to imitate, even down to the cheerful little inverted mordent, the parting wave that the text is simultaneously denying. The accompaniment then picks up and extends the sixteenth-note motion of the voice, in the process breaking the rigid four-bar mold of the previous phrases with a fifth bar containing a small surge of motion that will be the direct model for the larger ones to come.[8]

The third feature, involving the treatment of range in the vocal part, also announces itself in bar 11. Here the restricted circling gestures of the opening are expanded: the voice covers an eleventh in little more than a quarter note, again in seeming ironic portrayal of the motion denied in the text. A similar tension between text and musical motion, now amplified by the high d♯' on the "un-" of "unbeweglich," exists at the corresponding place at the end of strophe 2. Admittedly, the melodic motion in both places is still the same circling motion that had marked the opening phrases of the song, now decorating a simple cadential progression (ii$_5^6$ or iv^7–V–i). But the gestures themselves are becoming more concentrated and energetic.

The preservation of the draft of much of the first part of *Winterreise* enables to us to observe Schubert as he refines his initial ideas.[9] In the particular instance of bars 11–12, we can see him doing a bit of what might be called expressive fine tuning, by which he turns a vague, generically expressive musical gesture into a more sharply defined and specific one. His initial version of the voice part in bar 11 went up only to a c♯' on the fourth sixteenth note, then down only to a c✕ on the last eighth note. In reworking the passage he considerably expanded the energy of the gesture simply by changing its extreme notes. He also sharpened the musical expression of swelling, but suppressed motion in the piano interlude of bar 13 by revising the upper voice of the first four sixteenth notes, whose original static version is given in example 1. Again, the tiny initial detail grows in subsequent variation. The rise of a minor second in the upper voice at bar 13 becomes a major second upon repetition in bar 22, providing the starting note, g♯, for the lyrical upward expansion of the vocal part in the ensuing bars, just

Example 1

as the momentary rhythmic activity in the bar of extension-interlude becomes the source of the more consistent motion at the beginning of the next section.[10]

A contrast of motion, mode, and lyric style define this next segment as a contrasting middle section. The textual motivation for this contrast is the protagonist's switch at this point from description of an external situation in nature to description of a present action of his own—an action that he still, however, describes impassively, as if from the outside. In fact, the tone of the poem remains constant and rather cold across stanzas 3 and 4. The scratching of a *Rinde* with a *spitzen Stein* is neither a warm sound nor a friendly image, and the unpleasant aspects of this memory in Müller's poem (the "Tag an dem ich ging" and the "zerbroch'ner Ring") almost outweigh the pleasant ones. In Schubert's middle section, however, an increasing warmth comes over the protagonist as action stimulates memory.

Although the turn to the major mode announces this change in a conventional way, the development of the three features to which I have referred above gives individuality and evolving shape to the emotion expressed. First, the sixteenth-note rhythmic motion of the piano interlude is converted into a more consistently used and clearly directed motion of upbeat-loaded second beats, pressing across to the following downbeat.[11] Simultaneously the vocal line begins to rise in range. Moving upward in a conjunct lyrical style that replaces the triadic circling of the opening stanzas, it passes from the third, through the fourth and fifth, to the sixth degree of the scale (with harmonic support for each), at which point (bar 28) it frees itself from the accompaniment to overreach the d' with an appoggiatura e', the highest note of the piece so far. This high d' with upper appoggiatura occurs in the spot in the poetic and musical stanza (the third line and phrase) that corresponds to what I have called the musical-verbal kernel in the first two stanzas: the sinking motion to the D-sharp triad. The transformation of this kernel in the middle section gains expressive meaning not only from the rising swell of the musical gesture that it culminates, but from the contrast with the analogous moments in the previous stanzas. The frozen motion-emotion of stanzas 1 and 2 is warming and pressing to the surface. This expressive meaning is reinforced by the simultaneous failure of the rhythmic motion to stop on the downbeat of bar 28, as it had on those of bars 23–27. Instead, the sixteenth notes flow right through the first half of the bar, stop only momentarily on the second half, then flow continuously across bar 29 and the first half of bar 30, before breaking into the triplets at the beginning of stanza 4.

Though Schubert's setting of stanza 4 follows closely the model of 3, several details reveal that the protagonist's emotion continues to grow as he pursues his memory. As before, his vocal line rises in a single gesture to the high e', although to do so it must now ignore the emotional downward turn of Müller's "den Tag, an dem ich ging." With a subtle variation of this repeated musical climax, the coolness and distance of the beginning of the song disappear entirely: it is as if we were present at the action described. As the protagonist draws the ring around the names ("windet/Sich"), he must suddenly confront the realization that he cannot complete the action: the vocal line, after circling back warmly to the climactic high e', suddenly breaks, plunging down a gaping seventh. The attempted gesture has failed, and with it breaks the dream.

Although the dream has broken, Schubert's setting goes on to express through musical metaphor the idea that remembered passion cannot be so easily denied. The gap between stanzas 4 and 5 is full of unresolved tension. This tension is expressed by the bass line, where the move to the low E implied by the descent in bars 38–39 is interrupted at the beginning of stanza 5 in bar 41, and resolved only at the cadence in bar 54. Likewise, the rhythmic motion of the end of stanza 4—like that of stanza 3, more continuous than that of the beginning—now runs on even longer, across two full bars of piano interlude, before stopping abruptly at the rest in bar 40. This energy is not released in a downbeat accent, not dissipated or wound down; it is interrupted. And it bursts out again immediately in the jerky interjections of the voice in bars 41ff., then erupts with unprecedented force in bars 47ff.; here the phrase rhythms lose their four-bar regularity, not through extension as in stanzas 1 and 2, but through truncation, which imparts an impatient forward thrust.

The clearest musical expression of this unresolved tension is the handling of range in the vocal line. The failed gesture of bars 36–37 will not fully accept its failure. The vocal line in bar 37 rises once more to c♯', breaks once more ("zerbroch'ner Ring"), then rises again to b in bar 38 for its final note of the stanza. After the interlude and general pause, the accompaniment proposes a return to the repressed motion and emotion of the beginning. But the heart of our protagonist, the psychological heart of the literary convention, says no. He separates himself both from his own original circling melody and from the downward g–f♯ pull of the top voice of the accompaniment, and, beginning stanza 5 at the b♮ where he had ended the fourth, moves directly to the high e' of his previous climax. A tension had already been introduced between accompaniment and vocal line—voice pulling upward against downward-pulling accompaniment—when the voice overshot the accompaniment for its previous climax (bars 28 and 36). It became more striking when the voice refused to return to the g–f♯ cadential area of the accompaniment in bars 37–38, insisting on its own c♯' to b. The voice now stages a full metaphorical rebellion against the return proposed by the accompaniment and by the conventional A B A' form.[12]

Here again an examination of Schubert's draft reveals how he sharpened the expressive musical metaphor. In revising the draft Schubert changed the rhythmic figure of the accompaniment of bars 31–39 from sixteenth notes to triplet sixteenth notes, making more vivid the expression of mounting excitement across the middle section. In the draft, a c♯' on "sich" in bar 36—instead of the high e' of the final version—falls short of the wonderful immediacy created in the final version by the continuing upward swing of the climactic gesture right through bar 36 until the sudden break at the beginning of bar 37, the primary component in making us feel that we are present at the moment of the breaking of the dream. The vocal line of bars 37–38 originally proceeded as in example 2, which virtually

Example 2

fails to express the continued upward pull of the voice part against the descending accompaniment, embodied in the c♯' and b of the final version.[13]

As we have noted, the vocal part of the beginning of stanza 5 refuses the proposal of the piano part to return to the suppressed, frozen motion of the beginning of the piece. Instead, it pursues across the entire closing section the curve of mounting passion begun in the middle section, thus ending up in full tension with the conventional shape of the song, with the requirement posed by the narrative of the poetic cycle, and with the initial musical image of the song as proposed and reasserted by the accompaniment. The course of this curve of mounting passion is traced especially by the continuing development of the three elements already isolated: vocal range, rhythmic motion, and the kernel of bar 9.

After beginning the closing section in the same b−e' range occupied at the climax of the previous section, the voice climbs gradually higher across the remainder of the song. Annexing f♯' at the first question (bar 46), g' at the second (bar 53), and finally a' at the repetition of the second question (bar 59), it ends on the tonic an octave above its starting point.[14] After proposing a return to the rhythmic style of the opening of the song, the accompaniment is soon swept into bursts of thirty-second notes, completing the progression of the whole song from eighths to sixteenths to triplet sixteenths to thirty-seconds.

Simultaneously with this climax of rhythmic motion in the accompanimental figuration comes a wondrous revision of the functional-harmonic and the metaphorical-expressive meanings of the kernel of bar 9. The stage is set for this revision by an expansion in total range, as the voice part moves to the top of its range and the piano drops an octave to its lowest extremes, and by a tightening of the phrase rhythm, as this octave drop in the piano pushes to the subdominant of D-sharp minor a bar early according to the model of the opening stanzas, which has so far been followed. All this prepares a release of energy from the second beat of bar 47 to the downbeat of bar 48. Here the protagonist, as Schubert portrays him, takes his resolve and makes explicit his continuing passion. And at just this point the kernel of bar 9 is reinterpreted. Just as the "still" and "kalt" of stanzas 1 and 2 no longer convey the true internal situation of the protagonist (and perhaps never did), the kernel, as developed in bars 45ff., is no longer a tiny sinking gesture to the leading tone, made only to be revoked by a quick return to the tonic. Instead it becomes a real point of departure, a platform from which to vault upward by fourth to G-sharp minor.[15]

Here I part from Lewin's interpretation, which sees in the move to G-sharp minor a reference to the parallel major of the middle section and a ray of bright optimism in the bleak musical landscape. This is, of course, a possible interpretation of G-sharp minor in the abstract; but that is not the way the key area is presented here. Nowhere in this passage, or indeed in the entire song, does Schubert call attention to the possible mediant relationship between G-sharp minor and E major. The preparation and presentation of G-sharp minor here stress, and hence express, two qualities: first, the vigorous, overreaching quality of G♯, which lies above the expected G♮ of the E-minor scale and is approached by a leap of a full fourth from the leading tone, instead of by half step as in the model proposed by the opening stanzas; second, its quality of being minor, rather than the conventional relative major on G. Both these qualities will be reinforced in the following repetition of the entire poetic stanza.

At the beginning of this repetition the accompaniment pulls back, once more urging a return to the opening image. The answer this time is a still more extreme interpretation of the kernel. Schubert for the first time modulates up within the first phrase of the stanza, reminding us of the standard upward modulation in an E-minor piece: to G major not G-sharp minor. Then he uses the sinking half step—now to F♯—as a platform to vault up not one but two fourths. The voice then modifies its previous melodic line to pick up these upward-leaping fourths and move in sequence to an astonishing G minor, emphasizing with this second question of the repeated stanza the minor-ness of the gesture at the first setting of the question.

After the repetition of this last line—simultaneously the end of the vocal line and its climax in range—the accompaniment snaps back at once to the opening image of frozen motion. The hints of ironic tension between surface textual detail and musical representation in the first section of the song have developed into a wide gap between the denial of emotion required by the external situation and the warmth of emotion within, a gap never wider than at the juxtaposition of the last vocal phrase with the piano postlude.

IV

The accumulated tension flashes across this gap and is released only at the beginning of the next song, *Rückblick*, to which *Auf dem Flusse*, in this sense open-ended and unresolved, serves as a large upbeat.[16] There are other connections drawing together these adjacent songs. The stepwise ascent from the first to the fifth degree that opens the vocal line in *Auf dem Flusse* (and that returns throughout its final section) takes on two chromatic degrees to become the opening of the piano introduction to *Rückblick*. The shocking G minor in the last strophe of *Auf dem Flusse* (bars 64–65), and the final rocking back and forth between E and G in the piano postlude (bars 70–71) prepare the G minor of *Rückblick*. The broken octaves in the last bars of *Auf dem Flusse* ( ) are transferred to the opening of *Rückblick* ( ).

The connections between *Auf dem Flusse* and *Rückblick* are by no means the only such close structural connections between adjacent songs in Schubert's *Winterreise*. It is usually proposed that *Winterreise* is not a true cycle, even in the loosely connected, narrative tradition of the *Liederspiel*, such as *Die schöne Müllerin*. I should like to propose that at least the first part of *Winterreise* is indeed such a cycle, or was read as such by Schubert when he first encountered it as an independently published unit of twelve poems, and went about setting it to music. My arguments to this effect will proceed from the historical information surrounding *Winterreise*, to the cycle of poems, to the cycle of songs.[17]

1. The history of Schubert's encounter with the poems of Müller's *Die Winterreise* has been told many times.[18] Schubert encountered the twelve poems that were to become his part I for the first time (we do not know precisely when) in a periodical of 1823. They are printed there as a group and in the order and the versions in which he set them.[19] Only later (again, we do not know precisely when) did he encounter a publication of 1824, in which Müller had interspersed twelve additional poems among the dozen original ones.

Schubert may have encountered the larger version only after he had drafted his setting of the twelve-poem version. This seems to be indicated by the presence of the word *Fine* after the last song in Schubert's autograph of the first twelve songs. (It also appears at this point in the non-autograph clean copy used as printer's model; the first edition is the first source to delete this word.)[20] This autograph bears the date February 1827, but it is on the clean copy of the revised first song. The date thus may well indicate when Schubert replaced his original draft of this song with this recopied revised version, after the main work on all twelve songs had been completed. Robert Winter's investigations into the paper types used by Schubert show that the paper on which he wrote both the draft of the first twelve songs and all of the inserted revisions, save that of *Rückblick*, was a paper used by Schubert from October 1826 through May 1827.[21] (The revision of *Rückblick* is on a paper used in June through September 1827.) All this evidence conspires to indicate that the bulk of the work on these twelve songs was done in the winter of 1826–27, probably before March 1827.

The draft for the complete second part has disappeared, and only a clean copy in Schubert's hand, dated October 1827, survives. Drafts survive for *Mut* and *Die Nebensonnen*, however; that of *Die Nebensonnen* can be associated with events of September 1827,[22] and is on a paper used at the end of the summer of 1827.[23] In these drafts the two songs bear no number, and hence give no evidence of being yet firmly placed in a cycle.[24] All this indicates late summer and early autumn of 1827 for the major work on part II.[25] Schober, as reported by Kreissle, claimed that Schubert had found Müller's *Die Winterreise* in the little library that Schober had "set up for" Schubert.[26]

How can we reconcile this with the fact that Schubert had moved in with Schober only in March 1827?[27] Perhaps it was in the little library provided by Schober that Schubert found the second volume of Müller's *Gedichte aus den hinterlassenen Papieren eines reisenden Waldhornisten* (1824), containing the full twenty-four-poem version of *Die Winterreise*. Then in the summer or early fall of 1827 he set the additional twelve poems, thus modifying his original intent. (Whether the twenty-four-song set becomes a new whole is a question that I shall not take up here.)

2. The twelve poems published in the periodical of 1823 do indeed describe simple actions and have references back and forth that weave the group into a narrative sequence, however loose.[28] The dream of *Frühlingstraum*, for example, takes place in a building (cf. the reference to the "Fensterscheiben"), presumably the "Köhlers engem Haus" in which the protagonist has lain down to rest in the preceding *Rast*. The rest hoped for in *Rast* certainly leads to the dream of *Frühlingstraum*, and thence to the resumed walking (though "mit trägem Fuss") of *Einsamkeit*—walking that refers back to the beginning of the sequence and rounds it off. In *Der Lindenbaum* the protagonist refers to having passed the linden tree in deepest night and to being now many hours from it, establishing a relationship both with the action and with the time passed in numbers 1–4.

One can even construct a chronology along the following lines:

— The protagonist leaves at night (song no. 1); stands before his beloved's house (no. 2); weeps, perhaps at this time, perhaps later (no. 3).

— The protagonist escapes—he runs away from where he is (no. 4). That he is seeking footsteps in the snow seems to imply an external source of light, either moonlight or the light of the next day. In any case, since no. 5 mentions that the linden tree of the departed village is now several hours behind him, some considerable time has elapsed since no. 1.

— Two static songs follow: the protagonist weeps again (no. 6—cf. no. 3) and establishes the image of the frozen stream; he interrogates the frozen stream (no. 7).

— The protagonist escapes again (no. 8), now probably from

an imagined view of the towers of the village called up by his acts of recall in no. 5 and in the middle section of no. 7: the text of no. 8 is a complex mixture of memory and action, past and present, fleeing and returning. The protagonist next follows a false image of nighttime light (no. 9). He then lies down to rest (no. 10), on what would be the night after he had left the village, after walking and brooding for close to twenty-four hours. He dreams and wakes (no. 11).

— Subdued, dragging, he sets off in the clear morning of the second day (no. 12).

The whole, thus interpreted, is a unified and rounded slice of time and experience. But it is not a closed one; it circles back to resume the action of the beginning. For that very reason it is perhaps more unusual than *Die schöne Müllerin*.

A number of distinctive recurrent images tie the poems together as well:

— The frozen tears and melted stream of no. 3 connect with the hot tears and melting snow of no. 4, which connect in turn with the tears melting the snow that becomes a stream in no. 6, which connects in turn with the (frozen) stream of nos. 7 and 9.

Recurrent images are especially frequent in nos. 5 through 8:

— The linden tree of no. 5 connects with those of no. 8.

— The images of affection carved on the bark in no. 5 connect with the images carved on the ice in no. 7.

— The image of the stream's return to the beloved's house in no. 6 connects with the image of the protagonist's return in no. 8.

Images of memory-in-dream accumulate across the second half of the group, from no. 5 onward. In no. 5 comes a large block of memory, unmotivated by any particular event, and following a sharp break from the mood of no. 4; in the middle section of no. 7 the action of carving in the ice stimulates memory; in no. 8 the memory of the middle section is powerful enough to lead to the exceptional transformation of the original material at the close; a hallucination (a kind of waking dream) in no. 9 finally leads to an explicit dream-memory poem in no. 11.

One can also see an alternation of static poems with poems of motion, giving a distinct dynamic shape to the whole twelve-poem set.

— A poem of motion by the protagonist (no. 1) is succeeded by one of violent motion that is not his (no. 2), then by a static, almost timeless poem of weeping (no. 3).

— This is followed by another poem of vigorous and sustained motion by the protagonist (no. 4), which is followed by a sharp break leading to the three static poems of accumulating memory-dream images to which we have referred (nos. 5–7).

— The tension of this longest group of poems without motion by the protagonist snaps with the violent motion of the beginning of no. 8, which is followed by a poem of gentler, erratic motion without clear direction (no. 9), slowing toward the rest foreseen in no. 10, and the dream of no. 11.

— The whole closes with a reluctant return to motion (no. 12).

3. In poems, one must reconstruct types of physical motion from the verbal images. In songs, especially in songs by Schubert, types of motion are presented directly to the imagination, and are among the fundamental elements of the artwork.[29] It is thus no surprise that Schubert's music makes clearer and stronger the design of motion types implied by Müller's poems. He creates a clear growth in the songs of motion—from no. 1, through no. 4, to a climax in the violent, irregular, forward-stumbling motion at the beginning of no. 8. This song, for the first time, does not end in the style of motion with which it opened, but quiets markedly toward the end. Then the slower, erratic motion of no. 9 leads to a return in no. 10 of the regular eighths of no. 1, now with a gently upbeat-leaning, cross-slurred articulation. The dream song of no. 11 gives in microcosm the various motion types of the cycle. Finally, the regular eighth notes, now with dragging afterbeat slurs, recur in the main musical image of no. 12. The songs creating this archlike design of motion types interlock with those elaborating the principal static image of the cycle, the tears-snow-stream image of songs 3, 6, 7, and 9.

Discussion of overall tonal design in *Winterreise* is made exceptionally difficult by questions concerning transposition from the pitch level at which the songs were originally written. Songs 6, 10, and 12 from part I were transposed (see n. 28), as were songs 22 and 24 from part II. We have authorization in Schubert's hand only for the transposition of no. 10. Nos. 6

and 12 appear in new keys in the nonautograph printer's copy; nos. 22 and 24 appear in the autograph fair copy in A minor and B minor respectively, with directions for transposition in the publisher Haslinger's hand. There seems little doubt that Schubert accepted these transpositions, but there is also little doubt that he was forced to do so by a prohibition issued from some quarter against requiring a high a' in the vocal part. In nos. 6, 10, and 12, for example, he rewrote the vocal line, or decided to eliminate an alternative version when he revised his draft; these revisions resulted in requiring a high a', which in turn led to transposition.[30] If we accept that these transpositions were forced upon Schubert by the necessity of avoiding the high a', we should perhaps then regard them as compromises, potentially as far from the ideal as the sorry alternative ending of *Auf dem Flusse*.

Curiously enough, the transpositions do not much change the overall effect of tonality in the cycle, for in both *Die schöne Müllerin* and *Winterreise* Schubert uses tonality more to group and interrelate songs than to make overall architectural shapes.[31] The sharp breaks in part I of *Winterreise* remain between nos. 2 and 3 (which suggests that no. 3 is seen as happening at a separate time and place from no. 2), and between nos. 4 and 5 (inaugurating the dream-memory series to which I referred above). The apparent break between nos. 7 and 8 is bridged by the tonal preparation of G minor in no. 7, as we have seen. Whether no. 10 is in C minor or D minor, no. 9 is isolated on both sides, as befits its hallucinatory subject.[32] The tonal connections across nos. 5 and 7, on the other hand, are particularly strong. Thus the largest group of interrelated songs stretches from nos. 5 through no. 8.

Just as there are particular types of motion in *Winterreise*, so there are particular types of vocal range. The most striking of these is that which covers rapidly, often in a single gesture, an abnormally wide span—a tenth to a twelfth. In part I, nos. 6, 9, and 10 belong to this group, and are prefigured by the violent interval vocabulary of no. 2. Of the songs covering a range of more than a twelfth, only no. 7 does not handle a wide range in this way. Rather, as we have seen, it expands upward pitch by pitch, reaching a climax only at the last line of the song, and finally covering the widest range of any song of *Winterreise*—one half step short of two octaves.[33] Thus the songs with abnormally wide range (nos. 6, 7, 9, and 10) stand grouped around no. 8 in the center of part I, with no. 7, at their apex, unique among them.

Local motivic connections in this central group of songs tell the same story. There are close motivic connections between nos. 4 and 5 (thus bridging in an almost subliminal fashion across the clear break created by tonality and by type of motion), and between nos. 5 and 6.[34] I mention this only as a last item in this discussion of the many approaches by which part I of *Winterreise* emerges as a unified structure. All of these approaches place nos. 7–8 at the apex of this structure. It seems fair to conclude that what has caused several commentators to focus on the expressive intensity of *Auf dem Flusse* derives from its structural position in a musical whole larger even than the song itself.

Notes

1. I have discussed these matters in greater detail in "Sound and Feeling," *Critical Inquiry* 10 (1984):614–43, including a review of recent literature.

2. Thrasybulos Georgiades, *Schubert: Musik und Lyrik* (Göttingen: Vandenhoeck und Ruprecht, 1967); Ermudte Schwarmath, *Musikalischer Bau und Sprachvertonung in Schuberts Liedern* (Tutzing: Hans Schneider, 1969); Arnold Feil, *Franz Schubert: Die schöne Müllerin, Winterreise* (Stuttgart: Philipp Reclam jun., 1975); David Lewin, "*Auf dem Flusse*: Image and Background in a Schubert Song," this volume.

3. I disagree with Lewin (p. 130) that the latter possibility has no bearing on our interpretation of the poem. That the stream may be frozen through (a matter not of science, as Lewin proposes, but of practical observation) gives some meaning to the last question of the poem. As we shall see, however, it does not make the question a real, as opposed to a rhetorical one.

4. Lewin nowhere gives any evidence in this section that this is "Schubert's reading" of the text, as he claims on p. 131. His evidence is purely verbal, divorced from any discussion of the setting.

5. One may find a hint of the idea in the second stanza of Müller's *Wasserfluth*, but Schubert's setting takes no notice of this possible meaning. The music remains wintry and static throughout.

6. Georgiades, *Schubert*, p. 360.

7. H. H. Eggebrecht, "Prinzipien des Schubert-Liedes," *Archiv für Musikwissenschaft* 27 (1970):89.

8. Were it not that the composer makes clear the connection between the successive stages in the growth of rhythmic motion across the song (bars 20–22 are the source of the motion of bars 23ff., which in turn is the source

of that of bars 31ff., which in turn bursts out intensified in bars 48ff.), we might pass over this first instance. Since he does make each image of motion grow from this gesture, we must, at least in retrospect, accord it the proper weight.

9. The surviving primary sources for *Winterreise* and the variants among these sources are described in Franz Schubert, *Neue Ausgabe sämtlicher Werke* (Kassel: Bärenreiter, 1964–), series 4, vol. 4b, pp. 299ff. The autograph draft of part I, together with the autograph fair copy of part II, has been published in facsimile (Kassel: Bärenreiter, 1955).

10. The transcription of the revised draft of *Auf dem Flusse* is included in Schubert, *Neue Ausgabe* 4:4b, 242ff. It correctly records that Schubert did not write a trill in the vocal line of bar 11. The trill was present in the drafted vocal line in D-sharp minor and disappeared, presumably by careless omission, only when Schubert hurriedly renotated the passage in E-flat minor. It reappears in the fair copy and in the first edition.

11. This conversion of the neutral, undirected pulse of the accompaniment of the first section into a more forward-pressing figure is aided by another detail. From bar 23 onward Schubert writes an accent on the second half of the first beat of each bar, which prevents one from hearing it as a passive afterbeat, a simple second half of the beat, and tilts it forward toward the upbeat grouping of the second beat of the bar.

12. I do not mean to imply that the accompaniment represents always one dramatic character or force, the voice another. This claim would over-specify the musical metaphor. The dramatic relationship between voice and accompaniment has been explored with great sensitivity by Edward T. Cone in *The Composer's Voice* (Berkeley and Los Angeles: University of California Press, 1974). I use Cone's phrase when I say that the "expressive potential" of the relationship between voice and accompaniment in this song is broad and changes frequently. At the beginning of stanza 5, for example, the accompaniment pulls against the passionate rebellion of the voice by asserting the initial image of the song—metaphorically the force of convention and external situation. But only a few measures later it is in the lunge of the accompaniment that the suppressed rhythmic motion breaks out anew, prefiguring the decisive gesture of the voice.

13. While Lewin notes the upward leap of the voice to b in bar 38, he fails to see its expressive significance. This failure is bound up with, and may even have led to, a small musical misreading as well. I quote Lewin (pp. 137–38): "At bar 38 the voice, detaching itself from the right-hand part, leaps up to B at the cadence, rather than settling on F♯ once more." But the detachment of the voice from the right-hand part is not the remarkable thing here. The voice has already detached itself from the right-hand part, first momentarily in bar 28 and then definitively in bar 36. In bars 37–38 it occupies its own tetrachord, from e' down to b. From now on its area of activity will be separate from that of the piano part. Thus the leap—the detachment in bars 37–38 of which Lewin speaks—is the one downward from its own tetrachord to rejoin for a fleeting moment the area of the right-hand part, first with the f♯ at the beginning of bar 37, and then again with the e at the end of

the same measure. Schubert's change of the last note of bar 36 from c♯' to e' emphasizes this point.

About another change between draft and final version we shall probably never be entirely certain. In the accompaniment of bar 37, Schubert drafted a c♮ in the right hand on the second eighth note, as required by the original vocal line of example 2. Then he changed this vocal line, but, either intentionally or by oversight, did not change the piano part on the second eighth. (He did, of course, change the ensuing eighths, having first written a V⁷ chord on the third and fourth eighths of bar 37 and a tonic on the first of bar 38.) Thus the revised autograph has a c♮ here, producing an even more violent sense of reversal at the beginning of the bar and a heightened sense of tension between voice and accompaniment as the voice produces a striking cross-relation by insisting anew on the c♯' on the third eighth. The non-autograph clean copy used by the printer retains a c♯ before the right-hand chord on the fourth eighth note, but the implied natural before the c on the second eighth, originally present in this copy as well, was erased by someone ("Schubert?," as the editors of the *Neue Ausgabe* say), and does not appear in the first edition.

14. The alternative ending, which appears for the first time in the first edition—not in the autograph or the clean copy—seems an unacceptable compromise for the sake of avoiding a high a'. Schubert was willing to transpose entire songs rather than sacrifice the contour of the vocal line once he had settled on it (see the discussion of range in the entire cycle below). This alternative ending utterly changes the climactic gesture and the end of the song; it is hard to imagine that it comes from Schubert's hand. I have never heard a performance that incorporated it.

15. This same expression of a firming of resolve in the third line of stanza 5 is heightened by the declamation of this stanza, especially as Schubert revised it. The first line of the stanza is declaimed in breathless snatches. The second is at least delivered whole, although it enters late in the phrase and forces the phrase to finish early (according to the model of stanzas 1 and 2). The third was initially to be declaimed in a rushed snatch like the first:

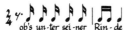

But Schubert revised this to return to the measured declamation of the previous stanzas, now changed in meaning (as is the original melody) by the vaulting modulation to G-sharp minor, by the new rhythmic motion of the piano part, and by the first *forte* in a whispered song. Variation in the rate of text coverage expresses the same resolve. Whereas at the beginning of the last stanza Schubert had halved this rate, covering only one line of text per four-bar phrase of the model (the second phrase is shortened to three, as the resolve of the protagonist takes shape), at the beginning of the third line of the stanza he moves back to covering one line per two-bar phrase. This impression of a decision taken is reinforced when the last line of the stanza is repeated—the first repetition of a textual unit in the song.

16. A linear analysis should, I think, acknowledge the exceptional nature of the case when a single, continuous vocal line resolves to a tonic an octave higher than the one from which it started. Schenker, in the analysis quoted by Lewin, has to concentrate the entire $\hat{3}-\hat{2}-\hat{1}$ *Urlinie* of the song in bars 53−54 in order to get it in the correct octave!

17. Jacques Chailley also proposes that parts I and II be seen as independent cycles, but scarcely concerns himself with defending or drawing conclusions from the hypothesis as regards part I. His concern is with what he sees as the revolutionary nature of part II. See Jacques Chailley, *Le voyage d'hiver de Schubert* (Paris: Leduc, 1975).

18. See Georgiades, *Schubert*, pp. 357−59; and Feil, *Franz Schubert*, pp. 26−29.

19. The last two lines of the first stanza of *Erstarrung*, for example, are quite different in the twenty-four-poem version of 1824.

20. Schubert's close friend Josef von Spaun reports in his *Aufzeichnungen über meinen Verkehr mit Franz Schubert* of 1828 that Schubert presented to his friends what Spaun called "die ganze Winterreise" (see O. E. Deutsch, *Franz Schubert. Die Erinnerungen seinen Freunde*, 2d ed. [Leipzig: Breitkopf und Härtel, 1966], pp. 160−61). The editors of the *Neue Ausgabe* (4:4a, XX) refer this to spring 1827, without stating their reasons. I can find no basis in Spaun's chronicle for fixing the date more closely than at some time after March 1827.

21. Robert Winter, "Paper Studies and the Future of Schubert Research," in *Schubert Studies*, ed. E. Badura-Skoda and P. Branscombe (Cambridge: Cambridge University Press, 1982), pp. 240−41.

22. See Schubert, *Neue Ausgabe* 4:4a, XXI.

23. See Winter, "Paper Studies," p. 246.

24. Is it significant in this connection that Schubert set the new poems of the twenty-four-poem 1824 publication in the order in which they occurred in that publication, simply skipping the ones he had already set from the 1823 publication—with the exception of *Mut* and *Die Nebensonnen*, whose order he finally decided to reverse?

25. Cf. Schubert, *Neue Ausgabe* 4:4a, XX−XXI.

26. Heinrich Kreissle von Hellborn, *Franz Schubert* (Vienna: C. Gerold's Sohn, 1865), p. 482.

27. See O. E. Deutsch, *The Schubert Reader*, trans. Eric Blom (New York: Norton, 1947), p. 931.

28. By way of reminder, I list here the twelve poems in the 1823 publication and the twelve songs of *Winterreise*, part I:

1.	*Gute Nacht*	D minor
2.	*Die Wetterfahne*	A minor
3.	*Gefror'ne Tränen*	F minor
4.	*Erstarrung*	C minor
5.	*Der Lindenbaum*	E major
6.	*Wasserflut*	E minor (orig. F-sharp minor)
7.	*Auf dem Flusse*	E minor
8.	*Rückblick*	G minor

9. *Irrlicht*	B minor
10. *Rast*	C minor (orig. D minor)
11. *Frühlingstraum*	A major
12. *Einsamkeit*	B minor (orig. D minor)

29. Georgiades and Feil have drawn attention to the variety and the importance of types of motion in Schubert.

30. The same is true of no. 22. The only case in which transposition was caused by something other than a required high a′ is no. 24. One can only speculate that this may have been a result of the transposition of no. 22 away from A minor, or perhaps a positive second thought that nos. 23 and 24 should have the same tonal center. (See n. 9 above for the various sources and variants.)

31. Georgiades (*Schubert*, pp. 194–99) and Feil (*Franz Schubert*, p. 30) discuss transposition in *Winterreise*. Georgiades advances the hypothesis that in Lieder, as opposed to opera or oratorio, the actual pitch location of a song—by which he means its particular place in a particular voice type—has no importance. The evidence often given for this is that Schubert copied songs from *Die schöne Müllerin* into different private song albums in different keys. Although this evidence may support Georgiades's hypothesis, it does not touch the matter of tonal interrelations in a larger whole, a matter with which Georgiades is not concerned, for individual songs copied into private albums are expressly detached from any larger whole. I shall have to put off until another occasion a development of the argument that the function of tonality within Schubert's cycle is especially to draw together some songs and separate others.

32. The new transpositions produce a rather different effect in nos. 10 through 12, which were originally related as i–V–i. After the transpositions, one can hear the G major of the end of no. 8 as the dominant of no. 10, functioning across the parenthesis of no. 9. The A major of no. 11 now appears even brighter, more dreamlike, and more sharply contrasting than in the original arrangement of keys. But Schubert seems deliberately to have avoided the subsequent return to the key of no. 10 in no. 12. Nothing required him to transpose no. 12 to B minor. He might have taken it to C minor and still avoided the high a′, while retaining the tonal connection with no. 10 that existed in the draft version.

33. This is undoubtedly why *Auf dem Flusse* could not be transposed as a way of eliminating the high a′.

34. The opening motives of the piano parts of nos. 4 and 5 are the same, save for the modal change; the arpeggios in barcarolle rhythm of stanzas 3–4 and 6–7 of no. 5 are slowed down and transferred to the introduction of no. 6.

Schubert's *Nähe des Geliebten* (D. 162):
Transformation of the *Volkston*

◆

WALTER FRISCH

I

The Lied should be the simple and comprehensible musical expression of a precise feeling, so that it can thereby encourage the participation of every voice capable of natural singing. As a small artwork, easily graspable at a glance, it must necessarily be a correct, complete whole, whose particular effect consists of the unity of the vocal part, and whose instrumental accompaniment, if not dispensable, should nevertheless serve only to support the voice.[1]

In 1786 Johann Friedrich Reichardt summarized thus the aesthetic ideals of the German Lied. He and the other composers of the Berlin school, including Krause, Schulz, and Zelter, attempted to practice what they preached, aiming for *Sangbarkeit* in their own songs. It is therefore not surprising that they turned frequently to the folk style, the *Volkston*, as their model. As Reichardt explained his preface to *Fröhen Liedern für Deutsche Männer* of 1781, "folksongs are truly that upon which the genuine artist relies when he begins to suspect his art is on the wrong track—as the sailor relies on the north star—and which he studies the most for his profit."[2] Most folksongs are, of course, simple strophic structures, in which one strain of music serves for all stanzas of the poem. The majority of the Berlin school songs follow that plan.[3]

In the late eighteenth century there was no shortage of poems to set in this style. Herder published two anthologies of collected *Volkslieder* in 1778–79. Major poets also began to cultivate the folk idiom: as early as 1773 Goethe published

"Heidenröslein," one of his most renowned and artful creations in the (ostensibly) simple style.

To a young, ambitious Austro-German composer in the
first decades of the nineteenth century, the folk idiom would not
have seemed an especially promising one to pursue. Schubert,
who began composing songs in about 1811, largely avoided it
at first. He concentrated instead on long, narrative ballads,
in which he could explore the dramatic styles of recitative,
arioso, and aria, derived from the more prestigious tradition of
opera seria. But three years later his allegiance shifted; between
1814 and mid-1816 he composed almost 100 simple strophic
songs, many of which capture the folk tone admirably.

In a work like *Heidenröslein* (D. 257) formal design and
melodic and harmonic content seem perfectly coordinated.
The song manages to attain sophistication without ever over-
stepping the aesthetic bounds of its folklike idiom. The same
could be said for many of the strophic songs of 1814–16. But
Nähe des Geliebten (D. 162), a strophic Goethe setting composed on 27 February 1815, manifests a compelling dialectic
between form and content. The harmonic and melodic aspects
of the song utterly transcend the folk style associated with a
strophic framework. *Nähe des Geliebten* is an appropriate subject for a critical-analytical study because its poetic and musical
background can be traced quite precisely and because its autograph sources reveal something of Schubert's endeavor to reconcile the conflicting demands of outer form and inner content.

II

The story of *Nähe des Geliebten* begins with neither Goethe nor
Schubert, but with "Andenken," a four-stanza poem written
in 1792 by Friedrich Matthisson:

> Ich denke dein,
> Wenn durch den Hain
> Der Nachtigallen
> Akkorde schallen!
> Wenn denkst du mein?
> Ich denke dein
> Im Dämmerschein

Der Abendhelle
Am Schattenquelle!
Wo denkst du mein?
  Ich denke dein
Mit süsser Pein,
Mit bangem Sehnen
Und heissen Thränen!
Wie denkst du mein?
  O denke mein,
Bis zum Verein
Auf besserm Sterne!
In jeder Ferne
Denk'ich nur dein![4]

> [I think of you, when the chords of the nightingales
> sound through the grove. When do you think of me?
>   I think of you in the twilight of the clear evening, at
> the shadow's source. Where do you think of me?
>   I think of you with sweet pain, with anxious longing,
> and with hot tears! How do you think of me?
>   O think of me, until we are united on a better star! In
> every distant place, I think only of you!]

The poem's device is clear: each stanza describes how the poet
reacts to, or is reminded of, his beloved. The first three begin
with "Ich denke dein"; the final one inverts the syntax with the
plea "O denke mein." The last line of each stanza shows a similar process working the other way around: the first three stanzas
conclude with "Wenn," "Wo," or "Wie" "denkst du mein?";
the last one with "Denk'ich nur dein!" Accompanying the
when–where–how progression is a kind of phenomenological
or sensuous sequence. The first stanza deals with aural perception (nightingales' chords), the second with visual perception
(twilight and shadows), the third with physical feeling (pain
and tears). Stanza 4 culminates this progression as the poet
imagines being united with his beloved. Yet in the final couplet
he acknowledges the real distance that separates them.

Matthisson's poem appeared in 1802. It was given modified strophic settings by Beethoven in 1809 (WoO 136, published 1810), and by Schubert in April 1814 (D. 99). Schubert's
first strophe (ex. 1) will suffice to give an idea of how well he

Example 1   Schubert, Andenken *(D. 99)*

could capture the naïve folk style. (Throughout this article I shall use "stanza" to refer to the unit of the poem, and "strophe" to refer to the musical unit.) The brief piano introduction evokes horn calls, a sonority often employed in the music of this period to connote memory and/or distance. (I return to this topic below.) The vocal melody consists of two symmetrical, eminently *sangbar* four-bar phrases, the second moving to the dominant. There follows a one-bar piano extension, then the two-bar "punch line," where the inquistive dominant seventh underpins the poetic query, "Wann denkst du mein?"[5] The changes in strophes 2 and 3 involve principally piano figuration. The final strophe begins like the others but becomes considerably expanded at the final couplet "in jeder Ferne/Denk'ich nur dein." This climax is beautifully achieved by Schubert, chiefly through melodic breadth and repetition. Yet it must be admitted that his setting does not quite capture the phenomenological progression of Matthisson's poem, especially the final acknowledgment of "Ferne," where we would expect something quieter, more inward. *Andenken* remains firmly—and charmingly—rooted in the *Volkston*; introspection and deeper reading of a poem are not part of its world.

Well before it attracted the attention of composers, Matthisson's poem inspired other poets. In 1792, very soon after its creation, it became the model for "Ich denke dein," a five-stanza poem by Frederike Brun, a friend of Matthisson's and herself a minor poet:

> Ich denke dein, wenn sich im Blütenregen
> Der Frühing malt,
> Und wenn des Sommers mildgereifter Segen
> In Aehren strahlt.
> Ich denke dein, wenn sich das Weltmeer tönend
> Gen Himmel hebt,
> Und vor der Wogen Wut das Ufer stöhnend
> Zurücke bebt.
> Ich denke dein, wann sich der Abend röthend
> Im Hain verliert,
> Und Filomelens Klage leise flötend
> Die Seele rührt.
> Beim trüben Lampenschein in bittren Leiden
> Gedacht ich dein;
> Die bange Seele flehte nah am Scheiden:
> Gedenke mein!
> Ich denke dein, bis wehende Cypressen

Mein Grab umziehn;
Und auch in Tempe's Hain soll unvergessen
Dein Name blühn.[6]

[I think of you, when spring is reflected in the bursting
forth of blossoms, and when the gently ripened yield of
summer shines upon the ears (of corn).
  I think of you when the ocean rises sonorously toward
the sky, and when the shore, moaning, recoils from the
violence of the pounding waves.
  I think of you when the reddening evening dissolves in
the grove, and when Philomel's lament, gently fluting,
stirs the soul.
  By the dim lamplight, in bitter suffering I thought of
you; my anxious soul implored you to the point of dying:
think of me!
  I will think of you, until the swaying cypresses sur-
round my grave; and even in Tempe's grove shall your
name bloom unforgotten!]

Though she draws upon both the general design and specific
features (but not the metrical scheme) of the Matthisson poem,
Brun has made a muddle of his elegant lyric. Even granted poetic license, her syntax is clumsy and awkward. Matthisson's
logical progression of imagery has become a chaos of meta-
phors. Each stanza now presents two different images (one in
each couplet), weighed down by excessive adjectives and par-
ticiples. The references to Philomel and Tempe seem especially
gratuitous amid the nonspecific natural and physical imagery.
The shift to past tense in stanza 4 also makes little structural
sense; it is not an effective preparation for the future-oriented
thoughts of the final stanza.
  None of these flaws prevented composers from setting
the poem. A simple strophic version of it by C. F. Zelter appeared in 1795 (ex. 2).[7] Schubert had conveyed the charm of
Matthisson's poem, even if he had not risen to its subtleties;
but Zelter descends directly to Brun's level of insipidness. The
chromatic neighbor and passing notes (A♮ and B♮, respectively) and the little roulades on "regen" and "Segen" seem as
superfluous as much of Brun's imagery. Neither "natural" nor
"simple," they violate the *Volkston* supposedly at the basis of
this style.

Example 2   Zelter, Ich denke dein

The historical significance of Zelter's *Ich denke dein* would be minimal if not for the fact that the song caught Goethe's attention. It is well known that Goethe admired Zelter's songs; indeed, he often praised Zelter's settings of his own poems, in which he found the "total reproduction of the poetic intentions."[8] In June 1796 he wrote to the wife of his publisher, "Zelter's melody to the poem 'Ich denke dein' had an inconceivable charm for me," adding that the song had directly inspired him to write his own poem, entitled "Nähe des Geliebten," to fit Zelter's melody:[9]

> Ich denke dein, wenn mir der Sonne Schimmer
> Vom Meere strahlt;
> Ich denke dein, wenn sich des Mondes Flimmer
> In Quellen malt.
>   Ich sehe dich, wenn auf dem fernen Wege
> Der Staub sich hebt,

In tiefer Nacht, wenn auf dem schmalen Stege
Der Wandrer bebt.
   Ich höre dich, wenn dort mit dumpfem Rauschen
Die Welle steigt,
Im stillen Haine geh' ich oft zu lauschen,
Wenn alles schweigt.
   Ich bin bei dir; du seist auch noch so ferne,
Du bist mir nah!
Die Sonne sinkt, bald leuchten mir die Sterne.
O, wärst du da!

> [I think of you when the sun's luster shines from the sea; I think of you when the moon's glimmer is reflected in the fountains.
>
> I see you when on distant paths the dust is raised, in deepest night when on the narrow bridge the wanderer trembles.
>
> I hear you when with a dull rushing the wave rises. In the still grove I often go to listen, when all is silent.
>
> I am with you; however far you might be, you are close to me! The sun is setting, soon the stars will shine for me. O, that you were here!]

The poem first appeared in 1795 in the *Arienbuch der Claudine von Villa Bella*. A few months later it was printed in Schiller's *Musenalmanach* for 1796, where a setting of the poem by Reichardt was added as a musical insert. In 1809 Reichardt published a revised setting in a collection of Goethe songs (ex. 3).[10]

Reichardt follows the Zelter/Brun model closely. There are two parallel musical phrases, corresponding to the paired lines of each stanza. As in Zelter, the first phrase cadences on the dominant, the second returns to the tonic. But Reichardt improves upon his predecessor's rather cramped song, allowing the poem more time to unfold. Zelter had virtually ignored the caesura (in Brun's poem) between the opening verb phrase and the dependent "wenn" clause. Reichardt creates a pause at this point and also wisely shifts the musico-poetic stresses. Zelter had placed "dein" on a downbeat; Reichardt moves the downbeat forward onto the verb "denke," and thus onto the new verb at the analogous spot in each succeeding stanza. (The verbs change only in Goethe's poem, not in Brun's.)

Example 3   Reichardt, Nähe des Geliebten

Reichardt also captures the folk idiom more effectively than Zelter. Even the chromatic E♭s and the roulade on "Schimmer" do not intrude upon the basic *Sangbarkeit* of the vocal part. But this is hardly a great song; indeed, the idea of greatness in such a context would have seemed inappropriate to Reichardt and his Berlin colleagues. As Wiora has noted, they were creating essentially *Gebrauchsmusik*, not art songs.[11] Although Reichardt prided himself on reading a poem aloud over and over before setting it to music, so as to catch every nuance,[12] in 1797 he thought nothing of publishing his original (1796) music for *Nähe des Geliebten* with the Brun poem substituted for the Goethe![13]

III

When Schubert sat down to compose *Nähe des Geliebten* on 27 February 1815, he thus had behind him, and probably in his mind's ear, a fairly extensive poetic and musical tradition—an "Ich denke dein" tradition, so to speak, to which he had himself contributed *Andenken*. It was a tradition he had already begun to transform four months earlier, with his first Goethe settings. There is, of course, little of the *Volkston* in the very first, *Gretchen am Spinnrade*, of 19 October 1814. But he soon turned to shorter Goethe lyrics that were suited—and intended by the poet—for the simple style. First came the strophic *Nachtgesang* and *Trost in Tränen* (both composed on 30 November 1814), in which Schubert achieves a synthesis of the naïve and the sophisticated. In *Schäfers Klagelied*, composed on the same day, the folk style is skillfully adapted to the discursive ballad or scena format.

There would have been every reason to expect that when Schubert turned his attention to *Nähe des Geliebten* later that winter, the resulting song would exhibit a similarly refined folk idiom. Indeed, on the same day in February he composed just such settings of Goethe's *Am Flusse* (D. 160) and *An Mignon* (D. 161). But what emerged in *Nähe des Geliebten* was far removed from any song he had yet composed, and light-years beyond the "Ich denke dein" tradition (see plate 1).

The tempo indication alone suggests that Schubert is attempting to capture a special mood: *Nähe des Geliebten* is the first song for which he used the phrase *langsam, feierlich mit Anmut* (slowly, solemnly, gracefully). (The metronome marking is his own, or was at least approved by him; such figures appear for all the songs of op. 5 in the first edition.) The conjunction of *langsam* and *feierlich* appears in a number of later songs; yet on only one occasion, in *Die Allmacht* (D. 852, 1825), is it specifically associated with the accompaniment pattern of full, repeated chords we find in *Nähe des Geliebten*. *Die Allmacht* is, of course, a fervent (if somewhat overblown) expression of religious feeling, for which the notion of "feierlich" and the grandeur of thick chords seem justified. But it is indeed remarkable that a small love lyric like *Nähe des Geliebten* called forth this style from Schubert. He makes of it a kind of secular *Allmacht*, an impassioned hymn to a beloved of human, rather than divine, dimensions.

Schubert wrote two drafts of *Nähe des Geliebten* on the same day.[14] Both have the same tempo/mood indication and es-

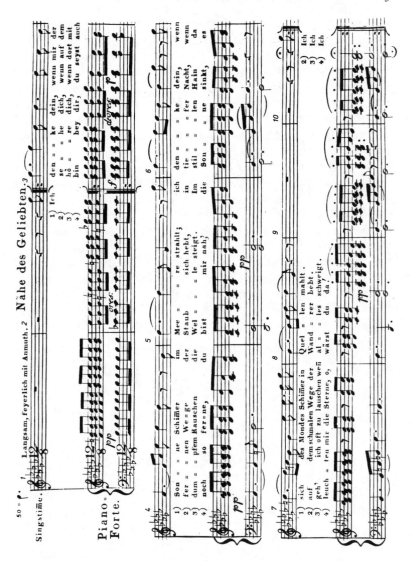

Plate 1   Schubert, Nähe des Geliebten (D. 162). Facsimile of first
edition (Vienna: Cappi & Diabelli, 1821), with bar numbers added, in
italics. By permission of the Music Division, The New York Public
Library at Lincoln Center, Astor, Lenox, and Tilden Foundations.

sentially the same musical design. But the first is cast in $\frac{6}{8}$ meter, and the accompaniment is subdivided into two chords per beat. As Schubert realized almost immediately, this pattern was too fussy, too busy to convey the grandeur and spaciousness he sought. He wrote "Gilt nicht" on the page, struck it through with several lines and took up another leaf, writing out the song in the version we know today (with a few small but significant exceptions, to be discussed below). This was published as op. 5, no. 2, in 1821.

Nähe des Geliebten is one of the earliest Schubert songs to display the special kind of intimacy between music and text analyzed by Georgiades in the 1823 *Wandrers Nachtlied*, a Goethe poem which Schubert "transformed . . . into a composition by penetrating, as it were, through the poem and beyond it to the deeper level that sustains it—to the language—and by drawing directly upon this." [15] Of course, "Nähe des Geliebten" is a folklike poem comprising four regular four-line stanzas, a very different kind of lyric from the terse, epigrammatic eight-line "Wandrers Nachtlied." Yet, as Georgiades has suggested, it too has a compelling deep structure:

> The content of the language, which in Matthisson and Brun contained only the latent possibility of becoming poetry, is here transformed into genuine poetry. The repetitions of "Ich denke" are replaced in each stanza with a new verb: "Ich denke dein" becomes "Ich sehe dich" and "Ich höre dich," each one linked with a physical realization. Matthisson's final strophe began with the inversion "O denke mein" instead of "Ich denke dein"; this is no more than a formal trick, a sentimental closing formula. Since in Goethe's version the sense of dialogue is eliminated entirely, there is no such inversion; but in its place in the final stanza Goethe brings about a synthesis of "ich" and "du," a deepening. No longer "denke"; no longer an image projected in the outer world, "sehe," "höre"; but the inner realm, "ich bin . . . du bist mir nah" and "O, wärst du da!," whereby the monologic character of the poem is stressed. This is also reflected in the new title: "Nearness of the Beloved," in spite of the actual distance. Thus in Goethe, as already in Brun—but not

in Matthisson—the "Ich denke dein" remains without a rhyme, without an answer from the beloved.[16]

Georgiades is perhaps too hard on Matthisson's poem (and not hard enough on Brun's). Although he does not change the opening verb in each stanza, Matthisson does, as I have suggested, trace a kind of phenomenological process, culminating in a "synthesis" in the first couplet of stanza 4, then an acceptance of the actual *Ferne* is the final couplet. He surely deserves credit for more than a "formal trick" ("formales Spiel"). Brun ignored this progression entirely; but Goethe builds upon it, makes it explicit. He absorbs several natural images from both his poetic sources—the stars, the grove, the twilight from Matthisson (the latter two also were also borrowed by Brun), and the sea and waves from Brun. But as he had done with the verbs, he fashions from these images a consistent pattern involving a contrast between the two couplets of each stanza. The opposition is perhaps clearest in stanza 1: in lines 1–2 the sun radiates, in 3–4 the moon shines.[17] Stanzas 3 and 4 show a similar pattern. In stanza 3 the rising wave of the first couplet is opposed to the still, silent grove of the second; in stanza 4 the immediacy and intensity of "Ich bin" and "Du bist" are opposed to the sinking sun, the shining stars, and the less emphatic conditional "wärst du." Even in stanza 2 one can detect something of this contrast, between the active image of the dust being raised and the darker, more passive one of the wanderer trembling in the dark night.

This device is Goethe's own inspiration; there is no hint of it in Matthisson or Brun. Nor is it captured in Reichardt's setting, where the two musical phrases of each strophe are parallel, and virtually equal in importance. But Schubert seizes on the poetic pattern of strong/weak or active/passive, and on the presence of the forceful verb phrase at the beginning of each stanza. The result is a musical strophe divided into two phrases of very different weight and shape. Schubert rejects the rather conventional Zelter-Reichardt plan of having the first phrase cadence on the dominant, the second on the tonic. Instead, both phrases close on the tonic (bars 5 and 8), but approach it in strikingly different ways.

Close in on—rather than close on—might be a better

term for how the tonic is first reached in *Nähe des Geliebten*. Most Schubert songs begin by defining the tonic and/or suggesting the principal thematic material. The piano introduction is usually harmonically rounded, ending with a half or full cadence.[18] *Andenken* (see ex. 1) is typical of many of the folk-like songs: in the first four bars the piano firmly establishes the tonic (though not, in this case, the thematic material) before the voice enters in bar 5. Nowhere in Schubert's Lieder, however, do we find an "introduction" quite like that of *Nähe des Geliebten*, which begins well away from the eventual tonic G-flat and offers no cadence. Indeed, the voice has virtually to force its way in at the end of bar 2.

The introduction begins over a pulsating dominant pedal in the key of E-flat minor, a dark and unstable sonority that is especially striking in the context of this ostensibly simple love lyric. (See ex. 4 for harmonic reduction.) The i_4^6 chord in the second half of bar 1 refuses to function cadentially. Instead the bass rises a half step to the flatted sixth degree, C♭, and the harmonic pace doubles as the right-hand chords ascend chromatically in parallel sixths.[19] On the final three beats of bar 2 the harmony coalesces into a German-sixth chord. We expect a cadence (as in ex. 4) returning to and resolving the i_4^6 chord abandoned in bar 1, and followed by the entrance of the voice.

Instead, the voice bursts in on the last beat of bar 2, above the dissonant augmented-sixth chord. It is near the very limit of its range (a difficult beginning, as any performer can attest), doubling the top line of the piano part. On the downbeat of bar 3 the bass B♭, the proper linear resolution of the C♭, is interpreted not as the dominant of E-flat minor, but as the third

Example 4

degree of G-flat major. As if stunned by its own arrival—by its own bold usurpation of the bass B♭—the first-inversion chord resonates for six full beats before descending (rather cursorily) toward the root. Above this the voice holds the G♭ on "den-" for five beats. As Georgiades points out, this remarkable extension of the first syllable of "denke" creates a durational proportion of 5:1 between the two syllables, considerably larger than the 3:1 at the opening of *Andenken* (and also much greater than the 2:1 of Reichardt's [ex. 3] and the 1:1 of Zelter's [ex. 2]). One could scarcely imagine more musical emphasis on the verb phrase.

Throughout the first three bars the bottom line of the piano part does not sound like a functional bass line; it is rather the lowest element of the throbbing chordal texture. But on the downbeat of bar 4 it begins at last to behave more conventionally. It detaches itself from the pulsating eighth-note motion, moves into the genuine bass register, and leads purposefully to a cadence on G flat through the first normal progression of the song, $ii^6_5-I^6_4-V^7-I$. In doing so, the bass also returns to and "explains" the C♭, the pitch that had proved so perplexing in bar 2. There it had dropped down a half step to the "false" dominant note and had failed to generate a satisfactory harmonic resolution; now it rises smoothly by half step toward the true dominant, D♭.

Like the bass line, the voice establishes its independence in bar 4. In the preceding two bars it too has been part of the dense texture, doubling the top line of the piano. But after the A♭ of "Sonne" it goes its separate way, arpeggiating up the ii triad to E♭, sitting on the dominant D♭ for five beats (by analogy to the tonic G♭ sustained for five beats at "den-[ke]") and rejoining the piano at the cadence on beat 7 of bar 4. The vocal phrase thus traces essentially an octave descent between the two G♭s.

The now-independent voice and bass line of bars 4–5 are also virtually mirror images, forming a splendid musical analogy to the sun's reflection in the sea. In bar 4 both parts move to D♭, the voice approaching from above (the appoggiatura E♭) the bass from below (C♭–C♮–D♭). In the next bar they both resolve the D♭ to the tonic, the voice again from above, the bass from below. (At "Mee-re" the D♭ certainly bears more weight than the leading tone; the temporal proportion is again 5:1, as in the opening "denke.")

Though it comes only halfway through the song, the cadence of bar 5 imparts a feeling of finality, of closure. It firmly resolves the harmonic ambiguity and marks the endpoint of octave descent in the voice. Where Reichardt and Zelter made of the first musical phrase a conventional antecedent, Schubert has thus fashioned a musical whole corresponding to the poetic sense of the active verb—a phrase in which enormous tension and dissonance are created and resolved within the space of five bars. This kind of compressed intensity is rare in early Schubert. What is unique is the placement of the musical climax within the piano introduction, or more precisely, at the moment where the introduction is overtaken by the entrance of the voice.

Everything that follows the cadence of bar 5 functions musically as a kind of coda, confirming the tonic. First, in bar 6, comes another cadence over a tonic pedal; then in bars 7–8 Schubert moves away to V^7 of vi, coming back to the tonic through vi, IV, I_4^6, V^7. Nothing unusual in common-practice music, this progression here has a very special function: it serves to reintegrate into the tonic region of G-flat major precisely the harmonies that had been made to seem so remote at the opening of the song: vi (E-flat minor) and IV (C-flat major). In bar 2 the C-flat harmony had been chromatically obliterated. In bar 4 it had returned and explained itself as ii_5^6 of G-flat major. Yet even there it had been approached abruptly, without preparation or smooth voice leading. Now at last the C-flat harmony is placed fully in context, embedded in a strong functional progression. The progression is given rhythmic emphasis by the accompaniment, which in bars 7–8 momentarily abandons the continuous, pulsating eighth-note motion. The first beat of each group of three is articulated only by the bass note. This waltz-like rhythm lasts only as long as the actual cadence; during the piano postlude Schubert gradually reintroduces the original pattern (thus preparing the next musical strophe).

Phrase 2 of the song, then, has retraced and clarified the harmonic course of phrase 1. In a similar way the vocal line of bars 6–8 retraces the octave descent of bars 3–6, almost as if in dreamy remembrance. As in bar 3, the voice moves at first from G♭ to D♭, but now the stark initial leap of a fourth is filled in by gentler stepwise motion. In the first phrase the unexpected G♭ had been articulated on both upbeat and downbeat (bars 2–3). Such emphasis is no longer needed in the second phrase; the pitch and tonality of G♭ have been established. The upbeat thus yields to an F♮ on the downbeat of bar 6. Despite the similarity of melodic profile, there are significant differences between the two phrases. The first is harmonically unstable, the second firmly in the tonic. The vocal line of the first phrase had refused to rest on the D♭ of "dein," pushing impatiently down the scale. Now it is more content to linger: it touches back to the high G♭, then rests before resuming the descent. At "Mondes Schimmer" the phrase regains the high G♭ one last time, then moves to the third degree, before cadencing from the fifth to the tonic.

The final note of the vocal part was a source of indecision for Schubert: it is different in each of the three autograph sources for the song. In the earliest (the first draft in $\frac{6}{8}$ meter) the voice concludes on the high D♭, which is sustained for five beats (ex. 5a). In the second autograph (the first copy of the final version, made on the same day) the vocal line descends to the third, B♭ (ex. 5b). Only in the third autograph (a copy of the final version, which Schubert made in 1816 for a volume of autograph songs sent personally to Goethe), and in the published version (plate 1) is there a conclusion on the tonic.[20] Each of these melodic cadences is plausible. Although it weakens the melodic parallelism between the two vocal phrases, a conclusion hovering on the dominant pitch D♭ suits the tranquil im-

Example 5

agery of the second couplet. The B♭ strikes quite literally (and effectively) a medium between openness and closure.

The G♭ Schubert ultimately selected does, however, seem the most effective conclusion. It confirms the parallelism of melodic profile between the two phrases and creates an elegant analogy between the emergence and departure of the vocal part; it brings the voice down to the same pitch as the top line of the piano (and the same register, if the song is performed by a soprano). The voice thus rejoins—blends back into—the accompaniment an octave below their original meeting point. More significantly, as Georgiades points out, the G♭ creates a direct motivic association between the opening and closing vocal gestures: the initial G♭–D♭ descent is completed by its inversion, the cadential D♭–G♭. The two complementary motives/intervals are then juxtaposed more immediately in the brief piano postlude, where the G♭–D♭ stepwise descent in the right hand is answered by the D♭–G♭ of the left. The postlude also serves thereby to prepare the opening vocal statement of G♭–D♭ in subsequent strophes.

Distance: this is another important quality of the second phrase. If by its intensity the first phrase strives to bring the beloved closer, the tranquillity of the second suggests the poet's acceptance of her actual remoteness. Schubert conveys this not only with the harmonic and melodic procedures already examined, but also with a specific musical image—horn fifths. In the second half of bar 5 the texture of the right hand of the piano, which has up to this point consisted mostly of full triads, thins out to two notes and assumes the unmistakable sound of a pair of horns. The sonority is evoked again in the second half of bar 6, then is absorbed once more into the thicker chordal texture.

Originally associated with hunting, of course, horn calls in early Romantic opera and Lieder often evoke the remote world of the German forest, as in Weber's *Der Freischütz* or Schumann's song *Waldesgespräch* from op. 39. In nonvocal and nonorchestral music, the musical metaphor becomes more generalized, suggesting separation and/or departure. The first movement of Beethoven's "Les Adieux" Sonata, op. 81a, is an explicit example.[21] In the finale of *Papillons* Schumann presents the *Grossvatertanz* tune in horn fifths. *Papillons*, of course, has

nothing to do with hunting or forests; here the gradual dimin-
uendo and fragmentation of the tune depict the departure of
the dancers from the ball. Schubert's own D-Major Piano
Sonata (D. 850) is full of horn sonorities (which is surely what
provides the "country" feel that has caused commentators to
associate the piece with Gastein, where it was composed in
1825). They are also prominent in the 1823 *Wandrers Nachtlied*
(D. 768), analyzed by Georgiades elsewhere in this volume,
where they are again associated with the forest world.

Schubert is undoubtedly drawing upon these kinds of
association in *Nähe des Geliebten*, where the horn fifths appear
in remote dynamics—*pianissimo* in the printed edition and an
even softer triple *piano* in the autographs—and introduce the
poetic couplets dominated by images of distance or darkness:
the flickering moon, the deep night, the silent wood, sunset
and starlight. In 1815 he would have known, of course, only
the Beethoven sonata from among the pieces mentioned. But
he need have looked no further than his own earlier works for a
precedent for using horn fifths in this context. It occurs in another song about absence, *Andenken*, the precursor of *Nähe des
Geliebten* already discussed. Here (see ex. 1) the horns lie in a
sense outside the song, appearing only in the four-bar introduction. They are thus somewhat gratuitous, contributing to
the general *Volkston*, but bearing no significant relationship to
the song or the poem. In *Nähe des Geliebten*, however, the horn
fifths literally grow from and blend back into the piano texture
and are intimately linked with the text.

They also serve to isolate the strongest motivic/intervallic
feature of the song, the fourth, which here (bars 5–6) ascends
stepwise through G♭–A♭–B♭–C♭. (The motive is at a different
pitch level than the initial and concluding G♭–D♭, but the association is, I believe, clearly audible.) In this stepwise form the
motive first appears distinctly at the end of bar 3, descending
in parallel tenths between outer parts. It is heard twice again in
the two subsequent bars, descending and ascending (respectively) in parallel sixths in the right hand of the piano part. In
the third statement (bar 5), the motive ascends through the
notes of the dominant chord, D-flat. At the long-awaited tonic
resolution in the second half of this bar we would expect another statement in parallel sixths. But it is precisely at this

point (beat 7) that the right-hand texture thins to support the ascending fourth with bare horn fifths instead of a thicker triad and parallel sixths. The motive is given further emphasis by the canonic echoes of the horn calls in the left hand of bars 6 and 7. What was a banal effect in *Andenken*, then, has become both evocative and structural. In *Nähe des Geliebten* the horn call serves purely musical functions: both to clarify the harmonic design (by coinciding with the tonic arrival) and to culminate the motivic process (by uncovering the basic motive).

To summarize, then: the musical design of *Nähe des Geliebten* comprises a piano introduction beginning off the tonic, which is then reached suddenly and unexpectedly at the same time the voice enters; a vocal part that begins in the extreme of its register on the highest pitch of the song and descends through an octave; a decrescendo leading to a strong, functional cadence halfway through the song; and a second, codalike phrase serving to confirm or stabilize the tonic. It was the shape of Goethe's stanza, as described above, that motivated this extraordinary plan. Schubert understood that each stanza has its moment of greatest emphasis at the very beginning, with the verb phrase. To capture this he needed to build musical tension *before* the entrance of the voice. The normal tonic-establishing piano prelude would not suffice: hence a piano introduction that builds up enormous musical tension, culminating in the entrance of the voice. To convey the softer or darker imagery in the second half of each stanza, Schubert creates for bars 6–8 a kind of echo of the first musical phrase, one that confirms the tonic and reintegrates the anomalous harmonies of the opening phrase.

IV

The preceding discussion has implied that the single musical strophe of *Nähe des Geliebten* is well suited to all the poetic stanzas. Not all critics are agreed on that point. Hans Gal has argued:

> The opening phrase, "Ich denke dein" . . . expands into a wonderfully noble melody. . . . This simple phrase has the same magical effect when it returns in the second and

third stanzas to the words "Ich sehe dich" and "Ich höre dich." But anyone who has a feeling for such matters will be disappoined by this phrase in the last stanza. Here the words are "Ich bin bei dir," and the false accent on "bin" can hardly be camouflaged; the spell is broken.[22]

There is some justice to Gal's broader point, though not to his specific reasoning. The vowel sound in "bin" may not be as broad as in "denke," "sehe," and "höre" (and thus not lend itself as easily to extension). But the *accent* is surely not "false": the word would be stressed in normal speaking, and in the poem it occupies the proper place in the iambic pattern. Gal might reasonably have objected to the less plausible stress on "noch" in this stanza (bar 4). He might also have claimed that Schubert failed to capture the different phenomenological status of the phrase "Ich bin bei dir," whose immediacy, as Georgiades points out, significantly alters the pattern of the preceding verb phrases. And yet, taking Schubert's side, we might argue that by retaining the same strophe for the final stanza he demonstrates musically that despite the apparent nearness—despite the "bin"—the beloved really remains equidistant throughout the poem. Indeed, the conditional "O wärst" in the last line implies that the nearness of the beloved is only in the poet's mind.

Good performers can (and should) compensate for some of the differences in nuance between the poetic stanzas, for example by softening the opening attack somewhat in strophes 2 and 3, then returning to a much grander *forte* for the "bin" of the final strophe. But the real strophic "problem" in this song cannot be solved by any performer, for it lies not in the relation of the musical strophe to the poetic stanza, as Gal would have it, but in the status of the "introduction" and "postlude." It is here that form and content come genuinely into conflict.

The introduction, one of the elements most indispensable to the shape of the musical strophe as I have described it, is not repeated in each strophe: bars 1–2 are heard only once. The postlude of bars 8–10 does service as the introduction for strophes 2–4, in which the high G♭ on the last beat of bar 2 ("Ich" in all stanzas) is to be sung without any accompaniment. The absence of the original introduction alters radically the relationship between the first and all subsequent strophes. No longer entering at the crest of a musical wave initiated by the piano, the first vocal phrase of strophes 2–4 must instantly create—or re-create—its own climax before subsiding to the cadence. Despite its motivic relationship to the opening vocal figure (both share the descending fourth), the postlude does little to prepare, or to mitigate, the rather violent attack on the high G♭.

Schubert himself was well aware of this situation. The status of the introduction is the most significant and suggestive issue raised by the autograph sources of *Nähe des Geliebten*. In none of the autograph manuscripts is bar 3 preceded by the beginning indication of a repeat sign: bars 1–2 are thus to be repeated with *each* strophe. This is also suggested by the last bar, bar 10, in which there is no separate upbeat for the voice ("Ich"); in the autographs the closing repeat sign is preceded in the vocal part by two complete half rests, the second with a fermata that corresponds to that over the G♭ chord of the piano (ex. 6). (Schubert did not use any dotted half rests in these autographs; the half rest thus can be interpreted as indicating a full half measure.) These notational features clearly imply a repetition of the full introduction: each strophe is to have its own introduction *and* postlude. Only in the published version of the song (as in plate 1), did Schubert (or the publisher, presumably with Schubert's approval) place the repeat sign before bar 3.

This change brings *Nähe des Geliebten* into line with other strophic songs that have a distinct introduction and postlude.

Example 6

For example, in *An Mignon*, a Goethe setting composed on the same day as (and on the verso of) *Nähe des Geliebten*, Schubert omits the introduction after the first stanza; the postlude then functions as prelude to subsequent stanzas. An apparent exception to this practice is *Tränenregen*, no. 10 of *Die schöne Müllerin*, a modified strophic song which also has a separate prelude and postlude. No autograph source for the song (or the cycle) survives, but in the first edition—as in the autographs of *Nähe des Geliebten*—there is no repeat sign at the end of the piano prelude, which is therefore to be repeated before strophes 2 and 3.[23] In *Tränenregen*, *An Mignon*, and other similar songs, however, the introductions are all self-standing harmonically and melodically. Their presence or absence is thus not as crucial a matter as in *Nähe des Geliebten*, where the "introduction" surges directly into the first strophe.

Although we should probably take the printed version of *Nähe des Geliebten* as representing Schubert's final thoughts on the matter, we can still ask which version is preferable—with or without the repetition of the introduction? On the one hand, bars 1–2 seem too magnificent, and too closely bound up with the architecture of the song, to be abandoned after only one hearing. On the other hand, their successive repetition could never re-create the initial harmonic ambiguity or the surprising emergence of the voice from the piano part.

That there is (or was) no fully satisfactory solution to the introduction "problem" points up the special nature of Schubert's *Nähe des Geliebten*. Reichardt experienced no difficulty in shifting his music between texts; and Goethe happily wrote his poem to fit a preexistent melody. But for Schubert, re-creating Goethe's poem in musical terms was not as easy. Indeed, it was something of a Procrustean effort, an attempt to fit into the conventional folklike strophic structure, implied by the poem's broader design and by the musical tradition, some very unconventional music, inspired by the content of the poem. To reiterate my initial point, then: the form and content of *Nähe des Geliebten* engage in a dialectic. That the dialectic remains unresolved is not a flaw; it is, rather, the reason why *Nähe des Geliebten* stands as one of Schubert's most compelling early songs.

Notes

1. Cited in Ernst Bücken, *Das deutsche Lied* (Hamburg: Hanseatische Verlagsanstalt, 1939), p. 43. (Translation mine. In this article, all translations from the German are my own unless otherwise noted.)

2. Cited in Max Friedländer, *Das deutsche Lied im 18. Jahrhundert* (1902; repr. Hildesheim and New York: G. Olms, 1970), vol. 1, part 1, p. 196.

3. The best modern survey of the aesthetics of the Lied in the late eighteenth and early nineteenth centuries (with an extensive bibliography of primary sources) is Heinrich W. Schwab, *Sangbarkeit, Popularität, und Kunstlied* (Regensburg: Bosse, 1965). On strophic songs, see esp. pp. 51–54. See also Walter Wiora, *Das deutsche Lied* (Wolfenbüttel und Zurich: Möseler, 1971), pp. 22–44.

4. The poem can be found in Friedrich von Matthisson, *Schriften* (Zurich: Orell, 1825), vol. 1, pp. 191–92.

5. In line 5 of stanza 1 Schubert altered Matthisson's "Wenn" to "Wann." Schubert's *Andenken* is discussed and compared with Beethoven's setting and with his own *Nähe des Geliebten* in Thrasybulos Georgiades, *Schubert: Musik und Lyrik* (Göttingen: Vandenhoeck und Ruprecht, 1967), pp. 40–55. I return to Georgiades's ideas below.

6. Stanzas 1, 2, 3, and 5 of the poem are given in Friedländer, *Das deutsche Lied* 2:459–60. The complete poem can be found in the original printing, *Musenalmanach fürs Jahr 1795*, ed. J. H. Voss (Hamburg: C. E. Bohn, 1795), p. 177.

7. The song is printed in Friedländer, *Das deutsche Lied* 1/2:212.

8. Goethe's remarks to or about Zelter are discussed in Jack Stein, *Poem and Music in the German Lied from Gluck to Hugo Wolf* (Cambridge, Mass.: Harvard University Press, 1971), pp. 41–42.

9. J. W. von Goethe, *Goethe's Letters to Zelter*, trans. A. D. Coleridge (London: G. Bell and Sons, 1892), p. 1. The original German is cited in Friedländer, *Das deutsche Lied* 2:201–2.

10. The 1809 setting is included in J. F. Reichardt, *Goethes Lieder, Oden, Balladen und Romanzen mit Musik*, ed. Walter Salmen. Das Erbe Deutscher Musik, vol. 58 (Munich: Henle, 1964), p. 22. The history of Goethe's poem is given by Friedländer (see n. 9).

11. Wiora, *Das deutsche Lied*, pp. 35–37.

12. See his remarks cited in Friedländer, *Das deutsche Lied* 1/1:190, and partially translated in Alfred Einstein, *Schubert: A Musical Portrait* (New York: Oxford University Press, 1951), p. 25.

13. See Friedländer, *Das deutsche Lied* 2:459. There were (and would continue to be) many other settings of *Nähe des Geliebten*, which I do not treat in this study. See the inventories by Willi Schuh, "Goethe Vertonungen," in J. W. von Goethe, *Gedenkausgabe der Werke, Briefe und Gespräche* (Zurich: Artemis, 1948–52), vol. 2, p. 700; and by Friedländer, *Das deutsche Lied* 2:201. Zelter's setting of 1808, which bears no relationship to his *Ich denke dein*, remained unpublished in his lifetime. It appears in C. F. Zelter, *Fünfzig Lieder*, ed. Ludwig Landshoff (Mainz: Schott, 1932), p. 32.

14. The first draft is included in both the old and new collected editions of Schubert's works. The two drafts are reprinted from the old edition in *Schubert's Songs to Texts by Goethe* (New York: Dover, 1979), pp. 47–48. In the new edition, see Franz Schubert, *Neue Ausgabe sämtlicher Werke* (Kassel: Barenreiter, 1964–), series 4, vol. 1, p. 276. See also pp. 14–15 of the critical report (*Quellen und Lesarten*).

15. See Georgiades, "Lyric as Musical Structure," included in this volume, p. 100.

16. Georgiades, *Schubert*, pp. 49–50.

17. Schubert changed Goethe's "Flimmer" (stanza 1, line 3) to "Schimmer," thus reproducing the word already used in line 1. This seems to me an unfortunate (and perhaps unconscious) alteration, which obscures (though it does not eliminate) the sun-moon opposition. In stanza 2, he similarly substituted "Wege," the last word of line 1, for the original "Stege" in line 3.

18. For a sensitive discussion of the musical and poetic aspects of Schubert's song introductions, see Joseph Kerman, "A Romantic Detail in Schubert's *Schwanengesang*," included in this volume.

19. In the first draft of the song (see n. 14) there is no quickening of the harmonic rhythm; each chord of the introduction lasts three full beats (in $\frac{6}{8}$ meter). In this respect, as in several others, the final version is much more effective.

20. For a discussion of the variants among these sources, see the critical report (see above, n. 14). Both autographs of the final version of the song have been reproduced in facsimile. The first one (dated 27 February 1815) is in Paul Gottschalk, *A Collection of Original Ms. of the World's Greatest Composers* (Berlin: Gottschalk, 1930), plate 21. The 1816 copy is included in the facsimile edition of the entire volume sent to Goethe, *Lieder von Goethe komponiert von Franz Schubert*, ed. Georg Schünemann (Berlin: Albert Frisch, 1943), pp. 18–19 (of facsimile proper). The introduction relates the story behind the preparation of this manuscript.

21. See Charles Rosen, *Sonata Forms* (New York: Norton, 1980), p. 183.

22. Hans Gal, *Franz Schubert and the Essence of Melody* (New York: Crescendo, 1974), pp. 78–79.

23. The editors of the *Neue Ausgabe* take a different position on *Tränenregen*, claiming that the publisher inadvertently left out the repeat sign before the last beat of bar 4 and that the error was not caught by Schubert's brother, who proofread *Die schöne Müllerin*. (See Schubert, *Neue Ausgabe* 4:2, p. 303.) There is perhaps some justice to their claim, since the song has a modified strophic form. The final strophe is written out separately and is *not* preceded by the original prelude. In the case of the *Nähe des Geliebten* autographs, however, as in most simple strophic songs, Schubert wrote out only one musical strophe, with the words of the first stanza underlaid. In the volume prepared for Goethe (see n. 20) he wrote out the poetry for stanzas 2–4 on the following page.

The Schubert Lied:
Romantic Form and Romantic Consciousness

LAWRENCE KRAMER

I. The Schubert Lied

In Schubert's hands the German Lied became the first fully developed genre of Romanticism in music. As Charles Rosen
affirms, without mincing words, Schubert's songs "are related
to the *Lieder* of the past only by negation; they annihilate all
that precedes. The classical idea of dramatic opposition and
resolution is completely superseded: the dramatic movement is
simple and indivisible."[1] The traditional way to explain why
the Lied, in particular, should form the breakthrough genre is
to observe that structural looseness and harmonic irregularity
can be persuasively justified as expressions of a text. Schubert
could support a Romantic style, as Schoenberg and Berg later
supported an atonal one, on fluctuations of feeling enforced by
poetry.[2] Traditional descriptions of Schubert's songs accordingly tend to focus on the new expressive resources of this music: the richness of the piano accompaniment in contrast to the
anemic chords and arpeggios of earlier Lied composers like
Reichardt, Zumsteeg, and Zelter, or Schubert's gift for lush
sonorities and inventive modulations.[3]

My purpose in this essay is not to declare these explana-
tions wrong, but to get beyond the limits imposed by their
static, merely descriptive rightness. As Rosen's comments suggest, it should be possible to approach Schubert's Lieder in
terms of musical processes rather than of musical traits: to
place them in contexts of tension between tradition and innovation, structure and texture, musical form and musical lan-

guage. Only in that way can we find convincing motives for Schubert's practice and open the possibility of a criticism that will not substitute the admiration of his innovative textures and harmonies for an understanding of how they work.

As a genre, the Lied as developed by Schubert seems to rest on two imperatives. The first is to break away from the harmonic contour of the Classical style, and especially to break the grip of the dominant and its dominants—the cadential circle of fifths—on musical structure. As Rosen notes, Classical music was based on patterns of "dramatic opposition and resolution." These were realized harmonically by taking tonic-dominant tension as the foundation of both local and large-scale form. Until fairly late in his career, Schubert could not depart from this model convincingly within the privileged framework of the Classical sonata. Before 1823–24, the years of the A-Minor Piano Sonata (D. 784) and the A-Minor and D-Minor Quartets, he filled out Classical forms with indirectly related tonalities in a straightforward manner, at the cost of harmonic urgency. As he eventually realized, the use of post-Classical harmony required a thorough recasting of Classical structure—a task accomplished in works like the late B-Flat-Major Piano Sonata, the C-Major String Quintet, and the last two symphonies.[4] But from the very beginning, Schubert was essentially un-Classical. As Martin Chusid has remarked, he seemed unable to tolerate long stretches in the tonic without some intriguing digression.[5] At the start of his career, his harmonic sense demanded a form that was burdened by neither the prestige nor the rigor of the Classical genres. And this he found in the Lied, which in the hands of its earlier practitioners was an empirical, indeed somewhat haphazard affair, loosely positioned between invocation of the *Volksgeist* and dramatic recitative.

The other imperative of the Schubert Lied is to align music with the widespread effort of literary and philosophical Romanticism to represent subjectivity in action. This expressly means that the purpose of Romantic song is not simply to enhance the emotional force of the text, nor even, as writers on the Lied traditionally claim, to evoke the meaning of the text, whether directly or ironically. The purpose is to represent the activity of a unique subject, conscious, self-conscious, and unconscious, whose experience takes shape as a series of conflicts and reconciliations between inner and outer reality. According to Wordsworth, this "mighty Mind" is the subject, in all senses of the term, of Romantic poetry. "Ever on the watch, / Willing to work and to be wrought upon" (*The Prelude* [1805], 13. 102–3), such a mind "feeds upon infinity," "exalted by an underpresence, / The sense of God, or whatsoe'er is dim / And vast in its own being" (13. 70–73). Schubert's songs literally give a voice to this historical expansion in the concept of the self. Perhaps that says something about song as a form: after all, the development of expressive monody in the Renaissance did the same thing, though the model of self involved was very different.

We start with a voice for the self, then. But whose voice? Edward T. Cone, in considering Schubert's *Erlkönig*, calls it the composer's voice: a presiding personality or "persona" that expresses itself through the music, "speaking" for the composer in the same indirect and partial way that the "I" of a lyric poem speaks for the poet.[6] Cone also makes the important point that this musical persona stands apart from both the vocal line of a song and the accompaniment: we hear it in the song as a whole. Even more important, the persona of the song stands apart from the persona of the text—a difference that Schubert expands into a generic distinction.

Like any song, a Schubert Lied evokes the persona of its text, which comes to life in the broad expressive character of vocal melody and accompaniment figuration. But Schubert's Lieder also negate that textual persona in favor of its musical counterpart. The musical persona affirms itself by recasting the rhetoric, rhythm, and imagery of the text, reinvesting the textual material with a new subjectivity. It is as if the music were exercising the "magical power" of imagination described by Samuel Taylor Coleridge, which "dissolves, diffuses, dissipates, in order to re-create."[7] The movement of the song corresponds to this re-creative process, which can range in its aims all the way from the musical persona's identification with, to its repudiation of, a textual alter ego.[8] Romantic poetry in both German and English is full of similar encounters between selves and personified self-images.

Schubert's approach to song through the Romantic subject is closely allied with his treatment of a larger musical issue: harmony. Schubert's music recurrently incorporates a conflict between Classical tonality and harmonic innovation, a conflict found in its most direct and concentrated forms among the songs. In its progressions, key relationships, emphasis, and chordal texture, Schubert's harmony repeatedly steps beyond Classical boundaries. Yet the music invokes the Classical context of these Romantic harmonies so strongly that the Classical style retains a substantial lingering authority. Harmony thus becomes a matter of clashing perspectives. Harmonic structure becomes dialectical rather than systematic, as Schubert's Romantic idiom evolves by negating, but never escaping, its Classical origins.

For Classical tonality, this dialectic entails a demystification at the hands of the musical persona. Schubert's mingling of harmonic idioms undermines the naturalness that Classical harmony seems to possess on its own ground, and exposes that harmony as a historically determined language that may attract, but cannot define or delimit, a Romantic subject. Both Mozart and Beethoven had earlier taken steps in this critical or "deconstructive" direction.[9] Yet if the dissonant introduction to Mozart's C-Major Quartet (K. 465) stretches Classical harmony to the limit, it still stays within that limit; and if Beethoven goes beyond the limit—one-upping Mozart, say, in the C-Major Quartet, op. 59, no. 3—he does so only to recommit himself to the Classical style more decisively.[10] Schubert is the first composer to set a Romantic harmony into play without assuming in advance its subordination to a higher Classical power.

Many of Schubert's songs seem to regard the affirmation of the musical persona and the dialectic of Romantic and Classical harmony as concurrent versions of the same general process—that is, of the representation of subjectivity in action. Sometimes, especially in strophic songs, Schubert forms blocs of contrasting harmonies and juxtaposes them—either to displace the structural effect of Classical fifth relationships with the coloristic effect of third relationships, or to spell out an antithesis between Classical and Romantic idioms. So *Der*

Musensohn proceeds by the impetuous juxtaposition of the tonic and the mediant major. The keys alternate without modulation as the vocal line moves from an upbeat in one to a downbeat in the other; Classical movement by fifths occurs locally, but not structurally. At the same time, Schubert writes recurrent hesitations into the lightly skipping $\frac{6}{8}$ melodic line, so that his musical persona admits to a slight but telling plaintiveness that Goethe's son of the Muses, who rapturously celebrates transience, tries to leave out.

More radically disjunctive is the collagelike design of *Am Meer*, from *Schwanengesang*. The accompaniment of this song alternates between doubling the voice over soft, gently rocking tonic-dominant harmony, and splitting off from the voice in dramatic tremolo swells. As the swells rise and fall, a plain circle-of-fifths descent in the tonic C major, V^7/ii–ii–V_5^6–I, is so distorted by dissonant intrusions that its cadential impact all but vaporizes (ex. 1; note especially the alteration of ii at *a*, and the unusual treatment of the dissonant F of the V_5^6/I, which disappears without resolving, then reappears as an appoggiatura to the tonic triad).

This clash of harmonic perspectives echoes the more radical one produced by the famous elliptical progression, German sixth to tonic, that both opens and closes the song. Joseph Kerman describes the frame passage as an "oracular" suggestion of "everything in the world that is inward, sentient, and arcane."[11] One thing that makes it so is a dim feeling that the German sixth has not really been resolved at all, that the elided sonority— the dominant—is obscurely missed. Schubert transforms the textbook movement from German sixth to tonic $\frac{6}{4}$ by doubling the C of the German sixth as a pedal tone, which turns the subsequent tonic chord into a root-position triad. But since the root in the bass is not reattacked, the upper tones act together as a kind of residual or pseudo $\frac{6}{4}$ chord, more a point of transition than one of rest. The pedal tone puts a familiar progression into a strange, even an uncanny, light. By framing the song with this subtle mystification, Schubert both extends and parodies, salutes and betrays, the circling movement at the heart of Classical tonality.

With the through-composed songs, Schubert often works by splitting the composition into disjunctive halves that are

Example 1

tenuously integrated at the close by a few perfunctory measures of tonal circling. *Einsamkeit*, from *Winterreise*, begins
pianissimo with a bleak, detached texture; the harmony is confined to the tonic, dominant, and submediant chords of B
minor. In the second half, there is a jagged and sonorous display of shifting dynamics, framed by swells on tremolos and
heavy chordal triplets. Twice the music drives to a climax on
the flatted supertonic, C, through a jangle of diminished chords
and fragmentary circle-of-fifths progressions. The tonic and
dominant are submerged, all but obliterated, as the submediant
G-major sonority that was naïvely prominent in the first half
aggressively redefines itself as the dominant of C major/minor.
The G–C progression is less an event within the orbit of B
minor than it is the articulation of a competing tonic-dominant
axis. Schubert underlines the point by refusing to interpret a
single C-major chord as a Neapolitan harmony in B minor.

Overall, the large-scale resolution of one tonic-dominant
polarity into another can be said here to replace the Classical

resolution of dominant to tonic. In particular, the setting of the final phrase, "so elend nicht," turns on the reinterpretation of G^7 as a German sixth of B minor. But the resolution itself is dubious. The closing return to the tonic, only four measures long, depends on a rhythmically feeble cadence and quickly peters out on the hollow sound of open fifths and sixths.

Auf dem Flusse, also from *Winterreise*, is similarly if more subtly designed. In the first half, the major harmonic event is the first modulation, a startling move from the tonic to the leading tone, E minor to D-sharp minor, after only eight measures; Schubert seems to seize on D♯, the third of the dominant major, as a kind of subversive secondary dominant. The second half of the song is antithetical to the first both in texture and harmonic design. The vocal melody that begins the work now disappears from the voice and migrates to the bass as an ostinato. As a concomitant, the D♯ dissonance, often in opposition to D♮, is presented on a wide variety of harmonic and melodic planes—as a tonic, a dominant, a mediant, a false relation, a leading tone—so that the closing return to the tonic coincides with the exhaustion of the imperious, heightened discord. This process becomes explicit in the closing phrase of the voice, which is nothing more than the melodic elaboration of D♯–E resolution. In its last incarnation, D♯ appears as part of a dominant-seventh chord, but the cadential resolution that follows is less significant in itself than as a medium for the long-term resolution of the polarized leading tone.[12]

Of course, not all of Schubert's more than six hundred songs are as disjunctive as these. *Am Meer* and *Einsamkeit* in particular represent only an expressive limit within the broad generic contour of the Schubert Lied. But a simple diatonic song like *Heidenröslein* does the same thing; its Classical qualities represent a limit, not a norm. The diatonic naïveté of the song is sophisticated, not innocent; it belongs to a musical persona who, like Goethe's narrator, declines to make anything of the irony implicit in his little fable.

II. Presentational Structures

In order to make the Romantic form and Romantic consciousness of the Schubert Lied available to criticism, two working principles will be necessary. The first is that the relationship of the text to the music must always involve a critical interpretation of the poetry; merely to recount what the poem "says" is not enough.[13] The persona of a Romantic song is rarely content just to echo a text. On the contrary, it actively appropriates the text, which is to say that it both identifies and substantially revises the poetic persona's pattern of consciousness. The familiar techniques by which the music mimics, emphasizes, or alludes to the text cannot automatically be taken as parallels; they must be thought through as parts of the musical persona's subjective drama.

The second principle is that Schubert's songs are likely to complement their movement around a central tonality—in some cases even to replace it—with harmonic structures of a different kind. I have suggested elsewhere that the Romantic style characteristically presents such independent harmonic structures in tonal contexts of varying strengths and prominence.[14] Edmund Husserl's phenomenological concept of "horizon," the tacitly apprehended context of lived experience, is helpful on this point. Classical music can be said to present harmonic patterns, both local and structural, that exemplify Classical tonality itself—the system of tonal relationships and musical forms that constitutes the horizon of the harmonies presented. Romantic music, in contrast, depends on the ever-present possibility of presenting harmonic patterns that sound within a tonal, even a Classical, horizon, but *do not* exemplify it.[15] In Schenkerian terms, this could be put as the quite un-Schenkerian proposition that Romantic music customarily establishes foreground or middleground structures that are detached from the composing-out of a background.

Die Stadt, from *Schwanengesang*, offers a skeletal, almost schematic example of Romantic presentation in Schubert. The song follows an *a b a' b' a* design. In the *a* sections, the piano creates an impressionistic haze by obsessively arpeggiating a functionless diminished-seventh chord. A nominally tonic pedal point pulses along underneath, but its effect is to cloud the sonority, not to clarify the harmony. The *b* sections answer this ambiguity with rigidity: they confine themselves to rudimentary tonic, dominant, and subdominant harmonies, as if to intimate that anything more would risk a tonal collapse.

This antiphony of harmonic idioms becomes a dramatic conflict when the voice, which enters the song with the first *b* section, is accompanied—overtaken—by the shivery arpeggio
during the second *a* section. For two measures the vocal line
retains its original orientation to the tonic, C minor. But with
the expressive entry of an A♮ that embitters the phrase "an
graue Wasserbahn," the vocal line commits itself to an extended falling articulation (C–A♮–F♯–E♭–C) of the ambiguous diminished-seventh chord that ripples beneath it.

   The only significant harmonic event in *Die Stadt* arises
unexpectedly as the vocal line draws to a close. Schubert recapitulates an earlier progression, ii^6–i$^6_4$–V, by altering the supertonic chord to a Neapolitan sixth and adding a subdominant: ♭II^6–iv^6–i$^6_4$–V. A small change—but it suddenly expands
the harmonic frame of reference and proclaims, though belatedly, that Classical tonality is not dead, only sleeping. Yet
this, the point of greatest tonal integration, is also the point of
emotional disintegration. The Neapolitan progression marks
the moment in the poem when the rising sun illuminates the
spot where the speaker has lost his beloved. The poem invites
us to recognize from this that the speaker has been making a
kind of pilgrimage to that very spot, where the visual illumi-
nation that greets him ironically takes on a psychological parallel. What the light of day reveals is that his homecoming is an
exercise in self-torment, a neurotic reenactment of his failure
in love. By ending the poem with the revelation of his loss, the
speaker imbues his ritual of return with pathos and nostalgia:
the force of his obsessiveness is blunted by the conventional
posture of the disappointed lover. Schubert echoes this effect
with the traditional pathos of his Neapolitan sixth, but he will
not let the pathos stand. The song closes with the solo piano
once more tossing up its haze of arpeggios, a move that reverses the speaker's effort to expose an obsession and explain it
away in the same breath. Instead of being glossed over, the feeling of psychological disturbance intensifies as the song ends
in vocal silence amid the tonal uncertainty of its gray water-
music.

   A much earlier song, *Geistes-Gruss* (D. 142, 1815–16), is a
match for *Die Stadt* in its dissociative form. *Geistes-Gruss* begins with soft tremolos in E major, moves to the dominant, B,

then turns without modulation to the lowered mediant, G, where it adopts a declamatory texture and moves to a close. The skewed key design is an extravagant gesture, not a radical one, but it has an expressive significance that is lacking in the tonal ramblings of Schubert's longer, balladlike early songs. The G-major section begins with a reiterated I-V$_5^6$ progression that is sequentially restated on vi. The sequence represents a moment of self-conscious reflection on the harmonic structure of the song. The chord on the sixth degree of G major is E minor, so that the sequence forms a diatonic version of the chromatic third relationship that shapes the piece as a whole. The E-minor triad and the E-major tonality even behave in the same way, each moving to its own sixth degree. Finally, the harmonies involved in the initial G-major sequence reappear near the close of the song (at "und du, und du") in retrograde order. The result is a resolution in G major via vi–V^7–I.

The song closes by echoing its final cadence over a tonic pedal. By thickening the sonority and sinking quickly from *forte* to *pianissimo*, the little epilogue mutes the feeling of arrival without disturbing the harmony. This both gives the spirit-greeting celebrated by the text, an injunction to fare ever onward, an appropriately open-ended feeling, and turns the greeting into an oracular justification for the split tonality of the song. Once again, the music becomes an allegorical reflection on its own design.

A look at the multiple versions of *Geistes-Gruss*, four of which appear in the old *Gesamtausgabe*, suggests that Schubert hesitated over just how disjunctive the song should be.[16] The idea of bluntly juxtaposing chromatically related key areas appears in the first version, but not in the second and third, where Schubert smoothes the transition to the closing key by moving through its dominant-seventh chord. In the final version, Schubert returned to his original idea and added the tremolo figuration. As the song now stands, the spirit-voice appears to enter through the breach in tonal nature represented by the abrupt appearance of G major. The shift in harmony becomes an act of conjuration.

Four full-scale critical interpretations will take up the rest of this essay. They are intended to give a feeling for the variety, complexity, and consistency of Schubert's presentational structures, and so to give a sketch—only that, by necessity, but one ample in particulars—of the Schubert Lied as a Romantic genre. The songs in question, *Meeres Stille, Pause, Der Doppelgänger,* and *Ganymed,* span Schubert's career, and all represent his song writing at its best and most inventive.

III. Meeres Stille (D. 216, 1815)

Marked *Sehr langsam, ängstlich,* with a metronome mark of $\downarrow$ = 27, *Meeres Stille* is music that barely moves. Schubert's tone painting of Goethe's calm sea involves immobility in every expressive dimension. Both the vocal line and the accompaniment are depressed in register; the highest note in the song is c′. There is no change in dynamic level and, in the accompaniment, no change in rhythm; the voice suspends itself over dull arpeggios, one to a measure, in steady *pianissimo.* Even the words fail to move in the usual sense; the singer's long notes make taffy of the text at the tempo indicated. Only the harmony is not static, but while the arpeggios vary in tonal function their sonority is monotonous, an almost unbroken succession of close-position chords and octave basses.

Meeres Stille is very nearly a continuous fabric of sound, but Schubert gives it a tripartite design by means of a short rest and a fermata. The work is constructed symmetrically. The first section consists of a modulation from the tonic C major to the mediant major, E. The middle section slips into the submediant, A minor, cadences on F, then initiates a return to the mediant major. The section closes on V of III, and the third section reverses the harmonic direction of the first by moving from the mediant back to the tonic, closing on a full cadence. The harmonic design, then, is based on a recursive principle of enclosure: C major surrounds E major, which in turn surrounds A minor. The rigidity of the pattern, with its conceptual image of envelopment, is quite possibly a piece of Bach-like musical symbolism on Schubert's part, a schematic portrait of the ship that the poem imagines enveloped by the "monstrous breadth" ("ungeheuren Weite") of ocean.

Considered abstractly, these harmonies are straightforward

Classical progressions. Heard concretely, they are tenuous and self-subverting. In the outer sections, the tonic is slackly profiled and the mediant major is surprisingly feeble. As the opening C-major chords are arpeggiated, their spacing divides them into a pair of distinct perceptual units, a tonic octave followed by a pseudo $^6_4$ chord. The result is a tenuous quality that disappears if the chords are played as simultaneities. More important, the mediant major starts off strongly and then disintegrates. The modulation that introduces it at the end of the first section (bars 6–8) includes a substantial cadence in E/e: ii^{o6}–V^7–I. The diminished ii chord points to E minor; E major emerges instead. It is rather bemusing to hear this new key dissolve instantly, but so it does; the middle section begins by dispelling it with a diminished-seventh chord from which A minor tentatively emerges.

Later on, the peculiar instability of the mediant major comes to make sense. The middle section draws to a close by initiating a new mediant modulation, which is held up by a fermata on V/III. The third section begins by completing the full cadence, but with E minor replacing E major. The outcome of this cadence both recalls and intensifies the major/minor clash implicit in the first section, and Schubert at once brings the conflict to the surface. He repeats the original mediant modulation exactly, then immediately corrects III to iii. In other words, the chromatically tonicized key of E major is twice reduced, demoted, to a diatonic step within C major. This permits the tonic to reemerge without modulation, as if it had never been left at all. The cadential descent to the mediant major is never answered; it is elided, left as a kind of concealed fissure in a surface that is seemingly all tonic.

Schubert's implicit and explicit juxtapositions of the major and minor triads of E call attention to an ambiguity that is ever-present in Classical tonality, the uncertain distinction between a scale degree and a key. The sense of ambiguity turns the song, like *Geistes-Gruss*, into a projected form of self-consciousness, a meditation on the slipperiness of harmonic meaning. The odd tenuousness of the seemingly firm mediant major bears out the difficulty, and helps to disturb the tonal clarity of the work as a whole.

Example 2

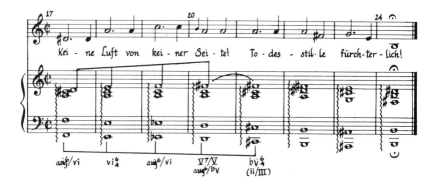

The middle section goes even further. Putatively in A minor with a hint of F major, it develops a Romantic presentation that reorients the song around an independent harmonic process that is antithetical to tonic resolution. The episode sounds indefinite and confused, and it should; its role is to create a dissonance of harmonic perspectives within a fuzzy, generalized tonic horizon.

Here again, an ambiguity inherent in Classical tonality is heightened and drawn into a pattern that comments on its own uncertainties. Once introduced, the submediant A-minor sonority shows an exclusive affinity for its own submediant, F, which gradually establishes itself as a new key area. At bar 17, the addition of a dissonant tone to the F-major triad produces a chord that is spelled as a German sixth of A and progresses to an A-minor $^6_4$ chord. The progression forms a partial resolution that would normally be completed by a move to the dominant of A minor. Instead, the augmented sixth reappears, abandons all thought of resolving, and leads to still another dissonance of the same type (ex. 2). This new chord is completely unanchored: it could be either a dominant seventh of G, which is how it is spelled, or an augmented sixth of F-sharp. For a moment, all tonal bearings are lost, and in that lies the crux of the song. As V^7/V of C, the dissonant chord seems to gravitate toward the tonic. As an augmented sixth, it points to the axial tonality of the tritone. So, in one sonority, maximum stability and maximum tension float suspended. As it happens, Schubert takes the chord as a function of F-sharp, which makes the asyntactic arbitrariness of its arrival a point of collision between harmonic idioms.

Two independent presentational patterns are exposed by this. First, a look at bars 17–21 shows that the F-sharp-minor triad is produced by a continuous semitonal modification of the initial augmented sixth of A, the semitones falling in the bass and rising in the upper voice (ex. 2). The process subordinates and skews tonal syntax, as its strangest product shows; the problematical chord of bar 20 is a kind of enlarged passing dissonance, but one with a tonal identity too strong to be submerged.

Behind this pattern—essentially one in which voice leading bluntly overrides harmonic coherence—there is a larger one. As it turns out, the presence of the F-sharp-minor chord clarifies every harmonic event in the song. The mediant modulations that frame the middle section begin with a diminished triad, the pivotal F♯–A–C, because the long-range reference point of the progressions is not the mediant (and indirectly the tonic) but the resolved form of that triad, F♯–A–C♯. Likewise, the mediant major evaporates into the submediant, and the submediant moves only toward developing its augmented sixth, because the submediant augmented-sixth chord is needed to provide the point of origin for the semitonal "osmosis" that generates the F-sharp-minor sonority. The F♯ can even be heard as a destructive "alter ego" that negates the harmonic authority of the F-major triad that comes to prominence in the middle section, whether as the subdominant of the song's tonic or as the submediant of A minor.[17]

In sum, all the lines of presentation are oriented toward the tritone rather than toward the tonic. And though the final mediant modulation tries to cover the breach thus opened by reclaiming the F-sharp triad as a predominant chord, no return from the irrational yet overdetermined central tritone can be fully convincing. It is no accident that the word set to the F-sharp-minor triad is *Todes*. Spelling out the ultimate suspension of vitality, the ultimate enclosure, the word marks both the point of maximum estrangement in the poem and the pivot for Schubert's subjective appropriation.

Goethe's "Meeres Stille" evokes a feeling of oppressive stillness by repeatedly making the same observation from different perspectives. The language of the poem, like its becalmed sailor, is held fast to the empty sea. Of the two stanzas, the first repeats itself and the second makes matters worse by repeating itself and the first stanza, too. Even the grammatical constructions are parallel:

> Tiefe Stille herrscht im Wasser,
> Ohne Regung ruht das Meer,
> Und bekümmert sieht der Schiffer
> Glatte Fläche rings umher.
>   Keine Luft von keiner Seite!
> Toddesstille fürchterlich!
> In der ungeheuren Weite
> Reget keine Welle sich.

>> [Deep stillness rules the waters, the sea rests without motion; and with anxiety the sailor sees a smooth surface surrounding him.
>> No breeze from any side! Terrible death-stillness! In the monstrous/enormous waste not one wave stirs.]

Between the two stanzas, however, there is a significant shift in narrative style. The speaker of the first stanza is detached, impersonal, and uncharacterized—more a function than a persona. The second stanza carries out a repeal of this neutrality. Description turns to exclamation; the first two lines of the second stanza sympathetically assume the perspective of the anxious sailor. And this movement from detachment to sympathy, from observation to identification, invests the oppressive seascape with a new meaning. Seen from within the sailor/speaker's anxiety, the scene becomes a metaphor. The stillness ("Stille") of the first stanza reappears as a death-stillness ("Todesstille"), while the connotation of monstrosity in "ungeheuren Weite" suggests a rift in nature from which neither the sea nor the sailor can emerge.

Schubert's song deletes the moral and imaginative dimension of sympathetic identification from the poem. The sectional division of the song pointedly ignores the stanzaic division of the text, the unvarying accompaniment reduces all difference to sameness, and the vocal line does nothing to distinguish between the abstract voice of the first stanza and the humanized voice of the second. The persona behind this music is a victim of his own anxiety from the start. Unable to make room for others, his subjectivity isolates him and fixates him on what is literally a dead end. All *bekümmert*, the song is also all metaphor: it forms a leaden epiphany of death that consummates with the F-sharp-minor triad and pronounces its vision to be unendurable with the succeeding three chords, which come to rest in unresolved dissonance. When the voice closes the bleak annunciatory phrase "Todesstille fürchterlich," it falls to its registral nadir, a low B, the dark sound of which marks a paralysis motivated by unconditional mortal terror.[18]

IV. *Pause* (D. 795, no. 12; 1823)

Like *Einsamkeit*, *Pause* from *Die schöne Müllerin* is divided into antithetical blocs of harmony. The song follows an *a b a' c* pattern with a short coda; the harmonic plan can quickly be summarized. The *a* section keeps to the tonic, B-flat major. The *b* section begins in the submediant, G minor, includes a strong cadential progression to C major/minor, proceeds through tonic-dominant harmony into the flat mediant, D-flat major, and ends with a half cadence on the dominant. The *a'* section recapitulates the harmony of *a* and the first part of *b*. It begins in the tonic, then moves quickly through G major to a pause in C minor. The *c* section begins in A-flat major, from which it twice moves chromatically onto F♭, then to the tonic.

This bare description alone brings to light a Romantic presentation based on tritone relationships. The submediant passage at the beginning of the *b* section lies a diminished fifth away from the flat mediant passage to which it leads; and the *c* section uses a flatted dominant, F♭, as a harsh and perplexing avenue to the tonic. Even if the song were worked out with impeccable Classical syntax, this design would put it under a strain. But the tonal syntax is a dialectical element here. Impeccable enough, even ingenious, through the close of the *a'* section, it becomes eccentric—not to say bizarre—in the *c* section.

The turning point comes as the *a'* section closes. After the cadence to G minor, C minor is approached abruptly via an

A-flat-major triad whose incongruous brightness seems to mock the word "bange" that it accompanies. This is not a mere casual detail, but a kind of tear in the Classical fabric of the music. For no apparent reason, the *c* section seizes on A-flat as a tonality and uses it to reprise the main motive of the song, which comes out sounding strangely remote and hollow.

Nothing is done to tonicize this intrusive chromatic region, and nothing to rationalize its materialization out of a stray wisp of dissonance. Nothing, in fact, is done to it at all. The A-flat-major triad remains an entirely static tonal level for seven measures, then turns fleetingly to the minor and disappears, along with the melody, into a sustained triad of F-flat. A painful, mystifying dissonance then follows, the upper tone of which is resolved as an appoggiatura to produce a lingering $G\flat^6_5$ chord (ex. 3). This new dissonance is overtly irrational, like everything in its surroundings, but its ambiguity is "decidable." By respacing the chord, Schubert forms an augmented-sixth chord of B-flat, the song's tonic. The tonic obligingly returns, but it has barely been established before the music lapses back into the tritonal area. The A-flat episode is reprised, but condensed into a mere three measures; A-flat is represented only by its minor before the F-flat swallows it up. When B-flat major returns again (via the triple dissonance) it peters out quickly, rattling off the much-repeated main motive in a weakly closural coda.

Like the F-sharp-minor tritonal chord in *Meeres Stille*, this remarkable passage forces Classical harmony to become incoherent by insisting on a counter-coherence all its own. It is easy enough to move up the circle of fifths from A-flat to

Example 3

B-flat. If Schubert's route is tortuous, even fantastic, the reason lies with a Romantic presentation that strips the tonic of its centralizing power. In particular, A-flat major intrudes on the song after a cadence to C minor; the A-flat harmony therefore represents a move to the local submediant area. Schubert then applies this movement recursively: the same distance is covered in the chromatic movement from A-flat to F-flat. And to go a step further, the dissonant tone that forms the appoggiatura to the pivotal $^6_5$ chord is C, so that the movement away from F-flat also involves a chromatic submediant relationship, here reduced to a melodic dissonance—one shared by the voice and piano.

The overall structure of the *c* section is determined by this preference for the lowered-submediant sonority. The chain of descending thirds, C–A-flat–F-flat, forms an independent, harmonically indefinite pattern. Still more important, the chromatic submediant relation A-flat–F-flat forms an antithetical exaggeration of the diatonic one, B-flat–G, that is prominent earlier. The condensed repetition of the A-flat passage focuses the antithesis: the movement from V^7 to I to vi in B-flat just before the last entry of the voice is immediately juxtaposed with a movement from V^6 to I to VI^6 in A-flat. And the fact that the tonic is ultimately regained through a chord of its augmented sixth assimilates it, too, to the grid of minor-sixth sonorities that governs the *c* section. In this, as in every other respect, the end of the song parodies and deconstructs its beginning.

Pause marks the turning point in the drama of *Die schöne Müllerin*, and the disjunction between the Classical and Romantic materials of the song draws the boundary line between the miller's illusion of happiness and his eventual misery and death. Since falling in love, the poetic speaker has been too joyous to sing, but the wind sometimes sighs through his neglected lute, and the sound disturbs him:

> Oft fliegt's um die Saiten mit seufzendem Klang,
> Ist es der Nachklang meiner Liebespein?
> Soll es das Vorspiel neuer Lieder sein?

> [Sometimes a sighing flutters at the strings. Is it the
> echo of my love-torment? Will it be the prelude to new
> songs?]

The closing question is twice set as a hushed antiphony, the first half suspended over the tritone, the second moving into the tonic. The distance between the harmonies forms the measure of self-estrangement. Unwilling to answer, the musical persona dwells on the dread that disturbs him in the form of an external sighing, the outward projection of a painful anticipation that he cannot suppress but wishes to disavow.

The texture of the whole final section, with its paradoxical combination of harmonic stasis and abrupt shifts of sonority, reinforces this suggestion of an anxiety that the speaker is unwilling to confront. The hopeful but unconvincing resolution for the final line of text is imbued with a feeling of self-deception, the nervous expectancy of a divided self in whom the wish to disentwine Romantic passion from suffering is contradicted by the sound of the word "Liebespein" set to the most painful dissonances in the song (see ex. 3).

V. Der Doppelgänger (D. 957, no. 13; 1828)

Der Doppelgänger belongs in a unique expressive category with the great concluding song of Winterreise, Der Leiermann. Both pieces find the extremity of despair in a confrontation between the halves of a divided self: the subject who desires, and a double who represents that subject's worst aspects—anxiety, self-torment, self-contempt. Both songs follow what must be called a minimalist aesthetic; they rest on a bare scrap of melody, a brief, dully repeated accompaniment figure. In the case of Der Doppelgänger, this minimalism forms part of Schubert's response to Heine. It is shared by at least two of the other Heine Lieder, Die Stadt and Am Meer, and it is reflected in both the bare octaves that form part of the accompaniment in Ihr Bild and in the texture of octaves and tremolos in the outer sections of Der Atlas. The sense of the text embodied by this stylistic choice is harsh. Heine's early lyrics, with their combination of willed naïveté, extravagant sentiment, and jeering irony, suggest a persona in whom the self has thinned out to a kind of linguistic diagram, a raggle-taggle bunch of clichés strung together by a self-consciousness that can neither accept nor exclude them. Schubert's minimalism poignantly exposes this feature of the poetry, and at the same time tacitly resists it.

By constructing his minimal forms from simple cadential material, Schubert suggests a last-ditch, antithetical force of coherence working against the dissociation set loose in Heine's poems.

Aside from this, the spare repetitiveness that Schubert associates with the spectral double has a generic basis. The speakers in the Heine poems that Schubert set in 1828 are victims of compulsive repetition who return endlessly to the scene of their worst loss. Similar compulsives, haunted by sexuality or guilt, are frequent in the music and literature of the Romantic period. A short list would include Coleridge's Ancient Mariner, Berlioz's persona in the *Symphonie fantastique*, Byron's and Schumann's Manfred, Wagner's Flying Dutchman, and Nathanael, the hero of E. T. A. Hoffmann's "The Sandman."[19] If Maurice J. E. Brown was right to suggest that the appropriate sequence for the Heine songs is not the posthumously published one, but the order in which the poems appear in Heine's *Die Heimkehr*, then the second half of *Schwanengesang* forms a coherent little song cycle that portrays the tragic lapse of the self into obsessive repetition as the result of sexual grief.[20] Schubert's concentrated, insistent song structures accept this repetition compulsion, as Freud called it, as their imaginative milieu. In this context, a double becomes the *reductio ad absurdum* of self-consuming repetition, and Schubert's musical texture in both *Der Doppelgänger* and *Der Leiermann* goes to the same limit.

In general, the impulse of Schubert's Heine songs is to bring musical structure *almost* to the point of disintegration. *Die Stadt*, which ends with a solitary C that stands for the tonic C minor but is not even securely tonal, is the extreme case; *Der Doppelgänger* is formally less desiccated, but far more insidious in its irony. The basic process in *Der Doppelgänger* is the steady erosion of Classical harmony as a source of musical meaning, the gradual exchange of a Classical for a Romantic presentation. Like *Pause*, the song unfolds by deconstructing itself, but continuously rather than abruptly. Two overlapping perspectives are involved in this, one centered on the depletion of the tonic, the other on a breakdown of harmonic syntax.

The essential element in each case is the accompaniment, which consists entirely of variations on a four-chord progression, "tolling," as Richard Capell long ago observed, "in the half-conscious fancy of the speaker."[21] The content of the progression is i–V⁶–III–V$_4^6$ (or V$_3^4$) in B minor—an extended half cadence. As example 4 shows, the texture of the chords is curious. All of the tonic and dominant triads are incomplete; the tonic and closing dominant, missing their thirds, sound especially barren in empty fourths and fifths. Only the dissonances, the dominant-seventh chords and some of the mediant triads, are filled out. Eventually, a few scattered B-minor triads do appear in complete form, but with steadily failing power to direct the harmony; the dominant triad remains incomplete except when the seventh is added.

Schubert's stilted chording is enough by itself to give B minor a spooky, desiccated feeling, but there is something more. The song leaves the tonic for only five measures, just before the close; the move, a wrenching nonmodulatory shift to the raised mediant minor, D-sharp, coincides with the point of crisis in the poem, where the speaker accuses his double of aping his love-torment (*Liebesleid*). As example 5 shows, the spell of D-sharp minor consists only of a pair of half cadences, i–V–i–V, a varied transposition of the obsessive B-minor progression. The apparent continuity actually marks a disintegrative gesture. As a concentrated and repeated half cadence, the D-sharp-minor progression is stronger and more focused than its B-minor counterpart. Moreover, all of the D-sharp-minor chords are complete, richly sonorous triads—a dissonant fulfillment, by chromatic heightening, of the full mediant triads that have been heard (with increasing emphasis) since the beginning. Add to this the tone weight of the longest

Example 4

Example 5

was äffst du nach mein Lie-besleid, das mich gequält auf die-ser Stel-le

stretch of *fortissimo* in the song, and it becomes clear that the raised mediant in *Der Doppelgänger* is a far more forceful tonality than the tonic. As in *Pause*, the structural dissonance of the music cannot be contained by the tonal architecture; it breaks the frame.

The brief remainder of the song, fading from *piano* to triple *piano*, helplessly concedes the point. Initiated by an eerie altered chord, the close is almost astonishing: the long unbroken chain of half cadences is not resolved by an antithetical perfect cadence, but by a tepid plagal one. More a surrender than a conclusion, the final cadence doubles its failings by moving incongruously to the tonic major. The Picardy third seems like a solecism in music so fixedly somber. Its D♯, subliminally echoing the dissonant D-sharp tonality, sounds the wrong note in both a figurative and a literal sense. This way of ending represents both a strained attempt to assert the integrity of the tonic and a confession that long-term dissonance resolution is impossible here. Impossible: not so much for the music, taken abstractly, but for the subject whose music this is.

The other harmonic contour of *Der Doppelgänger* involves the disintegration of the i–V⁶–III–V⁶₄ pattern by the alteration of its closing chord. The focus of the alterations is the establishment of C♮ as an unresolvable long-term dissonance independent of tonal orientation. This process occupies the second half of the song, where it grows more disruptive by degrees. The first chord affected is simply a dominant seventh with its fifth flattened from C♯ to C♮; left unresolved, the C♮ seems to

Example 6

be an expressive inflection evoked by "Schmerzen," the word it accompanies. With the second affected chord, things get more problematic. Introduced triple *forte* as the speaker first recognizes his double, the chord is the seventh C♮–E–G–A♯, reinforced with a C♮ in the bass. The spelling indicates a German sixth of the subdominant, E; the other possible function of the sonority, as a dominant seventh of the tritone F, is penumbrally suggestive. The chord, however, is resolved according to neither of these functions; its G is treated as an appoggiatura and resolved to produce another V^4_3 with a recalcitrant flattened fifth (ex. 6). The tonic then returns to begin another extended half cadence, but its initial movement to the dominant comes to grief against the next incarnation of the C♮ dissonance: a glassy measure filled by a bare C♮–F♯ tritone that announces the dread term "Doppelgänger." This is resolved to the bare dominant fifth F♯–C♯, but the failing progression is then disturbed again by the clangorous substitution of the raised mediant, D♯, for the closing dominant chord. For its final visitation, the "wild" C♮ returns with uncanny effect in a root-position C-major triad. Unlike the earlier C♮ seventh and C♮–F♯ tritone, this chord fails to lead to the dominant that it displaces. As if to parody the tonic, it moves instead to its own V^7/iii—which, as the song's V^7/iv, ushers the music to its nerveless plagal close. The final tonic triad remains polarized against the C♮ dissonance that it has failed to resolve on either a large or a small scale. It is less a point of rest than a disavowal of the paralysis that has overtaken the Classical harmony.

Like *Einsamkeit* and *Geistes-Gruss*, *Der Doppelgänger* is built from the confrontation of antithetical halves, though without a collision of textures. And here the confrontation has a special meaning: like the poetic speaker, the song is split into a "normal" half and a mirror image that mocks and distorts it. The music, too, has its doppelgänger. But Schubert's expressive design does more than simply absorb the self-punitive pattern of the text. When Heine's speaker encounters his double, he desperately resists acknowledging his identity with this other self. The crux of the poem is a sudden shift from description to direct address: the speaker turns to, turns *against*, the double with a question that is an accusation, an act half of defense and half of defiance:

> Da steht auch ein Mensch und starrt in die Höhe,
> Und ringt die Hände vor Schmerzensgewalt;
> Mir graust es, wenn ich sein Antlizt sehe,
> Der Mond zeigt mir meine eigne Gestalt.
>   Du Doppelgänger, du bleicher Geselle!
> Was äffst du nach mein Liebesleid,
> Das mich gequält auf dieser Stelle
> So manche Nacht, in alter Zeit?

> [There stands a man and stares on high, and wrings his hands in violent grief; I shudder when I see his face—the moon shows me my own form.
>   You doppelgänger, you pale companion! Why do you ape my love-torment, which tortured me in this place so many a night, in the old times?]

The difference—the saving difference—between the self and its shadow is manifested by the muteness of the double, which Heine's imagery stresses hard. Schubert's musical persona, in contrast to all this, accepts his identification with the specter passively and half-nostalgically. Most of the text is set in an overwrought, declamatory style, but at the thought of old times, with their many nights of tortured love, the musical persona breaks into eloquent, melismatic song (ex. 7).[22] With this gesture, he repeats and travesties his earlier grief for the ear, as the double has done for the eye: he gives the mute double a voice. The *Liebesleid* returns as a distorted *Liebeslied*, in an animation of Heine's submerged pun. Like the other vic-

Example 7

so man - che Nacht, in al - - ter Zeit?

tims of Romantic repetition, the musical persona surrenders his allegiance to the moment of erotic failure in which his inner life was formed.

VI. *Ganymed* (D. 544, 1817)

In an effort to capture a moment of supreme ecstasy, *Ganymed* carries presentational independence to a giddy, not to say reckless extreme. The song begins with the most elementary tonic and dominant harmony in A-flat major. By the time it ends, it has evolved into F major by means of a harmonic process that is little more than nonsensical from the Classical standpoint evoked by the opening measures. This melting away of tonal coherence follows closely from an appropriation of Goethe's poem that is both radical and emotionally urgent; so for this analysis, we have to begin with the text.

Goethe's Ganymed is an example of an image frequent in Romantic poetry, a figure who attracts—seduces—the divine through the richness of his consciousness.[23] Within the poem, he participates in a double transcendence. First, there is an ecstatic immersion of the self in nature; then, when this proves to awaken more desire than it can satisfy, there is a transcendence of nature into the presence of a divine principle. Both nature and the divine are personified, one in feminine form, as Spring, the other in masculine form as the "all-loving Father," Zeus, or, as Hölderlin would call him, "Vater Aether," the fertilizing origin of spring. Both personifications are also the objects of intense erotic longing—for that matter, are the imaginative products of that longing, which is Ganymed's only mode of consciousness. The transfer of desire from a female to a male love object, from nature to divinity, suggests a poem of radical disjunction, and Goethe marks the turning point when Ganymed recognizes that his ever-burgeoning desire is leading him somewhere, and asks where: "Wohin? Ach, wohin?" But a look at the poem reveals that this discontinuity is actually the articulation of an underlying continuity. Nature and the divine are woven together into a larger unity that humanizes both in a vision of answerable desire:

> Wie im Morgenglanze
> Du rings mich anglühst,
> Frühling, Geliebter!
>
> . . .
>
> Ach, an deinem Busen
> Lieg ich, schmachte,
> Und deine Blumen, dein Gras
> Drängen sich an mein Herz.
> Du kühlst den brennenden
> Durst meines Busens,
> Lieblicher Morgenwind!
> Ruft drein die Nachtigall
> Liebend nach mir aus dem Nebeltal.
>
> Ich komm, ich komme!
> Wohin? Ach, wohin?
>
> Hinauf! Hinauf strebt's.
> Es schweben die Wolken
> Abwärts, die Wolken
> Neigen sich der sehnenden Liebe.
> Mir! Mir!
> In euerm Schosse
> Aufwärts!
> Umfangend umfangen!
> Aufwärts an deinem Busen,
> All liebender Vater!

> [As in the glow of morning you beam all around me, Springtime, beloved! . . .
> Ah, on your breast I lie and languish, and your flowers, your grass, press on my heart. You cool the burning thirst in my breast, lovely morning wind! In you the nightingale lovingly calls to me from the misty valley.
> I come, I come! Where? Ah, where?
> Upwards! I am urged upwards! The clouds float down,

the clouds bend down to my yearning love. To me! To me!
In your lap, upwards! Embracing embraced! Upwards to
your breast, all-loving Father!]

As the poem proceeds, all the leading images associated
with Ganymed's springtime rapture evolve into complementary images that express his union with the Father. The earthly
rapture is, so to speak, transposed to a higher register. The
breast of the beloved spring becomes the Father's bosom; the
misty valley becomes the floating clouds; the morning wind
that answers to desire becomes the bending clouds that re-
spond to "yearning love"; Ganymed's repose on the grass becomes his upward striving; and the passive, heteroerotic desire
for spring, which begins with being enveloped and ends in a
responsive caress, turns to the active, homoerotic desire for the
Father, which posits a reciprocity of active and passive love
with the key phrase "embracing embraced!" The heavenly bliss
even subsumes the feminity that is left behind on earth, as
Ganymed yearns toward the "Schoss" of the Father: "lap"
in reference to a male, but also "womb." The poem achieves
closure as Ganymed's longing, a conflation of the erotic and the
metaphysical, reaches the threshold of both fulfillment and—
quite literally—sublimation in his ascent to the Father.

Schubert's song takes over the purposeful fluidity of the
poem without fully matching Goethe's extravagance and ambivalence. The music depends on two extended Romantic
presentations: a disjunctive one that evokes the overt gap between earth and heaven, female and male, and a continuous one
that weaves the divided forms into a larger unity. These patterns unfold simultaneously. Overlapping rather than colliding
with each other, they blend together in a kind of structural
polyphony.

The disjunctive presentation involves a contradiction between the ultimate establishment of a tonic key and an impres-
sionistically conceived harmony that floats unpredictably from
tonality to tonality. The song moves through a series of four
primary harmonic areas, each of which is associated with its
dominant: A-flat−C-flat−E/A−F. From a Classical standpoint,
the tonal sequence is arbitrary, even a little bizarre. There is
neither a harmonic descent nor a harmonic circle, neither a ca-

dential contour nor a central key. But the harmonic texture of the music is paradoxical. Though the series of primary areas is virtually phantasmagorical, the harmony within each area is unproblematical in Classical terms. In other words, long-range and short-range syntax have been hopelessly sundered. The harmony, as a result, has the moment-to-moment effect of a curious fragility, a crystalline or deliquescent quality, almost— given the lack of a tonic—a sense of illusoriness.

Yet a tonic *is* established: there is no sense at the end of the song that closure has not been achieved—quite the contrary. In part, Schubert manages this by weighing his proportions. Of 121 measures in the song, 46 are in F major, so that when the music cadences in that key and stays there till the close, the intention of tonic resolution, if not its Classical rationalization, is achieved. But something more radical is at work, too. As the four tonic-quality areas succeed each other, the synthesizing and organizing power of tonality is called on more and more fully. Each new area uses more dissonant, more complex harmony than the last, and each, as it emerges, resolves a greater degree of harmonic uncertainty. The eventual tonic thus evolves through a gradual, indeed seamless, process of intensification, rather than through the clearly directed, highly articulated harmonic movement demanded by the Classical style. In particular:

1. The A-flat harmony of the opening remains placid until the first big crescendo, when a jarring chromatic chord brings an interrupted cadence. Schubert takes the dissonance as a pivot for a cadential progression to C-flat (ex. 8).

2. Gb (V of C-flat) is respelled as F♯ and the music turns— or rather wanders, since the harmonic foreground is fairly volatile—down the circle of fifths to E. The new tonality takes charge for several measures; then a strong cadential progression leads into A major/minor.

3. The tonic F major is presented as a specific negation of the preceding E and A. Schubert announces that A is a transitional tonal area by restricting its triads to their first inversion, but it is not yet clear where the music is heading. E briefly seems to be a possibility again, but the allusion to it only confirms its inadequacy as a point of arrival. With dramatic abruptness, a $^6_4$ chord of E minor rises into a forcefully attacked

Example 8

C-major triad. After harping on the C-major sonority for several measures, Schubert interprets C as a dominant and cadences into F major. The strength of this final tonality is established by its referential control over the harmonies that follow,
the liveliest and most wide-ranging in the song. F major is
never left, but there is not another cadence on it for over thirty
measures. Its presence is contextual, centralizing—which is to
say that it acts like a strong tonic.

The overall shape of the fifty-odd F-major measures consists of a movement toward three progressively longer cadences—the first dominant, the others tonic—on the closing
phrase of the text, "All liebender Vater." The cadences con-
summate the song by calming its volatility; they all slow the
pace of the accompaniment and float the voice on a long, leisurely melisma. At these moments, too, a rhythmic resolution
supports the harmonic one. The sequence of primary tonal
areas is graduated rhythmically as well as harmonically. Each
new area brings with it an increase in rhythmic agitation, the
result of increasingly sensitive syncopation in the accompaniment and an increasing tendency for the voice to run phrases
of text breathlessly together. The F-major section carries this
rhythmic tension to a climax, but it also resolves it—precisely
in the serene contours of the three cadences.

The arrival at F major, then, splits the song harmonically
into a wandering half and a centered one, and so articulates
the gap between mundane and divine rapture that Ganymed
quickly, inexplicably, orgasmically crosses. In the poem, movement across this threshold is marked by an evaporation of self-

consciousness, but the song—perhaps defensively[24]—takes the opposite tack and chooses this moment to reflect on itself with a text-music parallel. The first cadence to F major occurs during the setting of Goethe's transitional question-and-answer, "Wohin? Ach, wohin?/Hinauf!" The repeated "wohin" is set to a dominant harmony; the resolving "Hinauf" divides its syllables between V^7 and I of F major. The cadence to the long-awaited tonic thus confirms Ganymed's discovery of his divine destination, while at the same time Ganymed's cry of discovery proclaims that the musical destination has been reached. Closure does not come within the framework of inherited discourse, either perceptual or musical: it comes where desire is quenched by the breaching of such discourse.

Schubert's realization of this consummating breach is distractingly effective, but it is, as we know, only half the story. The song also presents a realization of the seamless continuity that joins the mundane and the divine, the empirical and the transcendental ego. For this, it relies on a structural symmetry that both cuts across the divisions of the text and leaves the evolution of the tonic out of account.

The contradiction between immediate harmonic coherence and large-scale harmonic drift that governs the song as a whole also operates at a more intermediate level. Since each of the four primary harmonic areas is linked with its dominant, the overall fluidity of harmonic movement is locally contradicted by the strong contour of tonic-dominant harmony. What Schubert does with this situation is to create what might be called a denatured (in terms of the text, de-natured, transcendentalized) cadential pattern. The first two primary areas, A-flat and C-flat, move to their dominants; the second two, E/A and F, are produced from their dominants. In other words, the sequence of harmonies resembles—at a distance—the most basic pattern in tonal music: a large half cadence followed by a large full cadence, I–V–I–V//V–I–V–I. Conjoined by the fluid transitional movement from F-sharp major to the first E-major cadence, the half- and full-cadence groups complement each other as structural upbeat and structural downbeat.

This pattern of disembodied large-scale cadences is one among several sources of harmonic continuity in *Ganymed*, each of which uses a denatured fragment of tonal syntax to re-create the movement of transcendence found in the poem. A second pattern depends on the fact that each of the large half cadences lies a semitone apart from one of the full cadences:

$$
\begin{array}{cccccccc}
\text{A}\flat-\text{E}\flat & & & & \text{E}-\text{A} & & & \\
& \text{C}\flat-\text{G}\flat(\text{F}\sharp) & & & & & \text{C}-\text{F} & \\
\text{I} & \text{V} & \text{I} & \text{V} & // & \text{V} & \text{I} & \text{V} \quad \text{I}
\end{array}
$$

From this standpoint, *Ganymed* can be taken as a single enormous chromatic appoggiatura, F♯–F♮, once again marked off as such by the transitional area between F♯ and E. This relationship not only matches the transposition of images in Goethe's text—mist to clouds, mother earth to Father Aether, and so on—but also suggests that the tensions of Ganymed's earthly desire can only be resolved by restatement in a celestial embrace. The sense of longing associated with semitonal voice leading in both Classical and Romantic contexts becomes a diffuse presence in the musical texture, which imperceptibly transforms the longing into consummation.

Chromatic relationships also give a plausible meaning to the seemingly random sequence of primary tonalities. The first half of the song articulates a rising chromatic third-relationship, A-flat major to C-flat major. In the second half, this dissociative movement is balanced out by a falling diatonic third-relationship, A minor to F major. The means for this move is C major, the resolved form of the structural upbeat, C♭. Complementary movement by thirds thus replaces the same sort of movement by fifths as a cadential contour, and the resolution of large-scale harmonic tension comes to depend on the retrospective definition of C-flat as a chromatically lowered dominant.

The line of relationship between C-flat and F is drawn by a beautiful and unexpected melodic cross-reference. Such allusions are rare in this song, which makes a point of flouting surface coherence; until the repetitions at the close, melodic figurations melt away as soon as they have established themselves.[25] The fruitful exception to this is the melismatic setting of the phrase "unendliche Schöne," which anticipates in texture the pair of full cadences on "All liebender Vater" at the close of the song. As it happens, this early melisma occurs just as the music cadences on C-flat; the tone C♭ that emerges as the me-

Example 9

lodic goal of the voice belongs to the initial C-flat-major triad (ex. 8). The concluding F-major melismas, especially in their predominant B♮(=C♭)–C♮ appoggiaturas and in the closing melodic fall C–F, seem both a reminiscence and a correction of the critical tritone relationship on which this harmonic design turns (ex. 9).

The pattern of complementary thirds does not have the immediate clarity of a large-scale Classical progression. But its presence is established, more or less subliminally, when we accept the continuity of the song and hear the F-major ending as a full release of tension. The production of the tonic by intensification is supplemented by a new tonal syntax, formed for the moment, which depends for its effect on its dialectical relationship with the Classical harmony that it violates.

Overall, the impact of *Ganymed* depends on its smooth integration of seemingly irreconcilable elements. By keeping the harmony within each tonal area simple and Classical, Schubert makes the listener feel at home, yet by making the large form a kind of sublime non-sense, he makes a transcendental argument. There is a perceptual flux, a constant blurring and evaporating of relationships, in the music, yet it is pervaded by a peculiar feeling of direction, as if toward an unrecognized object of desire. This ambiguity is enhanced by the intricate overlapping of harmonic presentations, which coalesce in the presence of a tonic that comes from nowhere, potent but a little unreal. Perhaps this is felt more strongly after the closing cadence, which is not allowed to evoke any sense of

Example 10

rest or fixity. After the voice falls silent, the piano moves into the upper registers for the first time in the song. Three tonic triads and a subdominant-quality diminished triad sound and sound again, slowly ascending; then the song concludes with a dominant-seventh chord resolving over a tonic pedal (ex. 10). The strong resolution melts into air, as Ganymed's consciousness dissolves into the presence of the all-loving Father.

All of this represents a highly selective response to the text. It heightens the perceptual continuity of the poem while demoting its eroticism, though the song represents the erotic turning point of the poem with real intensity. The emphasis on perception is continued even after the dissolution of the final cadence when a fermata appears over a rest. The notation tells the performers to prolong musical silence by not relaxing for applause; the listener's musical perception must be allowed to fade slowly into an echo or blank.

What this amounts to in relation to the erotic material is a partial evasion, or more exactly a sublimation. And since sexual desire in song hardly needs sublimating as such (many songs actively *de*sublimate it), we seem led to conclude that what is being sublimated here is the homoerotic element in the poem. In saying this, I do not mean to suggest that Schubert is disavowing any homoeroticism of his own—nor, for that matter, that he isn't; I simply don't know.[26] But his song wants to idealize its rapture, and therefore declines to give direct expression to the erotically charged yearning of a male persona toward another male. Instead, it defuses the sexual radicalism of the text by assimilating it to a perceptual deliquescence so extreme that all ordinary connections—tonal, emotional, erotic—are abstracted and etherealized. In a sense, this means only that Schubert is less erotically sophisticated than Goethe, which hardly comes as a surprise. Goethe uses homoerotic desire in "Ganymed" to reinforce the presentation of an ecstasy that transcends the presumed boundaries of nature. Later, in *Faust 2*, he does so again, when Mephistopheles, gloating over the dead Faust, is suddenly overwhelmed with lust for the boy angels who come to fetch Faust's body away. "Der Geist der stets verneint" is forced into an affirmation of being through the desire awakened by the boys.

But Schubert is not working toward that kind of affirmation. What he is after instead is perhaps best suggested by Schoenberg's remarks on the finale of his own String Quartet no. 2 in F-sharp Minor, which contains his first stretch of fully atonal writing. The music is supposed to represent a movement of transcendence that purifies the self of earthly cares, of the gravity of life and the "gravity" of tonality: "passing through the clouds into thinner and thinner air, forgetting all the troubles of life on earth."[27] Schubert, presenting an abstracted form of harmonic motion in which the tonic is free-floating and the cadence is free of content, seems bent on evoking the same kind of release. The eroticism at the margins only heightens the feeling.

VII. Conclusion

As a Romantic genre, the Schubert Lied articulates a multiplicity of conflicts: between harmonic languages, between the Romantic subject and the force—the embodiment, direction, transformations—of its own desires, and between the musical and poetic personae. Perhaps the most striking thing about this process is its spontaneous quality; it seems to reflect the pressure of a subject working from within the expressive world of Classical tonality rather than the pressure of a subject intruding from without. Schubert accomplishes this by confining his harmonic innovations to an almost covert erosion of musical syntax. He does not often indulge in functionless symmetrical sonorities, chromatically overladen chords, mystification by semitonal part writing, or the suppression of root progression as an audible principle of structure. His discontinuities are produced with the Classical palette of dissonances and exotic chords. Dominant sevenths, diminished sevenths and triads, Neapolitan and augmented sixths are all put to uses that expose the rationality of Classical syntax as historically contingent rather than natural. Concomitantly, the static, reiterative accompaniment figures that are basic to Schubert's style help to isolate planes of sonority and set them in opposition to each other as diatonic progressions are simplified and stripped of the submerged traditions that tie them with seeming inevitability to certain standard dissonances. Schubert's habitual fondness for chromatic third relationships has the same effect. By loosening the specificity of harmonic tension, as embodied by the demand of the dominant for the tonic, they isolate disparate sonorities and make dialectic audible.

The history of the Lied after Schubert suggests the importance of positioning the music on the edge between paradigms. Schumann often follows Schubert's model in his songs, but with Wolf the authority of the Classical style is often so attenuated that the music—movingly enough—dissolves rather than reinterprets its bonds to the past. One dissolution, moreover, seems to lead to another. Anxious and ego-laden, the songs substitute the perfection of declamation for a transforming responsiveness to the text. Part of the great outpouring of vocal music in the early twentieth century—by the early Schoenberg and Berg, by Mahler, Debussy, and Ives—reflects the opportunity of renewing an exhausted argument between Classical and Romantic tonality on the borders between tonality and atonality. The Lied, at its most characteristic, is apparently a twilight form, with a peculiar eloquence that comes from a changing language. The Schubert Lied is its archetype.

Notes

1. *The Classical Style* (New York: Norton, 1972), p. 454.

2. See, for example, Ernest Porter, *Schubert's Song Technique* (London: Dennis Dobson, 1961), p. 34.

3. See the essays by Alec Robertson (esp. pp. 15–55) and T. C. L. Pritchard (esp. pp. 243–46) in *The Music of Schubert*, ed. Gerald Abraham (New York: Norton, 1947).

4. See Charles Rosen, *Sonata Forms* (New York: Norton, 1980), pp. 281–91.

5. Schubert, *Symphony in B Minor ("Unfinished")*, Norton Critical Score, ed. Martin Chusid (New York: Norton, 1971), p. 75.

6. Edward T. Cone, *The Composer's Voice* (Berkeley and Los Angeles: University of California Press, 1974), pp. 20–40.

7. Samuel Taylor Coleridge, *Biographia Literaria*, ed. George Watson (London and New York: Everyman Editions, 1965), p. 167.

8. I will risk throwing out the suggestion that pre-Romantic song keeps largely to various forms of identification, though often in terms that alter the textual persona.

9. By "deconstruction," I mean the effort to show that naturalness, immediacy, and self-evidence are effects produced by language, not properties of truth or presence, and are therefore of only limited authority. Deconstructive activity is not new, though the term, and a certain characterization of the activity it describes, has come to prominence recently through the controversial work of Jacques Derrida. The best short treatment of the subject is Christopher Norris, *Deconstruction* (London and New York: Methuen, 1982).

10. For a full analysis of the Beethoven quartet in this context, see my *Music and Poetry: The Nineteenth Century and After* (Berkeley and Los Angeles: University of California Press, 1984), pp. 57–75. On the Mozart, see William DeFotis, "Mozart, Quartet in C, K. 465," *19th-Century Music* 6 (1982):31–38.

11. "A Romantic Detail in Schubert's *Schwanengesang*," this volume, p. 52.

12. See the discussions of this song by David Lewin and Anthony Newcomb, included in this volume.

13. Such recountings or paraphrases are also interpretations—disguised ones—that are based on the view that one kind of meaning, identified as "literal" or "referential," takes precedence over all others. This view of meaning is a source of considerable dispute in contemporary literary theory.

14. In "The Mirror of Tonality: Transitional Features of Nineteenth-Century Harmony," *19th-Century Music* 4(1981):191–208.

15. I borrow the term "exemplify" from Nelson Goodman's *Languages of Art* (2d ed., Indianapolis: Hackett, 1976); for discussion, see Monroe C. Beardsley, "Understanding Music," in *On Criticizing Music*, ed. Kingsley Price (Baltimore: Johns Hopkins University Press, 1981), pp. 55–73; and Anthony Newcomb, "Sound and Feeling," *Critical Inquiry* 10 (1984):614–43.

16. *Franz Schubert's Werke* (Leipzig: Breitkopf und Härtel, 1884–97), vol. 20:3, pp. 189–92. Repr. in *Schubert's Songs to Texts by Goethe* (New York: Dover, 1979), pp. 85–88. Two additional versions or transpositions are mentioned in O. E. Deutsch, *Franz Schubert: Thematisches Verzeichnis seiner Werke*, ed. and rev. W. Dürr, A. Feil, etc. (Kassel: Bärenreiter, 1978), pp. 99–100.

17. I am indebted to Walter Frisch for pointing this out.

18. Some comparison between Schubert's setting and the one that appears in Beethoven's cantata *Meeresstille und Glückliche Fahrt*, also composed in 1815, seems obligatory. Beethoven's piece falls squarely within the Classical style. The music evokes a feeling of unrest and alienation through a vari-

ety of expressive devices: pitch repetition in all voices, liberal use of suspensions and anticipations, reiterated harmonies. There is also a certain
avoidance of the tonic in the first part of the setting. Beethoven begins with
an ambiguous third, D–F♯, which is only established as a tonic triad through
a deceptive cadence that moves away from it: I–V⁷–vi. This is followed by
another, more elaborate slippage from the tonic to the relative minor. There
is no cadence to a tonic triad until bar 31. All of this is highly effective, but it
is not problematical. Incidentally, Beethoven's appropriation of the text also
differs quite strikingly from Schubert's. Its emphasis, carried mainly by the
shocking *forte* attacks on "Weite," is on physical and spiritual isolation.

19. For a full discussion of Romantic repetition, see chapter 2 of my
Music and Poetry.

20. *Schubert's Songs* (1967; Seattle: University of Washington Press,
1969), pp. 59–61. See also Richard Kramer, "Schubert's Heine," *19th-Century
Music* 8 (1985):213–25. The original order of the poems is "Das Fischer-
mädchen," "Am Meer," "Die Stadt," "Der Doppelgänger," "Ihr Bild,"
"Der Atlas."

21. *Schubert's Songs* (1928; repr. New York: Basic Books, 1957), p. 256.

22. As Thrasybulos Georgiades points out, this shift from declamation
to song is articulated with a subtle rhythmic shift. Prior to "Was äffst du,"
the vocal line always begins after the accompaniment. From this point on,
each vocal phrase anticipates the accompaniment. *Schubert: Musik und Lyrik*
(Göttingen: Vandenhoeck und Ruprecht, 1967), p. 76.

23. For an account, see my "The Return of the Gods: Keats to Rilke,"
Studies in Romanticism 17 (1978):483–500.

24. See pp. 232–33 below.

25. Another exception, more felt than heard, is the motivelike use of a
falling whole tone in the voice, which tends to retard phrases as a mark of
yearning. This motive always appears as or in a dissonance—another demand
for requital. At the close, the whole tone is expanded into the third A–F (re-
capitulating the resolving third relationship), then expanded again into the
cadential fifth C–F.

26. On the question of Schubert's sexuality, see Maynard Solomon,
"Franz Schubert's 'My Dream,'" *American Imago* 38 (1981):137–54.

27. Arnold Schoenberg, "Notes on the Four String Quartets," in
Schoenberg, Berg, Webern: The String Quartets. A Documentary Study, ed. Ur-
sula von Rauchhaupt (Hamburg: Deutsche Grammophon, 1971), p. 48.

Appendix of
Longer Musical Examples

All the examples in the Appendix are reproduced from Franz Schubert's
Werke. Kritisch durchgesehene Gesammtausgabe *(Leipzig: Breitkopf
und Härtel, 1884–97).*

Example A Schubert, *Moment musical* in A-flat, op. 94, no. 6 (D. 780)

Allegretto D.C.

Example B Schubert, *Wandrers Nachtlied* ("Über allen Gipfeln," D. 768)

Example C Schubert, *Im Dorfe*, from *Winterreise* (D. 911, no. 17)

19 Je nun, je nun, sie haben ihr Theil genossen, und

22 hoffen, und hoffen, was sie noch üb-rig liessen, doch wie-der zu fin-den, doch wie-der zu

(25) fin-den auf ih-ren Kis-sen.

29 Bellt mich nur fort,⸻ ihr

(31) wa-chen Hun-de, lasst mich nicht ruh'n in der Schlum-mer.

Example D Schubert, *Moment musical* in F Minor, op. 94, no. 3 (D. 780)

Example E Schubert, *Auf dem Flusse,* from *Winterreise* (D. 911, no. 7)

The Contributors

Edward T. Cone, professor emeritus of music at Princeton University, is the author of numerous critical and analytical studies, including two books, *Musical Form and Musical Performance* (1968) and *The Composer's Voice* (1974).

Arnold Feil, professor at the University of Tübingen, has written two books on Schubert, *Studien zu Schuberts Rhythmik* (1966) and *Franz Schubert: Die schöne Müllerin, Winterreise* (1975). He is also an editor of the *Neue sämtlicher Ausgabe* of Schubert's works.

David Brodbeck, assistant professor of music at the University of Southern California, completed his Ph.D. at the University of Pennsylvania in 1984 on Brahms's editions of Schubert dances, and the influence of the dances on Brahms's own music.

The most recent works of Carl Dahlhaus to appear in translation are *Aesthetics of Music* (1982), *Analysis and Value Judgement* (1983), *Foundations of Music History* (1983), and *Music and Realism* (1985). His major study of nineteenth-century music, *Die Musik des 19. Jahrhunderts*, was published in 1980 and is due in translation from the University of California Press.

Walter Frisch, assistant professor of music at Columbia University, is the author of *Brahms and the Principle of Developing Variation* (1984) and a coeditor of the journal *19th-Century Music*.

Thrasybulos Georgiades, who died in 1977, was professor of music at Heidelberg, then at Munich. He was the author of wide-ranging studies on music, including *Greek Music: Verse and Dance* (1949; English translation, 1956) and *Music and Language* (1954; English translation by Marie Louise Göllner, 1982).

Marie Louise Göllner, professor of music at the University of California, Los Angeles, is a specialist in medieval and Renaissance music. A former student of Thrasybulos Georgiades, she translated his book *Music and Language* (1982).

Joseph Kerman, professor at the University of California, Berkeley, has been closely involved with both the theory and practice of criticism. His writings include *Opera as Drama* (1956), *The Beethoven Quartets* (1967), and *Contemplating Music: Challenges to Musicology* (1985).

William Kinderman, who teaches at the University of Victoria in British Columbia, is an accomplished pianist and has published analytical articles on Beethoven and Wagner. His monograph on the Diabelli Variations is forthcoming from Oxford University Press.

Lawrence Kramer, who teaches in the Humanities Division of Fordham University, is a composer and the author of *Music and Poetry: The Nineteenth Century and After* (1984).

David Lewin, professor of music at Harvard, has published many articles on music theory, as well as analyses of Schoenberg, Brahms, and Wagner.

Anthony Newcomb, on the faculty of the University of California, Berkeley, works in both Renaissance and Romantic music. He has published articles on Wagner, Schumann, and on more general topics involving aesthetics and analysis.

Thilo Reinhard, who holds an M.A. in composition from the University of California, Berkeley, is preparing *The Singer's Schumann*, a volume of translations and commentary intended to aid singers and vocal coaches.

Index of Composers and Works

Boldface indicates a more extended analysis.